THE MYTH OF COSMIC REBELLION

SUPPLEMENTS

TO

VETUS TESTAMENTUM

VOLUME LXV

THE MYTH OF COSMIC REBELLION

A STUDY OF ITS REFLEXES IN UGARITIC AND BIBLICAL LITERATURE

BY

HUGH ROWLAND PAGE, JR.

E.J. BRILL
LEIDEN · NEW YORK · KÖLN
1996

The paper in this book meets the guidelines for permanence and durability of the Committee on Production Guidelines for Book Longevity of the Council on Library Resources.

ISSN 0083-5889
ISBN 90 04 10563 8

PRINTED IN THE NETHERLANDS

To Michelle
For Her Love, Support, and Belief

הנך יפה רעיתי
הנך יפה עיניך יונים
אני לדודי ודודי לי

Song of Songs 1:15; 6:3

CONTENTS

PREFACE

This monograph had a humble beginning. In the Fall of 1986, I prepared a paper entitled, "Isaiah 14 Revisited," for the Hebrew 200 Seminar in the Near Eastern Languages and Civilizations Department at Harvard. My intention was to take a fresh look at the historical setting, thematic content, and prosodic structure of this lament against the king of Babylon. The faculty critic for my presentation, Prof. Frank Moore Cross, offered three observations: first, that he believed Isaiah 14 to be a "reflex" of a West Semitic myth of celestial rebellion; second, that there were other such "reflexes" in Canaanite and Hebrew literature; and third, that there were sufficient primary data now available to attempt a reconstruction of this myth from these extant "reflexes." These remarks led me to develop that paper into a doctoral dissertation entitled *The Astral Revolt: A Study of its Reflexes in Canaanite and Hebrew Literature* submitted some four years later. This monograph represents a revision and expansion of that initial work.

Special thanks are due Professor Cross, who served as my dissertation director. His sound guidance and confidence in my philological, exegetical, and hermeneutical skills freed me to develop my own agenda and reach my own conclusions, even when such disagreed with his own. His many suggestions have been invaluable. I also wish to express my gratitude to Profs. Paul Hanson and John Huehnergard, both of whom served as readers of the dissertation, to Prof. Joanne Hackett who provided valuable input in many areas, and the members of the Religion Department at Smith College in Northampton, MA (especially Prof. Quentin Quesnell, my departmental liaison) who served as hosts and colleagues during my tenure as Thomas C. Mendenhall Dissertation Fellow in 1988-89. Thanks are also due to the members of the Five College Biblical Studies Colloquium who invited me to share my research on Job 38 with them in academic 1988-89 and provided a wealth of input. A special word of thanks is due to Dr.'s Carol and Melvin Ember of Human Relations Area Files, Inc. at Yale University, where I worked as research associate from 1989-91. Their tutelage in cross-cultural methodology provided me with many useful insights and helped me to realize that a Semitic philologist must also be an *ethnologist* of antiquity. I must also thank my colleagues in the Theology Department at the University of Notre Dame. During the Fall 1993 semester, I presented part of this revised work to the Christianity and Judaism in Antiquity Seminar and received many helpful suggestions. Their assistance and support have been invaluable in this and other matters related to research and pedagogy. I wish to acknowledge a very special debt of gratitude to one of my senior colleagues—Dr. James VanderKam, Professor of Hebrew Bible at the University of Notre Dame—for his suggestion that I submit this manuscript to SVT, his meticulous reading of an earlier draft, and his sound advice on navigating the sometimes tempestuous waters of academic publishing.

Finally and most importantly I wish to thank my wife, The Rev. Michelle R. Thornton, whose steady and enthusiastic support led me to enroll in the NELC program at Harvard, sustained me while a student, and made possible the completion of this manuscript. I dedicate this work to her with love and sincere appreciation.

HRP, Jr.
May 1996

ABBREVIATIONS AND SIGLA

Abbreviations

AHw[1-3]	W. von Soden. *Akkadisches Handwörterbuch,* Band I, Band II & Band III.
ANEP	J. Pritchard, ed. *The Ancient Near East in Pictures.*
ANET	J. Pritchard, ed. *Ancient Near Eastern Texts Relating to the Old Testament, 3rd. Ed. with Supplement.*
ANT	*The Apocryphal New Testament*
AOAT	*Alter Orient und Altes Testament*
AOS	*American Oriental Series*
APOT[1, 2]	R. H. Charles, *Apocrypha and Pseudepigrapha of the Old Testament,* Vols. 1 and 2.
BASOR	*Bulletin of the American Schools of Oriental Research*
BDB	F. Brown, S.R. Driver, C.A. Briggs. *A Hebrew and English Lexicon.*
BHS	*Biblia Hebraica Stuttgartensia*
CAD[4, 10(II), 17(II)]	I. J. Gelb, et al. *The Assyrian Dictionary of the Oriental Institute of the University of Chicago, Vols. 4, 10 (Part II), & 17 (Part II).*
CC	Cosmic Commingling
CR[A]	Cosmic Rebellion (Old)
CR[B]	Cosmic Rebellion (Young)

CTA	A. Herdner. *Corpus des tablettes en cunéiformes alphabétiques.*
EHO	F. M. Cross, Jr. and D. N. Freedman. *Early Hebrew Orthography.*
GKC	E. Kautzsch, A. E. Cowley. *Gesenius' Hebrew Grammar.*
HALAT	*Hebräisches und aramäisches Lexikon zum Alten Testament*
HSM	*Harvard Semitic Monographs*
HSS	*Harvard Semitic Studies*
HTR	*Harvard Theological Review*
IOS	*Israel Oriental Studies*
JANES	*Journal of the Ancient Near Eastern Society of Columbia University* (New York)
JAOS	*Journal of the American Oriental Society*
JBL	*Journal of Biblical Literature*
JFSR	*Journal of Feminist Studies in Religion*
JNES	*Journal of Near Eastern Studies*
JSOT	*Journal for the Study of the Old Testament*
KAI	H. Donner and W. Röllig. *Kanaanäische und aramäische Inschriften.*
KTU	M. Dietrich, O. Loretz, J. Sanmartín. *The Cuneiform Alphabetic Texts from Ugarit, Ras Ibn Hani and Other Places* (KTU: second, enlarged edition).
LOJ[1, 5]	L. Ginzberg, *The Legends of the Jews*, Vols. 1 and 5.

LSJ	H. Liddell, R. Scott, H. Jones, R. McKenzie. *A Greek- English Lexicon.*
LXX[A,B,S,V]	Septuagint Codices—Alexandrinus, Vaticanus, Sinaiticus, Venetus
NRSV	*The Bible* (*New Revised Standard Version*)
OG	Old Greek
OTP[1, 2]	J. H. Charlesworth, *The Old Testament Pseudepigrapha,* Vols. 1 and 2.
MT	Masoretic Text
Proto-CR[A]	The Progenitor of the Old Cosmic Rebellion Myth
PRU	Ch. Virolleaud. *Le Palais royal d'Ugarit (II, III, IV, V, VI).*
RHR	*Revue de l'Histoire des Religions*
RSV	*The Bible (Revised Standard Version)*
SBLDS	*Society of Biblical Literature Dissertation Series*
SIMB	*Sabaean Inscriptions From Maḥram Bilqîs (Mârib)*
SMS	*Syro-Mesopotamian Studies*
TSSI[1-3]	J. C. L. Gibson. *Textbook of Syrian Semitic Inscriptions (Vols I-III)*
UF	*Ugarit-Forschungen. Internationales Jahrbuch für die Altertumskunde Syrien-Palastinas*
Ugaritica V	*Ugaritica V*, J. Nougayrol et al., eds.
UV	John Huehnergard. *Ugaritic Vocabulary in Syllabic Transcription.*

UT	C. H. Gordon, *Ugaritic Textbook.*
YOSR	*Yale Oriental Series, Researches*
ZAW	*Zeitschrift für die alttestamentliche Wissenschaft*

Sigla

ð	Transcription of the sixteenth letter of the Ugaritic alphabet—usually rendered ḏ
θ	Transcription of the twenty fifth letter of the Ugaritic alphabet—usually rendered ṯ
v	In the transcription of Ugaritic and Hebrew, a vowel of unknown quality
v̆̄	In the transcription of Ugaritic and Hebrew, a vowel whose quality is either long or short

CHAPTER ONE

INTRODUCTION

1.1 Overview

If one were to ask contemporary biblical scholars to compile a list of the issues that remain problematic in the study of ancient Israel, mythology would certainly be high on the list, particularly given the interpretive difficulties presented by the principal extant repository of Israelite myth—the Hebrew Bible. It is hardly an exaggeration to say that many of the more important questions about myth in ancient Israel remain unanswered, in spite of some substantial gains in the past.[1]

The present study aims to make a modest contribution to scholarly discussion about myth in ancient Israel. It explores a hypothesis articulated by Morgenstern (1939) in his analysis of the mythological background of Psalm 82—that there once existed an ancient Canaanite myth describing a revolt against the high god of the Semitic pantheon with at least two well developed alloforms that are discernible in Rabbinic and Pseudepigraphic literature. In these baroque alloforms the central character is Satan.[2]

---

[1] For surveys of scholarship on anthropological and folkloristic study of the Hebrew Bible since the nineteenth century see Eilberg-Schwartz (1990:1-30), Hahn (1956:44-118), Culley (1985:180-191), and Niditch (1993). One wonders, for example, if twentieth century scholarship has ever made full use of the resources left to it by Robertson-Smith (1969) and Frazer (1919).

[2] The theme of rebellion in heaven is an important part of the mythological tradition imported into Western literature from the ancient Near East. The first formal articulation of the theory within the modern academy might best be credited to Morgenstern, but one must not forget the contributions of John Milton and countless creative writers, theologians, folklorists, biblical critics, and others from the seventeenth century to the present who have been fascinated with Lucifer and his fall (cf. Fletcher 1926 and 1930 on Milton's familiarity with ancient Near Eastern and Jewish traditions). Recent treatments of the Satan tradition, its history, and development include those of Jeffrey Burton Russell (1977 and 1981), Forsyth (1987), and Pagels (1995). On the nature and shape of ancient Near Eastern combat mythology in the biblical book of Revelation, see Collins (1976).

Within the intellectual lineage[3] headed by F. M. Cross, Jr., the purported early form of this myth of cosmic rebellion has received considerable attention, though only insofar as it has been related to other areas of Canaanite and Hebrew lore. Cross' own interest may be traced to his teacher, W. F. Albright, who suggested in an early article that Isaiah 14:13 may be a quote from a Canaanite epic (1932-33:192 note 22) and later proposed an identification between Athtar and *hyll bn šḥr* of Isaiah 14:12 (1946:83, 84, 86 and 1969:187 note 73; 231-232). Clifford (1972) alluded to the myth in his study of the cosmic mountain in the ancient Near East as did Mullen (1980) in his monograph on the divine council. Hanson (1977) detected a more pervasive ancient Near Eastern revolt-in-heaven pattern that finds its fullest expression in 1 Enoch. Hendel (1987b) raised serious questions about Hanson's proposed pattern and concluded that it was an imaginary construct. While each of these scholars made an important contribution to the larger dialogue about the myth, none offered a reconstruction of its purported Syro-Palestinian prototype.

Two factors suggest that attention continue to be given to the possible existence of an early Semitic myth of rebellion against the chief administrative deity of the pantheon. First, the discovery and decipherment of the Ras Šamra texts have advanced our knowledge about the religion of ancient Canaan far beyond that of Morgenstern and his contemporaries. As a result, we have a more comprehensive picture of the Syro-Palestinian pantheon and a better understanding of the lore associated with certain of its members. Second, no study has been devoted *solely* to either the analysis of this myth as delimited by Morgenstern and others or the textual evidence used in its reconstruction.

In light of these data, seven principal objectives have been set for this study: (1) to reconsider Morgenstern's hypothesis that the myth of Satan's rebellion has an ancient Canaanite progenitor; (2) to review some of the more important scholarship on the myth of cosmic rebellion as constructed and analyzed within the F. M. Cross, Jr. lineage and to examine more closely the claim first made by W. F. Albright—that *hyll bn šḥr* in Isaiah 14 (cited by Morgenstern as the possible celestial rebel alluded to in Psalm 82) is to be identified with the god Athtar; (3) to compile a concordance of texts cited by Morgenstern and others in the reconstruction of the myth of Satan's rebellion and its alleged mythological ancestor (and that of the transgressing angels which is also dealt with by Morgenstern); (4) to con-

[3] I prefer *intellectual lineages* to the more standard *interpretive schools*.

sider the possibility that Athtar is the divine antihero in the earliest form of the myth of cosmic rebellion; (5) to provide an updated translation and close reading of a selected sample of Ugaritic and Hebrew texts which have informed discussion about this myth; (6) to reassess the value of these texts as witnesses to the most ancient version of the myth; and (7) to provide a reconstruction of this version based on the best evidence available.

1.2 Methodology

The method employed will be philological in foundation and exegetical in scope. Although it is hoped that this study will help to broaden our knowledge of ancient Near Eastern religion and mythology, these and other issues (e.g., the relationship between the revolt myth and that of Satan in early Christian theology) must be reserved for later studies.[4]

After a selective review of scholarship, the remainder of the monograph has been devoted to the analysis of selected texts from Ugaritic and classical Hebrew literature. For Ugaritic texts, the edition of Dietrich and Loretz (1976) has been used. The readings of this edition have been compared to that of Herdner (1963). An eclectic text has been reconstructed for each of the biblical sources. For all texts, account has been taken of prosodic structure and significant literary features have been cited when these have augmented the results of philological, historical, and comparative research.[5]

---

[4] For a recent study of the Satan in Israel see Day (1988).

[5] Since this is not a study devoted exclusively to matters of Hebrew verse, the description of prosodic structure has been kept to a minimum. Ordinarily attention would be called to significant grammatical, lexical, morphological, semantic, and thematic features of the text, the goal being to establish the extent to which all levels of language are operational in the determination of meaning. However, because the primary focus of this study is on the analysis of myth, this aspect of the study has been limited to scanning the number of syllables present in each constituent poetic colon and the assignation of the length of the colon. The opinions of Cross (1983b, 1983c) regarding the composition of Hebrew verse have been adopted, particularly with regard to the basic building blocks of Hebrew meter. In summary, it is his belief that basic components in the construction of Hebrew verse are the short metrical foot (consisting of between 4-6 syllables, corresponding to the two-stress colon in the more traditional stress-counting method) and the long metrical foot (consisting of 7 or more syllables, corresponding to the three-stress colon in the more traditional stress-counting method). Cross has adopted the practice of labeling the long foot as

This project is similar in aim (though certainly not in scope) to that of Ginzberg in his magisterial LOJ. In the description and retelling of Jewish legends, he employed three strategies: (1) giving one version in the main body of his text and discussing alternative versions in his notes; (2) fusing the disparate versions of a legend into a single legend; and (3) citing different versions of a legend at various points in his collection of materials. This study has adopted elements of (2) and (3). Careful attention has been paid to the sources chosen for close examination and an attempt has been

---

l(ongum) and the short foot as *b(reve)* in his scansion of Hebrew poetry. He is not of the opinion that Hebrew poets counted syllables in the oral or written composition of verse. He believes, rather, that the syllable counting method affords a more accurate view of the overall cyclic structure found in Hebrew versification. Inspiration for this method has been drawn from a number of earlier scholars, among whom is Roman Jacobson, whose article on grammatical parallelism (1966) has had profound influence on the work of both Cross and his students. Jacobson states that:

> on every level of language the essence of poetic artifice consists in recurrent returns. Phonemic features and sequences, both morphologic and lexical, syntactic and phraseological units, when occurring in metrically or strophically corresponding positions, are necessarily subject to the conscious or unconscious questions whether, how far, and in what respect the positionally corresponding entities are mutually similar. (Jakobson 1966:399)

The following terminology has been used in describing Hebrew versification and prosody: *colon*—a single line of poetry; *bicolon*—a poetic unit composed of two cola; *tricolon*—poetic unit composed of three cola; *quatrain*—poetic unit composed of four cola; *sestet*—poetic unit composed of six cola. In certain instances cola of six syllables may be labeled *l(ongum)* when they stand in parallel relationship to a colon of five or fewer syllables. A seven syllable colon may at times be considered *b(reve)* when standing in relationship to a colon of eight or more syllables. There are rare occasions when two cola of equal length will compose a bicolon, and in such an instance poetic license must be invoked in assigning relative values to either. These rules become particularly important when working with Qina meter which is regularly l:b, or 3:2 in traditional stress notation (cf. Isaiah 14:4b-20). Of course, there are other approaches to classical Hebrew poetry—some of which are at variance with that of Cross (see O'Connor 1980, Kugel 1981, Alter 1985, and Petersen and Richards 1992 for examples). It must also be remembered that there is always some degree of subjectivity in any form of poetic scansion for those who analyze verse and for those who are practicing poets (Petersen and Richards 1992:13; Skelton 1971:157).

made to reconstruct (in the final chapter) a single version of the progenitor of the myth of cosmic rebellion. Possible alloforms (and the sources that support them) have been discussed in footnotes.

The sources used have been taken from the Hebrew Bible and the alphabetic cuneiform texts from Ras Šamra. My interpretive posture toward them has also been quite similar to that adopted by Ginzberg in his treatment of Talmudic-Midrashic sources. I agree with him that: (1) ancient authors tend to elaborate legendary material that they find; (2) creations of popular imagination are preserved in the form impressed on them by poetic and scholarly imagination; (3) legends are rarely transmitted in their original shape; and (4) in the transmission of folklore, the purpose of the mediator is often to fuse (or establish a close connection between) a received tradition with creations of popular imagination—i.e., to contemporize older traditions—for purposes of intellectual stimulation, spiritual nurture, pedagogy, and entertainment (cf. LOJ:vii-xv). These could well be used as maxims for the study of the Hebrew Bible and the mythological literature from Ugarit—both being repositories of folklore.[6] However, the task of identifying the nature and scope of those traditions that the biblical authors (and their counterparts at Ugarit) attempt to contemporize is just as difficult as delimiting the connections between material found in the Hebrew Bible and that known from Talmudic-Midrashic, Apocryphal, Pseudepigraphic, and early Christian sources.

1.3 On The Vocalization of Northwest Semitic Languages

A close reading of any text involves analysis of all features which have direct impact on its primary meaning, setting, and subsequent place within a given mythological, historical, epic, or interpretive context. All information upon which assumptions have been made must be noted, so that the research design and methodological considerations central to the work are clear to readers. In order to appreciate the artistry used by ancient poets and

[6] The definition of terms in the study of folklore and mythology is problematic. I find it most useful to treat as folklore, "all the lore (myths, legends, folktales, ballads, riddles, proverbs, and superstitions) of a culture; generally orally transmitted, but may also be written" (Ember and Ember 1993:497). I understand myth as a sacred/religious tale of a social nature that is concerned with the genesis of socio-cultural, natural, or supernatural phenomena (Seymour-Smith 1986:203-204). For a definition of folklore in terms of "the traditional" cf. Niditch (1993:9-12).

bards to convey meaning, it is necessary to *vocalize* Ugaritic and Hebrew texts that bear witness to their collective genius. This study proceeds from the assumption that in any exegetical work, not only must the original text, setting, and meaning of a work be established, but the rules governing the language in which the text was composed must be noted as well. While this task should be adjusted to fit the specific requirements of particular lines of inquiry (whether philological, literary, comparative, historical, religious, social or political), one should attempt to convey as accurate a sense as possible of the languages involved. This should include attention to the actual pronunciation of the language. Only then may one consider the exegetical process complete.

It has been the practice of some researchers to give an increased measure of precision to their work by reconstructing the pronunciation of those Semitic languages which have been preserved in written form without vowels (as is the case with Ugaritic, early Hebrew, Phoenician, Ammonite, Moabite, early Aramaic, etc.); there are those who extend this practice to Biblical Hebrew, in an attempt to reach beyond the Masoretic system of vocalization for a more historically accurate sense of classical Hebrew pronunciation in its various stages of development. This process is imprecise at best, yet it is necessary when analyzing elevated speech/poetry. In such instances, one may not rely solely upon the Masoretic vocalization which is several centuries removed from even the latest Hebrew texts. Some seek to circumvent this problem by using transliterated/consonantal (non-normalized) texts, leaving it up to the reader to decode an author's assumptions about the phonology, morphology, grammar, and syntax of the language encountered. While it is an accepted convention in some circles to normalize Ugaritic texts, it is far less the norm to reconstruct historical vocalizations for those found in the Hebrew Bible.[7] Since material written in

---

[7] This is also the case with many critical editions of epigraphic Hebrew and other Northwest Semitic dialects (see KAI for example). One recent editor has recognized that this is a problem and has an introduction for each of his three volumes, describing briefly the phonological rules for Hebrew, Aramaic, and Phoenician respectively, which were operative/not operative during the period of time spanned by the texts in each volume (see TSSI$^{1\text{-}3}$). Numerous lexical items are normalized, but texts themselves are not. Cross (1973:21, with note 50) has adopted the practice of vocalizing Ugaritic and other Semitic languages based on comparative data. Pardee (1982) has vocalized epigraphic Hebrew according to Masoretic conventions. While the vocal-

Ugaritic and Hebrew has been drawn upon in this study, much of which is written in poetry and/or elevated prose, it has seemed prudent to adopt a uniform practice for the presentation of all texts. All have, therefore, been vocalized based on the author's understanding of these languages. The information given below is meant in no way to supplant that found in the grammars; it is given strictly for ease of reference, and to make less mysterious the actual grammatical and syntactic structure of each text as understood by the present writer.[8]

1.3.1 Ugaritic

The vocalization of Ugaritic, like that of any language written in an alphabetic script with limited attestation of vowels, is a speculative undertaking. Assumptions must be made about its relationship to other members of its language family, and its place in the historical development of those languages from a common progenitor. Gordon's Ugaritic grammar (1965) remains the standard, though now one must add that of Segert (1984). Both rely heavily on comparative data from other Semitic languages (particularly Arabic) in their treatments of morphology and syntax. In addition to the aforementioned, the unpublished notes of Huehnergard (1986) along with his recent study on Ugaritic Vocabulary (1987), and several works by Cross (1974b, 1973) in which he vocalizes selected epic and mythological texts from Ugarit, have been used to supplement data found in Gordon and Segert.

The following list contains the more important conventions adopted in the vocalization of Ugaritic in this study:

1. It is assumed that Ugaritic contained three short vowels (a, i, u) and three long vowels (ā, ī, ū).

2. The diphthongs -aw and -ay have contracted, yielding—ô and—ê respectively.

3. Prefixed prepositions b- and l- are vocalized bi- and li- (Huehnergard 1987:53).

---

ization of ancient Hebrew and Ugaritic is a highly speculative endeavor, failure to do so opens the door for the potential intrusion of errors in textual interpretation.

[8] For biblical passages I have also provided a reconstructed consonantal text.

4. The negative particle whose graphic representation is identical to that of the prefixed preposition l- is vocalized lā-.

1.3.2 Hebrew

The following phonological changes are assumed to have taken place during the period covered:

1. ā → ō

2. The monophthongization of final triphthongs

3. The loss of most final short vowels (those remaining being anceps [v̆̄])

4. Unbound -at > ā in unbound feminine nouns and 3rd, feminine, singular verbs

5. Stress has moved to the ultima in nominal forms and finite verbs with pronominal suffixes; stress is penultimate if an anceps vowel is present; construct forms are proclitic.

6. *i → a / ´vC(C)__G# (where G is a guttural consonant)

7. aw → ô (When diphthongs are unstressed)[9]
   ay → ê

Tonic lengthening of vowels in singly-closed syllables has occurred in nouns and in verbs with suffixes in exilic and later material (a > ā, i > ē, u > ō). Other developments, such as the resolution of final consonant clusters by anaptyxis, the weakening of laryngeals and the glottal stop and the resulting loss of doubling and the development of hateph (echo) vowels, vowel reduction, and vowel lengthening in tonic and pretonic syllables, are assumed to be late developments which do not apply to the corpus under examination (Harris 1939:79-80; Lambdin and Huehnergard 1985:8-14).

---

[9] *ay* regularly collapses to *ê* in all environments in Northern Hebrew.

CHAPTER TWO

REVIEW OF SCHOLARSHIP

2.1 Morgenstern's Hypothesis

In his study of the mythological background of Psalm 82 (1939:86-126), Julian Morgenstern established the existence of two independent myths which are reflected in biblical, pseudepigraphic, Rabbinic, and early Christian texts. The first is attested in the following sources:[10]

Hebrew Bible	
Genesis	6:1-4
Apocrypha	
Judith	16:7
Wisdom of Solomon	14:6
1 Baruch	3:26ff
3 Macc.	2:4
Pseudepigrapha	
Jubilees	5:1
1 Enoch	6-16;19; 39:1; 64; 69; 86:1-6
Testament of Reuben	5:6-7
Testament of Naphtali	3:5
2 Enoch	7
2 Baruch	56:12-15
New Testament	
Ephesians	6:12
2 Peter	2:4
Jude	6
Hellenistic Sources	
Jewish Antiquities	I.3.1

In it, a number of sinful angels descend of their own volition from heaven to earth and cohabit with mortal women. The offspring of their sexual union are giants. The deity is angered by this activity, condemns the angels to give up their divine nature, and forces them to live on earth as mortals

[10] Morgenstern noted possible additional connections between this myth and that of the phoenix, Genos and Protogonos (from Sanchuniathon), and Adapa.

with their consorts. The essentials of this myth are found in Genesis 6:1-4 while later sources contain forms of the myth that have been considerably embellished (1939:86-94).

The second myth, according to Morgenstern, existed in two versions. Allusions to it are found in Rabbinic tradition, early Christian writings,[11] and the following sources:

Hebrew Bible	
Genesis	6:4a
Job	4:18; 15:15; 28:5
Psalm	82
Isaiah	14:12-14; 24:21-23
Ezekiel	28:11-28
Apocrypha	
Sirach	16:7
Pseudepigrapha	
Life of Adam & Eve	13:1-16:1
1 Enoch	86:1; 88; 90:20-21
2 Enoch	18:1-6; 29:4-5
New Testament	
Luke	10:18
2 Corinthians	11:14
Hebrews	1:6
Revelation	12:7-9; 20:1-7

The first version tells of Satan, a rebellious angel who enjoyed special favor in the court of God, and his expulsion from heaven for refusal to pay homage to Adam—the primordial human created in the divine image. His punishment for this crime is to be cast from heaven and forced either to fly above or be imprisoned in an abyss. The second version, considered by Morgenstern to be the older of the two, relates the story of Satan and his angelic contingent who are cast from heaven for their rebellion against God and for Satan's attempt to establish himself as cosmic ruler in God's stead. The punishment for Satan and his rebels is exile on earth. According to Morgenstern, these versions were not originally linked. The first version is reflected independently in Hebrews 6:1 and the second is found in Rev.

---

[11] KTU 1.6 & 1.23, a Cappadocian tablet worked on by J. Lewy, the Adapa myth, the Atlas myth, the myth of the Titans, and portions of Hittite lore are cited by Morgenstern as possible corollaries.

12:7-9 and 2 Enoch 18:1-6. A composite form consisting of both versions is found in Life of Adam and Eve 13:1-16:1 (1939:94-105). Morgenstern identified the *npylym* of Genesis 6:4a with Satan and his rebels who were cast down to earth. He did not consider this reference to be an integral part of the information outlined in Genesis 6:1-3, but treated it instead as an editorial gloss intended to link the myth of the cohabitation of the gods with human women with that of the fallen angels (1939:107).

Morgenstern held that the myth of the fallen angels was one of great antiquity in Israel. He found evidence for this in the fact that Isaiah 14:12-14, a text that describes the fall of *hyll bn šḥr*, alluded to both versions of this myth of cosmic rebellion—the first (and younger version) describing the criminal's condemnation to an abyss and the second describing his being cast to earth—and by the fact that Ezekiel 28:11-28 referred also to this myth (1939:110-111). Thus, for Morgenstern, the stories of the fall of Satan and his followers (to earth or the abyss), in its earlier and later forms, and that of *hyll bn šḥr* reflected a single myth which had been present in Israel for a considerable length of time (1939:109).

However, Morgenstern was also convinced that the myth was not Israelite in origin. He believed that the Tyrian king featured as protagonist in Ezekiel 28, the location of this divine being's abode on Mt. Casius (home of the gods), the use of the divine names El and Elyon, and the name *hyll bn šḥr* found in Isaiah 14:12 pointed to a North Semitic origin (1939:111-112). He posited a similar origin for the myth of the gods and their sexual exploits with mortal women (1939:113). He believed that North Semitic mythology and cultic practices entered Israel through the mediation of the Galilean community (which enjoyed close contact with its Phoenician neighbors) and that Galilean festival pilgrims brought these elements to Jerusalem perhaps as early as the end of the 6th century B.C.E. (1939:80).[12]

---

[12] Here, Morgenstern has touched two areas of continuing debate in biblical circles: (1) possible repositories of Canaanite mythological material which emerge in the proto-apocalyptic literature of sixth-century Israel; and (2) the possible origin of North Semitic (by which Morgenstern appears to mean Phoenician) influence on the literature of early Christianity. Both are important in accounting for the generation, transmission, and diffusion of cultural elements common to several Mediterranean cultures. For a discussion of speculative thought during the 6th century in cross-cultural perspective, see Davison (1980:197-221).

Morgenstern's reconstructions are compelling, though his methodology has some minor problematic elements. First, it relies heavily on pseudepigraphic, Rabbinic, and Christian sources for details about the earliest of these myths—that which tells of Satan's rebellion. One could argue that his interpretations of earlier texts (e.g., Isaiah 14 and Ezekiel 28) are influenced by his reading of these later materials. Second, it does not deal adequately with the issues of transmission history and background (socio-cultural and mythological) of each of the texts cited. Only Psalm 82, the focus of his study, is given a thorough analysis. His generalizations about these other texts are astute, but critical editions, philological notes, and commentary would have allowed his readers to know exactly what he felt about the traditions that they contain. Third, his conclusion that the myth of heavenly rebellion is *not* of Israelite origin raises a slight problem since the bulk of his evidence is drawn from the Hebrew Bible and other literary sources produced by authors in the Jewish diaspora. Fourth, there is a lack of clarity about the relationship between the texts cited and the myths that he has reconstructed. For example, should these texts be called "reflexes," "citations," "adaptations," "allusions," "versions," "forms," or some other designation. Fifth, the protagonist of the earliest of the myths would almost certainly *not* have been Satan—a datum that he acknowledged—and *hyll bn šḥr*, whom he identified as the rebel, is an enigmatic figure whose identity needs clarification. Sixth, the data available from the textual witnesses are not as simple to classify as his system suggests—though it is an excellent starting point. The pseudepigraphic texts, in particular, show remarkable blending of these myths. The job of separating thematic strands is, therefore, not an easy task.[13]

---

[13] Cf. for example Ginzberg's reconstruction of these traditions in LOJ[1]:47-127 (and accompanying notes). He proposes at least three angelic falls: (1) the expulsion of the angel of truth from heaven to earth because of his opposition to the creation of man; (2) Satan's fall as a result of his refusal to worship the first man; and (3) the descent of angels to commingle with mortal women. He constructs a continuous narrative when dealing with the fall of Satan but acknowledges the existence of three alternate traditions: (1) that the fall was due to his jealousy toward Adam; (2) that it was the result of his misleading Adam; and (3) that it was the result of his attitude toward Job. Note should also be taken of Charles' reconstruction of what he refers to as the "demonology" of 2 Enoch that blends the traditions of the fall of Satan, the fall of the angels, and the liaison between angels and human women (APOT[2]:447, note 5).

In spite of these troublesome areas, Morgenstern's contributions are of considerable merit. He has provided, at the very least, a hypothesis that can be tested, outlines of three distinct and originally independent myths that can be examined further, and a body of texts that can be subjected to additional scrutiny. From this point on, the following sigla shall be used when referring to these three myths:

Siglum	Meaning	Myth
CC	Cosmic Commingling	Angels Take Human Consorts
CR^A	Cosmic Revolt (Old)	Satan Challenges God For Primacy of Place
CR^B	Cosmic Revolt (New)	Satan Expelled From Heaven For Refusal To Honor First Created Human

2.2 The Albright-Cross Lineage

2.2.1 Albright

Albright (1946:83, 84, 86 and 1969:187, note 73; 231-232) noted the relationship between Ugaritic Athtar and Isaiah 14. He considered Isaiah 14 to be a 6th or 7th century Canaanite mythological dirge which recalled Athtar's unsuccessful attempt to usurp Baal's throne, as described in KTU 1.6. He also proposed that the conflict between Baal and Athtar was indicative of tension between votaries of the two gods before the middle of the second millennium B.C.E. Albright identified the Athtar of Ugarit with South Arabian *Dhū-šamāwi*, who is Athtar/Venus in his manifestation as morning-star, with the ᶜ*Aštar-Kamoš* of the *Mesha Inscription*, Kemoš, god of Moab (in 2 Kings 3:26f. and Amos 2:1), and Canaanite *Ba*ᶜ*l šamêm*—whose cult he believed to have assumed dominance in Phoenicia in the 10th century B.C.E. (1968:228, 239).[14]

[14] Cf. Chase (1994) who has established conclusively the equation between *Ba*ᶜ*l Šamêm* and Haddu. Note should also be taken of the fact that Albright believed Athtar to be originally androgynous and identified with *hyll bn šḥr*. (1946:83-84).

2.2.2 Clifford

Clifford (1972:160-173) dealt with Isaiah 14:4b-21, Ezekiel 28, KTU 1.6 I, and KTU 1.23 in his treatment of the cosmic mountain in the ancient Near East. He argued that these texts (and Genesis 2-3) provide a glimpse of an attempted revolt against the divine head of the pantheon, the full extent of which is now impossible to recover. He also suggested that Isaiah 14 is a description of an unsuccessful attempt by *hyll bn šḥr* against the authority of El, and that the epithet "Conqueror of the nations" is either a misunderstood Athtar epithet or a reference to the god Šalim mentioned in KTU 1.23. He compared KTU 1.6 I 39-65 to Isaiah 14 and proposed that it is a variant of the same myth, but noted that in spite of Athtar's presumed violent nature, the focus of the version is on Baal and Mot, with Athtar being little more than a pawn on the side of Athirat and Mot. Athtar's attempt to take kingship belonging rightfully to Baal failed nonetheless. Clifford followed Gray in treating Šaḥar and Šalim in KTU 1.23 as hypostases of Athtar/Venus and considered the content of this text as indicative of the single myth underlying KTU 1.6, Isaiah 14, KTU 1.23, and other extant variants (Šaḥar being father of *hyll* in Isaiah 14). He postulated that in KTU 1.23, El's two newborn sons, when their ravenous appetites lead them to seek entry into El's field, are to be considered as rebels against El. He treated Šaḥar as an alternate name for Athtar, who breaks into El's paradise. As for Ezekiel 28:1-10, Clifford noted that the Tyrian prince laid claim to El's office and his home. For him, *blb ymym* (which he equated with Ugaritic *qrb ʾpq thmtm*) may allude at once to the dwelling of El and to the geographical location of Tyre. The prophet who authored the poem saw *ʾēl* as meaning simply "god," but the original reference was to the Canaanite God El. The stress on wisdom Clifford saw as suggestive of El and his abode. Ezekiel 28:11-19 he found to be less direct. He proposed that it described a rebellion against El by a wise being. The rebel's home was the mountain of El, equated here with El's garden, where he lived as a member of the divine council until palace intrigue, perhaps, led to his expulsion. Clifford suggested the possibility that the "stones of fire" are the equivalent of "the stars of El" in Isaiah 14:15 and the *banū ʾili* (members of El's council) cast as astral beings. He concluded that Isaiah 14 and Ezekiel 28 tell of conflicts against El in his garden on his mountain and suggested that they may be related to theomachies found in Hesiodic and Hittite sources as well in Sanchuniathon.

Many of Clifford's conclusions are quite convincing. The texts that he works with are difficult and subject to more than one interpretation. It seems clear that Isaiah 14 and Ezekiel 28:1-10, 11-19 have some relationship to a revolt against the chief god of the pantheon or to those involved in such a rebellion. His contention that Isaiah 14 and Ezekiel 28:11-19 indicate that the chief protagonist is an astral god (a "Shining One") is compelling, as is his observation that Athtar's failure on Ṣapon is secondary in importance to the conflict between Ba^{c}l and Mot in KTU 1.6 I. Equally convincing is his analysis of Canaanite and astral allusions in Ezekiel 28:1-10, 11-19. Both of these texts make clear reference to an attempted coup against El by a god who is a member of the council, an astral god, and one to whom wisdom has been ascribed.

A few words are appropriate at this point regarding areas mentioned by Clifford that are subject to more than one interpretation. First, the prophet's use of *ʾēl* as "god" can be seen in another way. The density of Canaanite mythological allusions suggests that the poet knew well the mythological content that he employed, and assumed the same of the intended audience. Such confidence would permit him to allow the tales to convey their truth without extensive editorial interference, thereby leading the intended audience to draw connections with their own life-situation and its unique Yahwistic theological underpinnings. Thus, *ʾēl* could refer to Canaanite El. Second, the activity of the two newborn gods in KTU 1.23, which Clifford sees as rebellious, can also be read differently. The two newborn gods might be treated as hungry and hyperactive, in possession of all of the energy associated with youngsters. Their actions do not appear to be as serious in nature as those narrated in either Isaiah 14 or Ezekiel 28. Finally, the Šaḥar/Šalim/Athtar equation made by Clifford seems somewhat less appealing than treating each as a fully independent divine entity. The astronomical manifestation of Athtar and Athtart during the early morning and evening hours might have led to the belief that they were offspring of Dawn and Dusk respectively.

2.2.3 Mullen

Mullen's treatment of the cosmic revolt (1980:35-39, 227-245), part of an exegetical analysis of Psalm 82, has been incorporated into his study of the divine council in Canaanite and Hebrew literature. Biblical reflexes of the revolt have been cited (Isaiah 14, Ezekiel 28) along with biblical passages that make use of a similar motif (Genesis 6:1-4; Genesis 2:4b-3:24) and post-biblical references to fallen stars (1 Enoch 86:1-6; 64-69; 3 Macc. 2:4; 2 Enoch 18:1-6) and gods in revolt (1 Enoch 6:7; 8:3-4; 69:2).

One of Mullen's concerns was the etymology of Ugaritic *šr*. He followed Cross in deriving it from the root √*šrr* (Proto-Semitic √*śrr*) "to shine, be brilliant" which is attested in Arabic and Akkadian (cf., *šarūru* "radiance"). The meaning of *šr* was critical for him because of the reference made to *mōtu wa šarru* ("Mot and Shining One") in KTU 1.23.8-9, and to the *šarrū puḫri* "Shining Ones of the Council" in KTU 1.23.57. Mullen treated the former reference as parallel to Hebrew *hyll* in Isaiah 14:12, and considered the latter as a reference to the cosmic forces of chaos and death. He acknowledged that little is known of the "Shining One" and "Shining Ones" but noted the striking similarity between *šr* and *hyll*, particularly since Isaiah 14:12ff. describes the fall of *hyll* and his fate in Sheol. He also mentioned, with caution, two possible references to "Shining Ones" in the biblical corpus—Psalm 89:15 and 58:1b. Of these, the former appeared to be a much stronger candidate for him than the latter.

Mullen's major interest in this study was the use of the revolt myth in Psalm 82. He has concluded that this psalm uses it to illustrate the coming fate of the gods who have been condemned by Yahweh in the council for their failure to maintain the foundation of the cosmos through the proper administration of justice. For Mullen, the rebellions described in Isaiah 14 and Ezekiel 28 are similar, the targets of the revolt being El and his authority. This put him at odds with Pope and others who contend that the scenes in Ezekiel 28 describe El's attempt to regain control of his own dominion. He did not, however, follow Morgenstern's interpretation of the cause for the fall of the gods in Psalm 82, and found no compelling evidence to justify taking vss. 2-5ab as an insertion to avoid mention of the actual reason for the condemnation (the intermingling of gods with mortal women described in Genesis 6:1-4 according to Morgenstern). He agreed that the aforementioned activity provided substantial justification for the condemnation. However, according to his interpretation, the failure of the gods to exercise their powers responsibly was also sufficient justification for the sentence which they received. He concluded that Psalm 82 is a unit which is complete in itself. Reference is made to the primordial revolt which led to rebel gods being cast into the underworld. Adam, the first human rebel, is also mentioned. For Mullen, these two rebellions set the tone for the judgment of inept and corrupt members of the divine council.

Most of Mullen's arguments are persuasive, but four issues require comment. First, the double name *mt wšr* is enigmatic. His translation "Death and Shining One" raises at least as many questions as it answers. Indeed, the "Shining One," if identified with Athtar, could be assumed to have been an astral and chthonic deity with warlike characteristics. However, one is left wondering what other shared aspects would make the relationship between Mot and Athtar so strong. One also wonders whether another interpretation might render the name more understandable in its context. The second issue is Mullen's interpretation of the background of Psalm 82. While vss. 2-5ab are understandable within a larger Hebrew-Canaanite framework involving the responsibility of government (earthly and divine) toward the community, it is possible that these failures may be explained within a broader framework that focuses attention on Canaanite El as the consummate ruler. If such were the case, the condemned gods could be seen to have failed because by nature and function they have proved less than worthy of their status. Vss. 2-5ab would have symbolic and literal importance. Failure to exercise divine duties would suggest that their time must have been spent in other, less productive, pursuits. Morgenstern's assumption that the Psalm has undergone considerable reworking is probably correct, though his connection of Psalm 82 with Genesis 6:1-4 is not equally convincing. One does suspect that a pre-Yahwistic setting is more strongly represented in the psalm than Mullen allows for. Third, the reading *šr pḫr* in KTU 1.23.57 has been revised in KTU 1.23.57.[15] The proposed reading of the latter edition is *yšr pḫr* "the council sang." Finally, Mullen's conclusion that the rebellion of the *šrym* and that of *ʾdm* in vs. 7 serve as background for the judgment of the unjust gods in Psalm 82 is very convincing. However, one wonders whether the condemnation of the gods might be *related sequentially* to the fall of the "Shining Ones" to which it is compared.

2.2.4 Hanson

Hanson (1977:195-233) proposed that there exists an ancient mythic revolt pattern discernible in a number of ancient Near Eastern myths. He focused his treatment on 1 Enoch 6-11, which he suggested is an expository narrative in which Genesis 6:1-4 (and 4-10 more broadly) has been interpreted from an eschatological apocalyptic perspective. The hermeneutical principle at work, in his opinion, is fundamentally typological. Primordial judgment and fall mentioned in scriptural references were treated as events which are

---

[15] Nonetheless, Mullen's observation that "Shining Ones" represent the forces of chaos and death is intriguing (1980:240). This datum is clearly demonstrated in several of the biblical texts treated later on in this study.

to take place at the eschaton when the elect will be saved and the unrighteous (angels and humans) punished.

According to Hanson, the mythic pattern assumed the following structure in the Šemiḥazah narrative of 1 Enoch 6-11(1977:197):

1. Plot of rebellion instigated by astral deities in heaven (6:2b-8)

2. Commingling of mortals and immortals, birth of giants, devastation by giants, plea by earth (7:1-6; 8:4 [minus 7:1de])

3. Intercession (angelic) before the Most High, Noah's deliverance, punishment of rebels and their offspring who are bound and cast to earth, ultimate punishment to be suffered in the abyss of fire (9:1-10:15 [minus 9:6, 8c, and 10:4-10])

4. Restoration of cosmic harmony and the kingship of the Most High (10:16-11:2)

Hanson argued that the narrative revived a pattern in mythopoeic thought concerned with explaining the polarities at work in the most fundamental of human experiences. Within the crucible of post-exilic trauma accompanying the loss of national independence in Israel, a disenfranchised band of visionaries reached back for archaic elements once transformed in an early period (presumably having undergone a primary transformation of some sort which rendered them accessible for use by these visionaries) and put them into a Yahwistic interpretive framework. These archaic elements have, as a result, been re-enlivened, given a second birth. The line separating primordial reality from the linear perception of events in so-called "real-time" has, thereby, been shattered, allowing a full flowering of mythopoeic piety. Hanson accounted for this resurgence by proposing that an uninterrupted stream of mythopoeic thought concerning the disruption of cosmic equilibrium by the rebellion of a select number of gods in the pantheon existed in the ancient Near East and hailed ultimately from mythic development in the second millennium B.C.E. It was this theme that re-emerged in the sectarian circles which produced the Šemiḥazah cycle (1977:202-203).

Hanson also attempted to isolate the origin of the concept that the forces of chaos in the cosmos originated in the rebellion of members of the divine council. Since this strain of thought is common in the ancient world, he used the structure of the revolt pattern found in 1 Enoch 6-11 as an analytical control in the assessment of comparable ancient Near Eastern mythological sources. He made his starting point the corpus of Hurrian myths extant in Hittite translation, and acknowledged agreement with those specialists who see this Hittite material as one of the sources influencing Hesiod's *Theogony* and *Works and Days.* He also noted that Hesiod, in turn, was one of the sources behind the myths of titanic rebels (including Prometheus) in Greek and Hellenistic sources. This, he argued, provided sufficient ground to consider a possible ancient Near Eastern origin for the aforementioned myths and their reflexes in second-temple-period Jewish sectarian literature. Hanson found evidence of the rebellion-in-heaven pattern in the Hurrian Kumarbi mythology (*Kingship in Heaven*), the *Song of Ullikummi*, the older version of the *Myth of Illuyanka*, the myth of Athtar's abortive attempt to secure Baal's throne (KTU 1.6 I 57-65), the *hyll bn šḥr* episode in Isaiah 14:5-21, Isaiah 24:21-23, the apparent rebellion against El alluded to in KTU 1.23, Anat's defeat of the rebel dragon in 1.83.8-10, *Enūma Eliš*, Ezekiel 26:19-21, Ezekiel 28:1-10, Ezekiel 28:11-19, Ezekiel 32, Genesis 6:1-4 (a fragment), and Psalm 82.[16] In Isaiah and Ezekiel, the rebellion-in-heaven pattern has been historicized, the major referents being Israel's concrete enemies. He suggested further that illicit procreation caused by the mixing of divine and human seed violated established bounds set in primordial times. Unauthorized activity of this sort was considered rebellion against the divine council (1977:204-218).

Hanson concluded that: (1) the Ugaritic texts and *Enūma Eliš* reflect the astralization and adaptation of the myth of heavenly rebellion which is later reflected in the Šemiḥazah narrative; (2) zoomorphic and anthropomorphic allomorphs of the myth have been reflected in the Isaiah and Ezekiel passages; (3) the myth's function in the latter setting, which is directly related to the genre in which the references are found (chiefly oracles, taunts and judgments against foreign rulers), seems not to have involved ritual reenactment or other cultic functions which were part and parcel of the original *Sitz im Leben* of the archaic material; (4) the four-part pattern, is, nonetheless, observable in Isaiah 14:5-21; 24:21-23; Ezekiel 26:19-21; 28:1-10;

[16] Hanson also cited the following texts in his discussion of the rebellion in heaven pattern and the culture hero tradition as reflected in biblical and pseudepigraphic literature: Isaiah 27:1; 51:9; Ezekiel 29:3-4; 26:17-21; 38:4; Psalm 74:13-14; 82; Job 40:25-26; Revelation 12:7-9; the myth of *Enki and Ninmaḫ*; *Atraḫasis*; the late astral version of *Enuma Eliš*; and the Sumerian myth of *Ninurta and Kur*. He also suggested that the material found in Hesiod's *Theogony* and *Works and Days* along with the Greek myths of Prometheus and the Titans share a common ancient Near Eastern background.

28:11-19; 32; and Genesis 6:1-4; (5) elaborations on the theme of the place of punishment (the pit, where the fallen gods of antiquity dwell) and the agent who punishes the rebels (Ezek. 28:16; *Song of Ullikummi*) point in the direction of 1 Enoch 6-11; and (6) Genesis 6:1-4 specifies the mode of birth of the rebels found in 1 Enoch. For Hanson, the ubiquity of the rebellion-in-heaven pattern in ancient Near Eastern literature implied that there seems to have been a continuous line of influence from archaic mythological traditions through biblical sources (pre-exilic and post-exilic) and on into the 3rd century B.C.E. Šemiḥazah narrative (1977:218).

Many of Hanson's conclusions are quite credible and the points of disagreement noted below result, for the most part, from the fact that the data are difficult and open to myriad interpretations. For example, it is clear that revolt myths are characteristic of ancient Near Eastern folklore. It is equally apparent that the rebellion theme runs through biblical sources of various periods. With regard to research design, Hanson's use of as highly developed a form of the myth as that of the Šemiḥazah narrative as a control for earlier reflexes of the revolt—clearly necessary given the primary focus of his treatment—poses some difficulties. Undoubtedly, several streams of mythological tradition have converged in 1 Enoch 6-11, thereby accounting for the full development of the rebellion-in-heaven pattern. The separation of these separate mythological traditions so as to allow individual analysis suggests itself as a reasonable and worthwhile task for the future. It also seems prudent to shift the locus of any corpus of texts used as analytical controls to an earlier period, preferably to the first or second millennium B.C.E., while allowing oneself to be informed by later reflexes. The need to compile a *universe* of purported reflexes and to develop criteria for sampling and testing texts within it suggests itself as well.

On another note, the interpretation of the commingling of divine and human species as rebellion is expressed clearly in 1 Enoch 6-11 but less so in Genesis 6:1-4. The motif of divine/human sexual relations is also absent from Isaiah 14, Ezekiel 28:1-10, 11-19, and Psalm 82. Evidence is present in each text of a theme involving the overstepping of bounds and punishment by means of a radical reversal of fates, but the full embodiment of Hanson's revolt-in-heaven pattern is found only in 1 Enoch 6-11.

Finally, Hanson is correct in treating zoomorphic, astral, and anthropomorphic allusions in these texts as alloforms of one myth, so long as Ginzberg's observations (LOJ:vii-xv) are kept in mind. Thus, Isaiah 14, Ezekiel 28, etc. might best be understood as contextual redefinitions or elucidations of the content of a single myth. In other words, one could argue conceivably for the existence of a single myth with a more or less standard form, portions of which have been used by biblical writers for particular programmatic aims.[17] The biblical sources cited by Hanson show evidence of this—they are literary masterpieces in which one can witness the encounter of poet, tradition, and cultural context. As mediators of tradition and creative innovators, the poets shaped and transmitted archaic material and provided it with an appropriate setting (historical, mythological, etc.). Moreover, through the intentionally engineered coalescence of cyclic and linear time, they made it possible for those who heard the oracles and other constructions to be reminded of the conflict raging continually between the forces of order and the powers of chaos. The socio-political environment for Israelites before and after the exile contributed to the formation of such a conceptualization. The Yahweh Speeches in Job, for example, suggest that unjust suffering and misfortune on the earthly plane are proof positive that cosmogonic conflict continues steadily. They also indicate that there are some manifestations of disorder that Yahweh himself is powerless to tame (Cross 1973:344-345). As audiences listened, for example, to Ezekiel's oracle against the Tyrian prince in 28:1-10, they may have drawn on their knowledge of the mythological battle between the highest of all gods (Yahweh or El) and a divine usurper who tried to take his throne. They may also have recognized and contemplated the similarities between Yahweh and El. Furthermore, they may have made the historical connection between the outcome of this mythological story, the timeless truth which it communicated about challenges to authority, and, perhaps, the implicit dangers of the institution of kingship (all kings, foreign and Israelite, being predisposed to excesses in the exercise of power). The recitation of any one of these poems may well have been perceived as a participatory reenactment of the central theme(s) of its constituent myth(s) in much the same way that the reading of any contemporary poem requires that those who hear enter the symbolic universe of the poet and engage her/his plot and character(s).

---

[17] Contextual redefinition is one of the tasks undertaken by artists. Literary artists can take an existing body of tradition and use it to construct new motifs and forms (oral and written) that reflect their agenda (political, theological, philosophical, etc.) and *Sitz im Leben*.

2.2.5 Hendel

In his treatment of Genesis 6:1-4 (1987b:13-26), Hendel focused primarily on that text's origin. He disagreed with Wellhausen and Gunkel, both of whom held it to be erratic and fragmentary in its present setting. He also disagreed with those who suggested that the Yahwist had suppressed more extensive mythological material than that which had been included. For him, the inclusion of Genesis 6:1-4 in the Primeval Cycle of Genesis 2-11 indicates that the Yahwist did not find the material objectionable and that the myth originated in Israel. Internal evidence suggested to him that the story has a purpose which extends beyond that of a simple etiology of the *npylym.* He was also highly critical of attempts like those of Hanson (1977) and Speiser (1964) to follow the lead of pseudepigraphic sources in deriving a rebellion-in-heaven pattern into which Genesis 6:1-4 may be placed. It is his contention that the discovery of the Hurrian Kumarbi cycle (*Kingship in Heaven, Song of Ullikummi, Myth of Illuyanka)* encouraged this kind of interpretation. Hendel found two problems with the method. First, the sons of god have not been conceptualized as rebels in Genesis 6:1-4. Second, there has been no clear condemnation of the sexual commingling of the gods and mortal women within the text. Furthermore, the gods themselves have received no punishment for this supposed crime; this has been reserved for humanity. Therefore, the connection of Genesis 6:1-4 to the revolt-in-heaven pattern has, for Hendel, been based on unconvincing conjecture. In his opinion, it was originally attached to the flood story, where it served as motivation for the flood. The Yahwist removed it from its original place in order to give the flood a motive rooted in moral theology—i.e., anger at humanity's evil (1987b:13-17).

Hendel also suggested that, somewhere in the continuum between Babylon and Greece, a myth originated that involved a connection between the birth of demigods and a deluge. This myth now survives only in fragments. He cited the Atraḫasis myth, the Greek tradition of the Trojan War, particularly that of Hesiodic origin (Hesiod's *Catalogue of Women*, fr. 204 M-W), the sacrifice of Prometheus and the birth of Pandora (*Works and Days* 53-105; *Theogony* 570-616), and the myth of five ages (*Works and Days* 53-105), in support of this thesis. The word *hēmitheoi* "demigods" occurs in Hesiod (myth of five ages and fr. 2044 M-W) and in Homer (*Iliad* 12.17-33, esp. 23). In the latter instance it occurs in a passage describing the destruction of the Achaean wall by flood. Hendel concluded from all of this that the Trojan War functions similarly to the Semitic tradition of the flood, and may have come to Greece by way of oral tradition from a Semitic provenance (1987b:17-20).

As far as the Nephilim (and related Rephaim and Anaqim) are concerned, Hendel submitted that their function in biblical tradition (Genesis 6:1-4, Num. 13:33, Deut. 2:11; 2:12; 20-33; 3:11, Joshua 11:21-22, 12:4-6; 13:12; 15:14, Judges 1:20, 2 Samuel 21:18-22=1 Chr. 20:4-8, and 1 Sam. 17) is to be destroyed by Israel's heroic figures and god. They are similar, in this regard, to heroes in the Greek tradition. Ezek. 32:27, a text of comparable tone describing the Nephilim as fallen warriors, was cited by Hendel in support of the proposal that the function of the Nephilim is to die. He concluded that the original motive for the flood was the destruction of the Nephilim. He also cited the Late Bronze Age as the period most likely to have witnessed the oral diffusion of this myth to Greece (1987b:20-23).

The major thrust of the flood tradition in Israelite thought according to Hendel was the elimination of hybrid life forms and the restoration of cosmic balance (hybrid forms threatening the equilibrium of the cosmos). He followed Mary Douglas, who has suggested that ancient Israel was preoccupied with dietary laws and kinship regulation, and that this excessive concern functioned to maintain categories established at the point of creation. Hendel proposed that a similar concern is in evidence in Genesis 6:1-4, and concluded that the Yahwist displaced Genesis 6:1-4 (and added the punishment of mankind in v. 3) so as to highlight human culpability in the deluge account. For him, this fit the overall pattern of boundary transgression found elsewhere in the Primeval Cycle (human and divine mixing in the tale of Adam and Eve, the human desire to be gods in Gen. 3:5, 22, the human desire to penetrate the heavens in Gen. 11:4, possible primordial violation of the incest taboo in Gen. 2:3, and the confusion of roles and overstepping of bounds evident in the Cain and Abel story), a pattern which he interpreted as dialectical in nature. Oppositions are generated and resolved in the midst of the evolution of human cognition and culture from the world of myth to that of the author's present context (1987b:23-26).

Hendel is correct in noting the continuity of flood tradition throughout the ancient Near East and in Greece. His identification of the overstepping of boundaries as an operational motif in the Primeval Cycle and his characterization of the Yahwist as a literary artist of considerable merit are also convincing. His criticism of the revolt-in-heaven hypothesis of Hanson (1977) is justified to an extent. However, it must be remembered that the mythological construct which Hendel proposes is just as conjectural as that of Hanson and others. Regardless of what one believes about Genesis 6:1-4, one thing remains troublesome for the interpreter—its brevity. A convincing hypothesis of any sort cannot rely on this passage as its focal point. Too much is left open to question and there is insufficient internal information to draw literary comparisons with Akkadian, Hurrian, Hebrew, or Greek sources because the basis of comparison in Genesis 6:1-4 is rather minimal. Although Hanson's use of a highly advanced form of the myth as a control is problematic, his approach is illuminating nonetheless because a discernible pattern is present in his control text. Hendel's reconstruction of an original myth and subsequent comparison of it to related traditions is equally problematic and instructive. Much of his argument rests on the presence of demigods as motivation for the flood. In the overall cycle of events dealing with the flood, the issue of demigods is confined to their brief mention in Gen. 6:1-4. Hendel relies heavily on the reconstruction of an Israelite reflex of a mythic pattern more completely attested elsewhere in the Mediterranean cultural continuum as the basis for his thesis. This method argues strongly against an Israelite origin rather than in favor of one. With regard to the diffusion of this mythological tradition in the larger Mediterranean world, Hendel's suggestion that the myth of the demigods' destruction by flood possibly originated in Semitic tradition and spread during the international era of the Late Bronze Age is quite attractive. However, it is equally possible that what this era witnessed amounted to a subsequent rather than an initial diffusion of the tradition. The existence of strikingly similar threads of tradition involving creation, the divine council, rebellion-in-heaven, and the deluge found throughout the region suggests that some of these may have been transmitted earlier than the Late Bronze Age. The point is that data and conclusions presented by Hendel invite further investigation and discussion.

2.3 Dissenting Opinions

2.3.1 Pope

Marvin Pope (1955) addressed the nature and location of El's abode and his status and significance in the Ugaritic texts. He concluded that El resided in a watery abyss in the underworld. His findings were based on the following (1955:61-81):[18]

---

[18] Pope uses the text numeration found in PRU. These sigla have not been retained in this summary of his position for the purpose of maintaining continuity with

1. The expressions *mbk nhrm* and *apq thmtm,* which suggest that El's home is subterranean and aqueous (in KTU 1.6 I 4-10; KTU 1.4 IV 20-24; KTU 1.2 III 4-6; KTU 1.3 IV 13-16; KTU 1.17 VI 46-51)

2. The use of the root *gly* (the proposed meaning of which is "to penetrate" a secret subterranean chamber), based on its use in KTU 1.16 VI 3-5, its general OT usage in connection with the uncovering of secret things and hidden places, and its specific usage in reference to underworld regions (as in 2 Sam. 22:16=Psalm 18:16; Job 12:22; and 38:16-17)

3. KTU 1.4 VIII 1-9 and KTU 1.5 V 11-16, which indicate that access to the netherworld must be gained by the lifting of mountains

4. The meaning of *ðd* and *qrš,* which Pope tentatively translated "domain" and "pavilion" respectively, but which he suggested, "with the utmost reserve" (1955:67) may have to do with coolness and, if so, would prove valuable (as an ancient counterpart) in understanding the history of the "refrigerium" (state of bliss experienced by the deceased)

5. KTU 1.2 I 19-20 in which El's location is said to be *tk ǵr ll*[19] "in the midst of Mt. Lil(?)," to which Mt. Lalapaduwa in the Hurrian *Song of Ullikummi* myth (which appears to have some connection with divine rule) and *ikunta luli* (a place name meaning "cool pond," where Kumarbi had a sexual encounter with a huge rock), in the *Kingship in Heaven* myth[20] may be compared

---

the treatment of Ugaritic material throughout this study. Instead, KTU numeration is followed.

[19] Pope has identified this Mt. Lil with Mt. Ṣapān in Isaiah 14:13-15, the OT designation (as received from Canaanite-Phoenician mythology) for the meeting place of the divine council.

[20] For Hittite mythology the translations of Goetze in ANET (120-126) have been consulted.

6. KTU 1.1 II 23 and KTU 1.1. III 21-25 which mention *ḫršn*, an underworld cosmic mountain next to sources of cosmic waters similar in essence to that found in Akkadian mythology

The earthly locus of El's cosmic abode, Pope identified with *Khirbet Afqa* in Syria—roughly twenty-three miles northeast of Beirut. It is situated at the source of the *Nahr Ibrāhīm* several miles away from lake *Birket el Yammūneh.* Pope proposed that the geographical setting fit most closely the description of El's abode. He also cited the tradition found in late classical mythology that associated Afqa with Adonis and Aphrodite and late Phoenician mythology which associated lake *el Yammūneh* with the amorous pursuit of Astarte by Tryphon. Moreover, he suggested that lake *el Yammūneh* may have been the site of the *hieros gamos* in KTU 1.23 and that it was the prototype of the myths and rites that were associated with *Afqa* well into the Common Era.

Pope suggested that El's exalted status is titulary and that he is either in the process of being displaced, or has already been displaced from his position as head of the pantheon. He cited the following evidence in support of this contention (1955:80-94):

1. KTU 1.12, in which El sets in motion a plot to rid himself of Baal, and laughs as the plot is initiated

2. KTU 1.2 IV, the battle between Baal and Yamm, in which the appearance of an indirect conflict between El and Baal is given

3. KTU 1.2 I, in which El is willing to hand over Baal to Yamm, an indication that no firm alliance exists between Baal and El

4. KTU 1.1 IV 24, in which El seems to commission Yamm to drive Baal from his throne, a plot similar to that found in the Hittite *Kingship in Heaven* and *Song of Ullikummi* texts.

5. KTU 1.1 V, which seems to indicate violence taking place between El and Baal (may be the episode mentioned by Cassuto[21] in which El is deposed by Ba^{c}l)

The testimony of Hurrian mythology (*Kingship in Heaven, Song of Ullikummi*), in which Kumarbi was deposed by the storm-god, and that of

[21] See Cassuto (1951:55).

Phoenician mythology in which Ouranos was deposed and castrated by Kronos (El) and Kronos was defeated (and castrated in some versions) by his son Zeus (Baᶜl-Hadad) provided for Pope added evidence of the motif in the ancient Near East. He suspected that the episode was actually found in KTU 1.1 V, but the text's fragmentary state prevented him from proving this decisively. He remained, however, untroubled by his adoption of the suggestion of Cassuto and Kapelrud that such an account should be reflected in the Ugaritic texts, and concluded that the demise of El at the hands of Baal provided the background against which El's status as reflected in most of the Baal Cycle should be understood. Pope also surmised that prior to his banishment, El ruled from "supernal regions, on his holy mountain" (1955:95), as indicated in KTU 1.2 I 19-31 and in KTU 1.6 VI 24-25.

Pope agreed with Morgenstern's conclusion that a single myth was the source of the mythology of deposed gods in the Greek myth of the Titans, OT, NT, the Book of Enoch, Isaiah 14:12-14, Psalm 82, Ezekiel 28:2-10, 12-19, the *Kingship in Heaven* text and *Song of Ullikummi* (both extant in Hittite), and the evidence of El's fallen state in Ugaritic mythology. However, for him, the myth, pre-Israelite in origin, involved not a revolt against El, but a revolt by him to regain sovereignty from Baal who had deposed him (1955:96-97). Pope suggested that El used Yamm to fight against Baal in the same manner that Kronos used the Titans to battle Zeus on his behalf, and in the same way that Ullikummi was used by Kumarbi to battle the storm god. El's plot, like the others, failed, and he remained in the underworld. The two poems found in Ezekiel 28:2-10, 12-19 respectively were taken by Pope to refer to the myth of El's failed attempt to regain his throne (1955:97-100). In addition, he described Isaiah 14:12-14 as "a theomachy or Titanomachy" (1955:103) similar to the versions in Hurrian and Greek, and deriving ultimately from the same background as the poems in Ezekiel 28, in which El and his champion Yamm are exiled to the underworld after their defeat by Baal.

Cross (1974a:245-253) differs markedly with Pope's interpretation of El's status in the lore of Ugarit, and his characterization of El as the lusty patriarch of the divine council is convincing.[22] His study raises serious doubt about Pope's characterization of El as a forcibly retired god. Pope's contention that a revolt by El to regain his sovereign prerogatives from

---

[22] Cf. Mullen's summary of the basic weaknesses in Pope's treatment of El (1980:92-110).

Baal, found perhaps in KTU 1.1, provides the mythological background against which Isaiah 14, Psalm 82, and Ezekiel 28 should be understood is less than convincing. More will be said regarding specific points at which the present author disagrees with Pope in the exegesis of these texts.[23] The fundamental problem with Pope's reconstruction is that he seems to have based both his characterization of the myth of El's dethronement and his understanding of El's status at Ugarit largely on the Hurrian Kumarbi mythology and Greek Kronos lore.

2.3.2 Wilson

Wilson (1987:211-218) attempted to clarify some of the obscurities in Ezekiel 28 which Pope's mythologically-based analysis left unresolved. He supported, in principle, Pope's interpretation of the El material at Ugarit and found his treatment of Ezekiel 28 on firmer ground than attempts made by other scholars whose conclusions are based on reconstructed mythological evidence.[24] Pope's interpretation of Ezekiel 28 was more acceptable for him because it was based on a myth which, if not actual, could at least be plausibly reconstructed from Ugaritic sources (1987:214). While having admitted undeniable mythological influence on the oracles in Ezekiel 28, he found, nonetheless, that no single approach was satisfactory in addressing all of the text's interpretive problems. Of these, the so-called editorial additions proved to be the most intriguing for him and he posited that by understanding these secondary additions as essentially Israelite in origin (alluding to events best understood in an Israelite context) a more satisfactory solution could be found to many of the interpretive cruxes in the text. Among these secondary additions he listed 28:3-5, 28:13 (the list of gems), 28:16, 18a (references to trade as the source of the ruler's sin), 28:19 (the king as the defiler of his own sanctuaries, and the fire of judgment), and 28:12, 17 (wisdom insertions similar in tone and originating from the hand which inserted 28:3-5). Wilson concluded that 28:1-10 and 28:11-19 originally had different functions. 28:1-10 was initially an oracle against a Tyrian prince whose pride led him to suppose that he was a god. The wisdom addition of vss. 3-5 modified the intent of the oracle, making it appropriate for an Israelite setting and reminded the leaders of Israel that their

---

[23] It should also be noted that the myth of El's dethronement as reconstructed by Pope is at variance with Morgenstern's reconstruction of the ancient prototype of the Satan myth.

[24] He has cited a number of these studies on p. 213, notes 10 and 11.

kings were not immune to such inappropriate presumption. He also concluded that 28:11-19 need not be treated as a composition laced with secondary additions. Most of these could be treated as an integral part of its original form. The dirge, whose original form is largely preserved by MT, dealt largely with the Israelite High Priest thinly veiled as the Tyrian king. The priesthood is charged therein with defiling the temple and thereby drawing Yahweh's wrath on both the priesthood (which was exiled) and the temple (which was destroyed). For Wilson, it did not occupy its present location in the Ezekielian corpus. The dualistic thrust of the original dirge was lost in the process of transmission and later editors saw only its obvious connection with a Tyrian king. It was for this reason that they attached it to an authentic oracle against another Tyrian leader. Secondary editorial work may have then taken place to make the two compositions more compatible in their new literary environment.

Wilson's conclusion that 28:1-10 and 28:11-19 had different functions originally is intriguing but ultimately unconvincing. In form and function, both are concerned with the usurpation of prerogative which rightfully belongs to the chief administrative deity. There is also no reason to suppose that 28:3-5 is a wisdom addition, the intention of which is to make the oracle palatable to an Israelite audience. El's wisdom is well known from Ugaritic lore. Furthermore, the oracle, with or without vss. 3-5, would convey to any socially aware, literate, and urbane sixth-century individual or group, that no ruler is immune from divine judgment should such ruler be found guilty of abrogating divine rights. Wilson's argument that 28:11-19 need not be treated as a composition laced with secondary additions is well-founded and his suggestion that the main character in the dirge is the Israelite High Priest, veiled thinly as the King of Tyre, is also intriguing. However, within a sixth-century socio-cultural and religious context, other suggestions are also plausible.

2.4 Additional Contributions

2.4.1 Grelot

Grelot (1956:18-48) sought to identify Athtar and to describe his relationship to the mythological program of Isaiah 14:12-15. He examined Greek, Hebrew, and Ugaritic texts in an attempt to solve some of the more vexing problems surrounding this god. His goal was to move beyond the inconclusive findings of Gunkel, Gray (who proposed that *hyll bn šḥr* in Isaiah 14 is the hero of an astral myth with whom the Tyrant of Babylon is partially compared and identified), Skinner (who saw evidence in it of a Babylonian astral myth), and others (1956:18-19). Grelot concluded that the Ugaritic texts reflect a Canaanite prototype of the Athtar myth found at Ugarit which has also spread to Greece and Israel. His examination of the Greek material (*Odyssey* 23:246 and Hesiod's *Theogony* 986ff.) led him to suggest that *hyll bn šḥr* is the same personage as Phaeton, son of Eos. Both reflect the deification of the morning star, Venus. The translation of the divine name in the Old Greek translation of Isaiah 14:12 (*heōsphoros*), the Vulgate (*Lucifer*), and the paraphrase of the Targum support this identification (1956:30). As for the prototype of the myth, he proposed that it was transmitted (from Phoenicia) to the Greek world where it splintered, developed several alloforms, and was imitated by the biblical writers—cf. Isaiah 14 and Ezekiel 28 (1956:32).

Grelot also suggested that at Ugarit the exploits of Athtar occupy but a minor part in the overall mythological scheme. In addition, there is no evidence whatsoever of his fall, though it is attested in Isaiah 14. Evidence of his ambition and his excess, however, have been preserved (1956:42). Grelot concluded that the biblical writers' attitude to this mythological material was critical and selective in that they rejected elements at variance with Israel's faith as they perceived it, and accepted elements which were not contradictory to Israelite faith as they understood it. As a result, the moral lesson of the Phaeton and *hyll* myths is identical. In both, hubris assumed tragic proportions. With regard to the relationship between Athtar and Satan, Grelot proposed that at some point in the history of religion, Athtar/*hyll bn šḥr* became the poetic prototype of the fallen angel who carried the name Lucifer in Christian tradition (1949:48).

Grelot's Athtar = *hyll bn šḥr* identification is convincing. His identification of the two with Phaeton is questionable. More research is needed to corroborate data outside of the immediate Syro-Palestinian area before conclusions of this sort may be drawn. Grelot's assertion that *hll* in KTU 1.24 is not to be identified with the *hyll bn šḥr* of Isaiah 14 also requires further investigation.[25]

[25] It is quite possible that this *hll* is to be identified with both the *hyll* of Is. 14:12 and Athtar of Ugarit. If so, this text could represent one of two stages in the historical development of Athtar theology. It could represent either a point in time when the names Athtar and *hll* were used interchangeably, or a point in time when the name *hll* became an independent hypostasis with its own integrity. One suspects that the for-

Finally, Grelot has argued convincingly for an Athtar/*hyll bn šḥr* identification and his effort to establish a prototype for the story of his fall from early sources is laudable. However, if one is ever to recover the Semitic prototype of the myth, the majority of primary data used in the reconstructive process must come from a Semitic provenance.

2.4.2 McKay

Another intriguing proposal was made by McKay (1970:463-464). He accepted Grelot's conclusion that there existed a connection between *hyll* and Phaeton because a close similarity could be noted between Šaḥar, the parent of *hyll*, and Eos, parent of Phaeton (1970:20). He rejected, however, the possibility of any connection between Athtar and Athirat and *hyll* and Šaḥar, although he agreed that they may have had similar aspects (1970:463). He suggested that the Greek Phaeton Myth entered Israel through the mediation of Phoenicia and proposed a five-part solution to the problem. First, in pre-classical Greece, Phaeton son of Eos and Cephalus became confounded with Heosphoros (the morning star) son of Eos and Astraios. He also became confused with the solar child who attempted to drive the chariot of his father across the sky. Second, in the Heroic Age, the Phaeton myth entered Syria-Palestine, where the myth of Athtar son of Athirat and his failure to occupy Baal's throne already existed. Third, because of similarities between Phaeton and Athtar, the two myths became confused and Phaeton's attempt to scale the heavens was translated in terms of an attempt to occupy the throne of the chief deity. Fourth, the names Phaeton and Eos were never modified—instead they were simply translated "because they corresponded so well with the astral phenomenon of Venus as the dawn star which never reaches the summit of heaven but is always compelled to return to earth as a 'weakling above the nations,' eventually descending below the horizon into Sheol" (1970:463). Finally, the goddess Šaḥar became firmly established in Hebrew mythology, after *šḥr* came to be used as a masculine noun signifying "dawn." The myth of her son being remembered, she retained some features of Greek Eos, but in Biblical Hebrew only the masculine noun for "dawn" remained and the image as dawn goddess was only a poetic symbol representing no active cultus. The exact reason for this is not known. It is possible that the noun enjoyed

---

mer is more likely the case than the latter. Unfortunately without additional primary evidence this must remain an untested hypothesis.

wider usage. This process resulted in the alteration of the Greek myth so that it assumed its present form in Isaiah 14:12-15.

McKay's suggested confusion between Phaeton and Athtar mythology does not agree with what is known of the transmission process of cycles of tradition. To propose that the guardians of tradition could make such a major mistake would be to question their sophistication and competence. The choice of pre-classical Greece as a starting point for his investigation is one that is also questionable. Furthermore, Šaḥar is masculine in Ugaritic (UT:489) and Hebrew (BDB:1007).[26] There is no evidence from these languages that this god was ever understood as female.

2.4.3 Craigie

Craigie (1973:223-225) sought a moderate approach. He argued in favor of Greek borrowing from the ancient Near East and saw this as more likely than the reverse. He was also of the opinion that the primary evidence supported the idea that Greek and Hebrew authors adapted an earlier Athtar myth—differences in regional renditions being the result of poetic license.

This proposal is much more attractive than McKay's, though one need not see poetic license as a major force in the regional adaptation of the myth. It can be attributed to conscious programmatic aims of a socio-political, religious, or ideological nature.

2.5 Summary

The foregoing review of scholarship has demonstrated the applicability of several *maxims*. First, exegesis and synthesis are complementary processes. The relationship between the two is seen clearly in Morgenstern (1939), Pope (1955), Hendel (1987), Grelot (1949), and McKay (1970). One might conceivably argue that sources should be allowed to speak for themselves without the imposition of external interpretive frameworks. However, all analytical work—even exegesis—is influenced by the paradigms of the researcher.

Second, it is important to establish reliable controls when conducting comparative research on culture, literature, or folklore. Wilson (1987) has accomplished this by limiting his discussion to the so-called secondary additions in Ezekiel 28 and Hanson (1977) has done likewise by isolating a

---

[26] Compare also Akkadian *šēru* A ($CAD^{17(II)}$:331-335) and Old South Arabian *sḥr* (see the reference in UT:489 under the *šḥr* entry and SIMB:Texts 550 and 664).

developed thematic and structural pattern with a definable spatio-temporal focus that can be used in assessing related materials of early or late date. Without a set of controls, interpretation, comparison, and reconstruction become highly speculative.

Third, the particularist and comparative perspectives must be held in creative tension when examining folklore. Craigie (1973) sought a *via media* in the debate about the point of origin of the Athtar myth and proposed a solution which would account for the uniqueness of alloforms in Greece, Ugarit, and Israel. Albright (1968), Clifford (1972), and Mullen (1980) have made careful use of Canaanite parallels in the reconstruction of the myth of the revolt against Yahweh/El and in the analysis of the texts that contain its alleged reflexes. Until more is known about localized manifestations of this myth (i.e., those found in Greek, Hittite, Ugaritic, and Hebrew sources respectively), it will be difficult to justify anything more than tentative movement from simple comparison to the type of synthesis attempted by Craigie. This is due, in large part, to our incomplete knowledge of the dynamics of cultural exchange between Israel and its Mediterranean neighbors. In the meantime, studies like those of Albright, Clifford, and Mullen, which help to define Israel's place within its more immediate Canaanite environment, should be undertaken to continue the dialogue about the shape that the myth may have assumed in Israel and Canaan respectively. For this reason, a grand synthesis of the disparate related materials in Greek, Rabbinic, pseudepigraphic, and early Christian sources seems less than judicious at this stage. Instead, focusing attention on a more discrete textual corpus —e.g., one composed of Ugaritic and Hebrew texts—is a more reasonable alternative.

Fourth, research on myth in the ancient Near East should be treated as a holistic ethnological enterprise. In addition to the basic philological and textual work already at home in biblical and cognate studies, a larger disciplinary framework is needed so that the forces that cause the generation, adaptation, and transmission of folklore can be appreciated. It is hoped that this study will lay a foundation that will make such efforts possible in the future.

At this point a few words about the proposals of Morgenstern and Albright are in order. Morgenstern's theory is credible and worth further exploration. The delimitation of the progenitor of CR^{A} (Proto-CR^{A} hereafter)—the focal point of the remainder of this study—is clearly a worthwhile endeavor. Unlike its more fully developed reflexes in Talmudic-Midrashic sources, textual evidence suggests that its basic outline described a revolt against the high god of the Syro-Palestinian pantheon, and that the rebel was a member of that pantheon. The Athtar = *hyll* theory of Albright and his students is equally credible. However, in order to analyze either of these proposals further, Ugaritic evidence about Athtar must be gathered and compared to data concerning *hyll* in Isaiah 14 and all other purported reflexes of CR^{A} must be assembled, analyzed, and critiqued (re., their general content and overall value as reflexes of Proto-CR^{A}). Such is also necessary for the remaining tasks of this study to be completed—i.e., consideration of the possibility that Athtar is the divine antihero of Proto-CR^{A}, a close reading of a selected sample of Hebrew and Ugaritic texts that have informed discussion about the myth, a reassessment of the value of these texts as witnesses to the myth, and a reconstruction of Proto-CR^{A} based on the best evidence available.

CHAPTER THREE

CONCORDANCE OF TEXTUAL EVIDENCE

The texts cited by Morgenstern and others as sources are quite numerous and represent a variety of cultural settings and genres. Those coming from the Hebrew Bible, Apocrypha, and Pseudepigrapha are often fragmentary and difficult to interpret. Furthermore, arriving at terms to describe the content of these texts relative to Morgenstern's three myths (i.e., CC, CR^A, and CR^B) is equally troublesome. As mentioned above, *recension, reflex, allusion, adaptation,* and *version,* suggest themselves as possible descriptives. The major difficulty with each of them is that these myths have no single fixed form that could be used in establishing recensional or other relationships. For this reason, the term *reflex* seems most appropriate in this context since the others have more precise meanings in textual criticism. In the pages that follow, a reflex is best understood as *a purported literary witness to a hypothetically reconstructed myth.*

The following is a list of biblical and other texts thought to contain reflexes of CC, CR^A, and CR^B. It should be treated as a tentative *sampling universe.* It is a composite list consisting of texts gathered from the studies reviewed in the previous section, suggestions made by F. M. Cross, Jr. in personal communications, passages recommended by independent scholars with whom portions of this study have been shared since 1989, and texts added by the author.[27] The editorial notes in LOJ, APOT, and $OTP^{1\,\&\,2}$ have also been consulted for additional reflexes.

For the sake of simplicity and as a hypothetical starting point, CC, CR^A, and CR^B, as outlined by Morgenstern, are used exclusively as theoretical referents in the section marked Myth-Code(s) for most entries.[28]

[27] Neither this list, nor that of any of the other scholars mentioned, can claim to be exhaustive. The nature of the enterprise mitigates against this. This project has many of the features of the *detective story* genre in popular American literature. A theory has been proposed, a small amount of preliminary work has been done, and a few tantalizing suggestions have been made by several investigators. At this stage in the process, my principal research tasks consist of: (1) sifting through what others have said and (2) searching the Hebrew Bible and other sources for additional reflexes that may have been overlooked.

[28] My assessment of the texts' mythological content is usually (though not always) in agreement with that of Morgenstern. Again, the data in this chart should not be

Sources that (in the author's opinion) do not seem to qualify as reflexes of one of these three myths are designated as unclear. Information concerning mythological content[29] and semiotic mode has also been provided. Question marks following a code indicate that there is some aspect of classification that remains unclear. A question mark without an accompanying code indicates that a final decision about classification could not be reached by the author.

3.1 Anatolian Sources

Text	*Kingship in Heaven*
Myth—Code(s)	Unclear
Semiotic Mode	Other
Text	*Myth of Illuyanka* (Older version)
Myth—Code(s)	Unclear
Semiotic Mode	Anthropomorphic, Zoomorphic
Text	*Song of Ullikummi*
Myth—Code(s)	Unclear
Semiotic Mode	Anthropomorphic, Other

3.2 Sumero-Akkadian Sources

Text	*Adapa*
Myth—Code(s)	Unclear
Semiotic Mode	Zoomorphic (?), Anthropomorphic
Text	*Atraḫasis*
Myth—Code(s)	Unclear
Semiotic Mode	Other

understood as fixed and immutable. The chart represents: (1) a starting point for further examination of CC, CR^A, and CR^B; (2) a preliminary corpus of texts for attempting to reconstruct these myths and their progenitors; and (3) a frame of reference for assessing the value of other alleged reflexes.

[29]In some instances, my assessment of mythological content disagrees with that of the authors cited in the review of scholarship.

Text	*Enūma Eliš*
Myth—Code(s)	Unclear
Semiotic Mode	Other

Text	*Enūma Eliš* (Late Astral Version)
Myth—Code(s)	Unclear
Semiotic Mode	Astral

Text	*Enki and Ninmaḫ* (On the Creation of Humans)
Myth—Code(s)	Unclear
Semiotic Mode	Other

Text	*Ninurta vs. Kur*
Myth—Code(s)	Unclear
Semiotic Mode	Zoomorphic, Other

Text	*Descent of Inanna*
Myth—Code(s)	Unclear
Semiotic Mode	Astral, Other

Text	*Ištar's Descent*
Myth—Code(s)	Unclear
Semiotic Mode	Astral, Other

3.3 Ugaritic Sources

Text	KTU 1.2 III 12-24
Myth—Code(s)	Unclear
Semiotic Mode	Polysemous

Text	KTU 1.6 I 43-67
Myth—Code(s)	Unclear
Semiotic Mode	Polysemous

Text	KTU 1.23.8-11, 52-56, 61-64
Myth—Code(s)	Unclear
Semiotic Mode	Astral (?)

Text	KTU 1.24.24-30
Myth—Code(s)	Unclear
Semiotic Mode	Astral (?)
Text	KTU 1.83.8-10
Myth—Code(s)	Unclear
Semiotic Mode	Zoomorphic

3.4 Hebrew Bible

Text	Genesis 1:26-27; 2:7
Myth—Code(s)	CR^{A} (?), CR^{B} (?)
Semiotic Mode	Other
Text	Genesis 2:4b-4:26
Myth—Code(s)	CR^{A}, CR^{B}
Semiotic Mode	Anthropomorphic
Text	Genesis 6:1-4
Myth—Code(s)	CC, CR^{A}, CR^{B}
Semiotic Mode	Anthropomorphic
Text	Numbers 13:33
Myth—Code(s)	CC(?)
Semiotic Mode	Anthropomorphic
Text	Numbers 16:1-35
Myth—Code(s)	CR^{A}(?)
Semiotic Mode	Anthropomorphic
Text	Isaiah 14:1-20
Myth—Code(s)	CR^{A}
Semiotic Mode	Anthropomorphic, Astral
Text	Isaiah 24:21-23
Myth—Code(s)	CR^{A}(?)
Semiotic Mode	Astral

Text	Isaiah 27:1
Myth—Code(s)	(?)
Semiotic Mode	Zoomorphic

Text	Isaiah 51:9
Myth—Code(s)	(?)
Semiotic Mode	Zoomorphic

Text	Ezekiel 26:17-21
Myth—Code(s)	(?)
Semiotic Mode	Other

Text	Ezekiel 28:1-10
Myth—Code(s)	CR^{A}
Semiotic Mode	Anthropomorphic

Text	Ezekiel 28:11-19
Myth—Code(s)	CR^{A}
Semiotic Mode	Anthropomorphic, Astral

Text	Ezekiel 29:3-4
Myth—Code(s)	(?)
Semiotic Mode	Anthropomorphic, Zoomorphic

Text	Ezekiel 32:2-8
Myth—Code(s)	(?)
Semiotic Mode	Zoomorphic

Text	Ezekiel 38:4
Myth—Code(s)	(?)
Semiotic Mode	Anthropomorphic (?)

Text	Obadiah 3-4
Myth—Code(s)	CR^{A} (?)
Semiotic Mode	Astral

Text	Zephaniah 3:2-3
Myth—Code(s)	CR^{A} (?)
Semiotic Mode	Anthropomorphic (?), Zoomorphic

Text	Zechariah 3:1-2
Myth—Code(s)	CR^A (?), CR^B (?)
Semiotic Mode	Anthropomorphic, Astral (?)
Text	Psalm 8:6
Myth—Code(s)	(?)
Semiotic Mode	Anthropomorphic, Astral
Text	Psalm 68:21-23
Myth—Code(s)	(?)
Semiotic Mode	(?)
Text	Psalm 74:12-17
Myth—Code(s)	CR^A (?)
Semiotic Mode	Zoomorphic, Anthropomorphic
Text	Psalm 82
Myth—Code(s)	CR^A (?)
Semiotic Mode	Anthropomorphic, Astral
Text	Job 4:18
Myth—Code(s)	CR^A(?), CR^B(?)
Semiotic Mode	Other
Text	Job 15:15
Myth—Code(s)	CR^A(?), CR^B(?)
Semiotic Mode	Astral
Text	Job 22:12
Myth—Code(s)	CR^A (?)
Semiotic Mode	Astral
Text	Job 28:5-6
Myth—Code(s)	CR^A(?), CR^B(?)
Semiotic Mode	Other, Astral
Text	Job 38:1-38
Myth—Code(s)	CR^A
Semiotic Mode	Astral

Text	Job 40:25-41:34
Myth—Code(s)	(?)
Semiotic Mode	Zoomorphic
Text	Daniel 8:10-12
Myth—Code(s)	CR^{A} (?)
Semiotic Mode	Astral
Text	Daniel 11:11, 21, 36-39, 45; 12:1
Myth—Code(s)	CR^{A}
Semiotic Mode	Anthropomorphic, Astral

3.5 Apocrypha

Text	3 Maccabees 2:4
Myth—Code(s)	CC
Semiotic Mode	Anthropomorphic
Text	Judith 16:7
Myth—Code(s)	CC(?)
Semiotic Mode	Anthropomorphic, Astral
Text	Sirach 16:7
Myth—Code(s)	CR^{A}
Semiotic Mode	Anthropomorphic
Text	Wisdom of Solomon 2:24
Myth—Code(s)	CR^{B} (?)
Semiotic Mode	Other
Text	Wisd. of Solomon 14:6
Myth—Code(s)	CC (?)
Semiotic Mode	Anthropomorphic
Text	1 Baruch 3:26ff.
Myth—Code(s)	CC
Semiotic Mode	Anthropomorphic

3.6 Pseudepigrapha

Text	Jubilees 4:14-15, 22; 5:1-19
Myth—Code(s)	CC
Semiotic Mode	Anthropomorphic
Text	Life of Adam & Eve 9:1
Myth—Code(s)	CR^{A} (?)
Semiotic Mode	Astral
Text	Life of Adam & Eve 13:1-16:1
Myth—Code(s)	CR^{A}, CR^{B}
Semiotic Mode	Anthropomorphic, Astral
Text	1 Enoch 6-16
Myth—Code(s)	CC
Semiotic Mode	Anthropomorphic
Text	1 Enoch 19
Myth—Code(s)	CC
Semiotic Mode	Anthropomorphic
Text	1 Enoch 39:1
Myth—Code(s)	CC
Semiotic Mode	Anthropomorphic
Text	1 Enoch 64
Myth—Code(s)	CC
Semiotic Mode	Anthropomorphic
Text	1 Enoch 69
Myth—Code(s)	CC
Semiotic Mode	Anthropomorphic, Astral
Text	1 Enoch 86:1
Myth—Code(s)	CR^{A}
Semiotic Mode	Astral
Text	1 Enoch 86:2-6
Myth—Code(s)	CC
Semiotic Mode	Astral, Zoomorphic

Text	1 Enoch 88
Myth—Code(s)	CR^{B}
Semiotic Mode	Astral, Zoomorphic
Text	1 Enoch 90:20-21
Myth—Code(s)	CR^{B}
Semiotic Mode	Astral, Zoomorphic
Text	Test. of Reuben 5:6-7
Myth—Code(s)	CC
Semiotic Mode	Anthropomorphic
Text	Test. of Naphtali 3:5
Myth—Code(s)	CC
Semiotic Mode	Anthropomorphic
Text	Testament of Benjamin 3:4
Myth—Code(s)	CR^{A}(?), CR^{B}(?)
Semiotic Mode	Anthropomorphic (?)
Text	2 Enoch 7
Myth—Code(s)	CC
Semiotic Mode	Anthropomorphic
Text	2 Enoch 18:1-6
Myth—Code(s)	CR^{B}. CC
Semiotic Mode	Anthropomorphic
Text	2 Enoch 29:4-5
Myth—Code(s)	CR^{A}, CR^{B} (?)
Semiotic Mode	Astral, Zoomorphic
Text	2 Enoch 31:3
Myth—Code(s)	CR^{A} (?)
Semiotic Mode	Anthropomorphic
Text	2 Baruch 56:12-15
Myth—Code(s)	CC
Semiotic Mode	Anthropomorphic

Text	Ascension of Isaiah 4:2; 10:29
Myth—Code(s)	CR^{A}(?), CR^{B}(?)
Semiotic Mode	Anthropomorphic (?)
Text	Apocalypse of Sedrach 5
Myth—Code(s)	CR^{B}
Semiotic Mode	Anthropomorphic

3.7 New Testament

Text	Matthew 11:21-24
Myth—Code(s)	CR^{A} (?)
Semiotic Mode	Astral (?)
Text	Luke 10:13-15
Myth—Code(s)	CR^{A} (?)
Semiotic Mode	Astral (?)
Text	Luke 10:18
Myth—Code(s)	CR^{A}
Semiotic Mode	Astral
Text	John 12:31
Myth—Code(s)	CR^{A} (?), CR^{B} (?)
Semiotic Mode	Other
Text	2 Corinthians 11:14
Myth—Code(s)	CR^{A} (?)
Semiotic Mode	Astral
Text	Ephesians 2:2; 6:12
Myth—Code(s)	CR^{B} (?)
Semiotic Mode	Astral (?)
Text[30]	2 Thessalonians 2:2-12
Myth—Code(s)	CR^{A}(?)
Semiotic Mode	Anthropomorphic, Astral

---

[30] This text was suggested to me by Prof. Karl Donfried of the Religion Department, Smith College, Northampton, MA.

Text	Hebrews 1:6-7
Myth—Code(s)	CR^B
Semiotic Mode	Astral, Anthropomorphic
Text	2 Peter 2:4
Myth—Code(s)	CR^A (?), CR^B (?)
Semiotic Mode	Anthropomorphic
Text	Jude 6
Myth—Code(s)	CR^A (?), CR^B (?)
Semiotic Mode	Other
Text	Jude 9
Myth—Code(s)	CR^A (?), CR^B (?)
Semiotic Mode	Other
Text	Revelation 12:7-9
Myth—Code(s)	CR^A
Semiotic Mode	Anthropomorphic
Text	Revelation 20:1-10
Myth—Code(s)	CR^A (?), CR^B (?)
Semiotic Mode	Zoomorphic

3.8 New Testament Apocrypha

Text	*Questions of Bartholomew* 4.25-60
Myth—Code(s)	CR^B
Semiotic Mode	Other

3.9 Apostolic Fathers

Text	Justin Martyr, *Dialogue* 79
Myth—Code(s)	CR^A (?)
Semiotic Mode	Other
Text	Justin Martyr, *Dialogue* 124
Myth—Code(s)	CR^B (?)
Semiotic Mode	Zoomorphic

Text	Justin Martyr, *Apology* 1.5, 2.5
Myth—Code(s)	CC
Semiotic Mode	Other
Text	Irenaeus, Against Heresies 4.40.3
Myth—Code(s)	CR^{B}
Semiotic Mode	Anthropomorphic, Other

3.10 Rabbinic Sources[31]

Text	*Bereshit Rabbati*
Myth—Code(s)	CR^{B}
Semiotic Mode	Anthropomorphic
Text	*Targum Job* 28:7
Myth—Code(s)	CR^{A} (?)
Semiotic Mode	Anthropomorphic, Other
Text	*Alphabetot* 93-94
Myth—Code(s)	CR^{A}
Semiotic Mode	Anthropomorphic
Text	*Tehillim* 82, 369
Myth—Code(s)	CR^{A}
Semiotic Mode	Anthropomorphic (?)
Text	*2 Alphabet of Ben Sira* 32a
Myth—Code(s)	CR^{A} (?)
Semiotic Mode	Other, Anthropomorphic
Text	Sode Raza in *Yalkut Reubeni*, Gen 1:27
Myth—Code(s)	CR^{A} (?)
Semiotic Mode	Anthropomorphic (?)

---

[31] Most of the texts in this section are cited and briefly summarized in LOJ^{5}:70-71, 84-85, 153). The only exception is Tuf. haarez which is cited and translated in $APOT^{2}$:447. Decisions concerning the appropriate myth code and semiotic mode have been based on the information provided in LOJ^{5} and $APOT^{2}$.

Text	*Midrash Aggada* Gen 5:18
Myth—Code(s)	CC
Semiotic Mode	Other (?)

Text	*Aggadat Bereshit*, Introduction 37
Myth—Code(s)	CC
Semiotic Mode	Other (?)

Text	*Tuf. haarez* f.9.2
Myth—Code(s)	CR^A(?), CR^B(?)
Semiotic Mode	Anthropomorphic (?)

3.11 Other Ante-Nicene & Post-Nicene Christian Sources

Text	Pseudo-Clementines, *Homilies* 7.13
Myth—Code(s)	CR^A (?)
Semiotic Mode	Astral (?)

Text	Pseudo-Clementines, *Homilies* 8.11-15
Myth—Code(s)	CC
Semiotic Mode	Anthropomorphic, Astral, Zoomorphic, Other

Text	Commodian, *Instruct.* 3
Myth—Code(s)	CC
Semiotic Mode	Other

Text	Clement of Alexandria, *Stromata* 5.1.10
Myth—Code(s)	CC
Semiotic Mode	Anthropomorphic, Other

Text	Tertullian, *De virginibus velandis* 7
Myth—Code(s)	CC
Semiotic Mode	Anthropomorphic, Other

Text	Tertullian, *De idololatria* 9
Myth—Code(s)	CC
Semiotic Mode	Other

Text — Tertullian, *De anima* 54
Myth—Code(s) — CR^{A}(?), CR^{B}(?)
Semiotic Mode — Other

Text — Tertullian, *Adversus Marcionem* 5.18
Myth—Code(s) — CC
Semiotic Mode — Other

Text — Tertullian, *De patientia*
Myth—Code(s) — CR^{A} (?), CR^{B} (?)
Semiotic Mode — Anthropomorphic, Other

Text — Lactantius, *Divinae institutiones* 2.14-15
Myth—Code(s) — CC
Semiotic Mode — Other

Text — Augustine, *De civitate Dei* 15.23
Myth—Code(s) — CC
Semiotic Mode — Anthropomorphic

Text — Augustine, *De Genesi ad litteram* 11.18
Myth—Code(s) — CR^{A} (?)
Semiotic Mode — Other

Text — Eusebius, *Praep. evang.* 1.10.1-42
Myth—Code(s) — Unclear
Semiotic Mode — Other

3.12 Classical Greek Sources

Text — Hesiod, *Works and Days* 42-105
Myth—Code(s) — Unclear
Semiotic Mode — Polysemous

Text — Hesiod, *Theogony*
Myth—Code(s) — Unclear
Semiotic Mode — Polysemous

Text	Aeschylus, *Prometheus Bound*
Myth—Code(s)	Unclear
Semiotic Mode	Polysemous

3.13 Roman Sources

Text	Lucan, *De Bello Civili* 9.1-5
Myth—Code(s)	CR^{A}(?), CR^{B}(?)
Semiotic Mode	Astral (?), Anthropomorphic (?)
Text	Ovid, *Metamorphoses* 1.750-2.400; 4.245;
Myth—Code(s)	Unclear
Semiotic Mode	Astral
Text	15.371-405
Myth—Code(s)	Unclear
Semiotic Mode	Zoomorphic

3.14 Hellenistic Jewish Sources

Text	Philo, *De Gigantibus*
Myth—Code(s)	CC, CR^{B} (?)
Semiotic Mode	Anthropomorphic, Astral
Text	Josephus, *Antiquities* 1.3.1
Myth—Code(s)	CC
Semiotic Mode	Anthropomorphic
Text	Josephus, *Antiquities* 1.1.4
Myth—Code(s)	CR^{B}(?)
Semiotic Mode	Astral

3.15 Qur᾽ān

Text	Suras 2:33-34; 7:11-18; 15:27-44; 17:61-65; 18:50-53; 20:116-127; 38:71-85
Myth—Code(s)	CR^{B}
Semiotic Mode	Other

CHAPTER FOUR

RATIONALE FOR SELECTED SAMPLE

The principal objectives of the remainder of this study are to examine selected literary reflexes of Morgenstern's CR^A, to test Albright's theory that *hyll bn šḥr* in Isaiah 14 is to be identified with the god Athtar, to consider the possibility that Athtar is the divine anti-hero in the progenitor of CR^A (hereafter Proto-CR^A), to offer a translation and close reading of a selected sample of Ugaritic and Hebrew reflexes of Proto-CR^A, to reassess the value of these texts as reflexes of this myth, and to provide a reconstruction of Proto-CR^A based on the reflexes selected.

In light of these objectives, the following texts have been chosen for translation, analysis, and close reading: KTU 1.2 III 12-24; KTU 1.6 I 42-6; KTU 1.23.8-9, 57; KTU 1.24.24-30; Genesis 6:1-4; Isaiah 14:1-20; Ezekiel 28:1-10; Ezekiel 28:11-19; Psalm 82; Job 38:1-38; and Daniel 11:11, 21, 36-39, 45; 12:1-3.

All Ugaritic texts providing definitive or purported data about Athtar have been included. Biblical texts were chosen based on their ability to meet one or more of the following criteria: (1) frequent citation in secondary literature (particularly in the Albright-Cross lineage) as a possible reflex; (2) the presence of motifs and/or characters that bear resemblance to Athtar; (3) the description of circumstances that are suggestive of an attack against Yahweh or Canaanite El; (4) reference made to the *npylym* in which their nature appears to be non-human; and (5) presence of a sufficient literary context within which to interpret the text. Taken together, these texts contain the best available evidence for a reconstruction of Proto-CR^A.

Texts cited in sections 3.5—3.15 of the concordance almost certainly contain some traces of older traditions.[32] A closer examination of them must be left to future studies that can address both their folkloristic content and other critical issues that affect their interpretation. The texts in sections 3.1—3.2 contain traditions similar to those found in biblical and Ugaritic sources. Examination of these must also be postponed for the present.

---

[32] Any selection of texts will be somewhat subjective. Others (e.g., Isaiah 24:21-23) could have been included but these contain additional mythological motifs that deserve focused studies of their own.

CHAPTER FIVE

ATHTAR—AN OVERVIEW

Several studies have attempted to reconcile the varied and conflicting data about the Semitic god Athtar. Of these, the examinations of Gray (1949, 1965), Gaster (1950), Caquot (1956), Dahood (1958), Roberts (1972) Heimpel (1982), and Smith (1994, 1995) deserve mention. A brief review of their contributions helps one to appreciate what can be said with confidence of Athtar's place in the religion of Canaan and elsewhere in the ancient Near East.

Gray (1949:72-76, 80; 1965:169-174) accepted the hypothesis of Nielsen (1936) and suggested a Canaanite Athtar = Venus = South Semitic Athtar identification.[33] Note should be taken of the manner in which he accounted for the compensatory effect of cultural isolationism on the rate of societal change.

> We accept Nielsen's theory on the grounds that the lapse of time in this case is discounted by the isolation and natural conservatism of the Semitic communities of South Arabia and the oases, where life was for so long immune from extraneous influences (1965:169).

Gray established that the province of Athtar was irrigation. He also addressed the problem of why it is that Athtar's name is absent from the lists of gods at Ugarit. He concluded that he was assimilated to Šaḥar and Šalim

---

[33] According to Gray, Nielsen suggested that Athtar tradition from South Arabia reflects an early stratum of Semitic religion. Nielsen posits that the Athtar of the Ugaritic texts is to be identified with the Athtar of the South Arabian pantheon. In this setting he is the son of the moon-god Il and the sun-goddess Athirat, and the deification of the Venus star—the brightest of celestial bodies after the sun and moon. Nielsen suggested that at Ugarit two cultural strains had merged leaving their mark on the pantheon. These consisted of an archaic stratum whose origins were in the essentially nomadic culture of the desert, and a younger level which was fundamentally agricultural in character. There is a pervasive bias that undercuts the type of analysis offered by Nielsen. He implies that the rate of social change in primitive cultures is so slow as to be almost undetectable. This allows him to bridge the temporal gap existing between Ugaritic and South Arabian sources. However, it is well known that all cultures change.

"the twin deities manifest in the star of Dawn (*Šḥr*) and Completion (*Šlm*) of Day" (1965:170). In addition, he posited that the name Ashtar-Kamosh found in the *Mesha Inscription* indicated that the gods Ashtar and Kemosh could be assimilated with little difficulty if not actually identified with one another. He extended the identification process to Ammon and found Milkom to be yet another Athtar hypostasis. His final identification equated Athtar, Kemosh, Milkom, and Šalim. This, for him, was indicated by the failure of 1 Kgs. 11:7 to mention Athtar by name (only his hypostases Kemosh and Milkom are mentioned), the reference to astral worship as background to Josiah's reform in 2 Kgs. 23:5ff., and indications congruent with information in the account of St. Nilus that Athtar was worshipped with human sacrifice (2 Kgs. 23:11, 16:3, 17:17, 3:27, and 2 Chron. 28:3). He also believed that worship of Athtar was centralized at Jerusalem at least since the 18th century B.C.E. and cited Zephaniah 1:5, 2 Kgs. 25:4, Neh. 3:15, 2 Kgs. 21:18-26, the names of David's sons (Absalom and Solomon), and the name "Jerusalem" in the Egyptian *Execration Texts* as evidence of this.

While I acknowledge the *extremely remote* possibility that Šaḥar and Šalim might possibly be hypostases of Athtar, there are significant problems with Gray's reconstruction. First, by adopting Nielsen's hypothesis he has constructed an interpretive paradigm for the primary data that is built on questionable anthropological and social theory. All cultures change. As an observer of cultural phenomena or an analyst of artifacts—physical or ideational—one must be sensitive to both the indicators and rate of such change. Furthermore, the Athtar/Milkom equation and the proposition that Jerusalem was a center of Athtar worship from ancient times are unconvincing. One suspects that the title *mlk* is most appropriately applied to El. One would have to build a more convincing case than Gray has to prove that a national deity in Canaan, other than El, could be called "King."

Dahood (1958:85-90) noted that Athtar usually heads lists of South Arabian deities and is considered to be the head of the pantheon in the region. For him, this datum and supporting evidence from ancient Mesopotamia indicated that Athtar was an astral god identified with the planet Venus. He noted that in Arabia he is known as "the eastern one," and that in Mesopotamia, Akkadian Ištar was equated with Sumerian *DIL.BAT*, the name by which Venus was known. Dahood also cited the Ugaritic text KTU 1.43.1, which reads *k ᶜθtrt ᶜrb* "when ᶜAthtart sets" as evidence of Athtar's astralization, and compared this with KTU 1.78, where the root √*ᶜrb* is used to describe activity of the sun goddess, *b šš ym ḥdš ḫyr ᶜrbt špš θǵrh ršp* "during the six days of the new moon of the month Ḫiyar, Šapš sets, her porter being Rešep." He also cites similar usage in KTU 1.46.9 *ʿrb špš wḥl.* He criticized Caquot, who treated this astralization as a secondary development, and believed that the Ugaritic personal names *ʿθtr ab* " ʿAthtar is my father" and *ʿθtr um* "ʿAthtar is my mother" suggest that as early as the fourteenth century B.C.E., Canaanites and the first wave of Semites entering Mesopotamia in more ancient times believed Athtar to be androgynous.

Dahood took astralization and the duality of gender as original divine traits belonging to Athtar and used these data to refute Gray's argument that Athtar/Athtart were assimilated to Šaḥar and Šalim. That Athtar appeared in personal names established for Dahood that this assimilation had not taken place by the fourteenth century B.C.E. His proposal was that Athtar was worshipped as morning star and Athtart as that of the evening. He did not believe that ʿAthtar was identified with deified Dawn and Dusk. With regard to KTU 1.6 I 43-67, Dahood was also critical of Caquot. He argued that Caquot's belief that astralization was not a primary phenomenon, his adoption of the theory that Arab nomads did not worship stellar gods, and his view that settled Semites would not be as inclined to worship astral gods as would their non-sedentarized counterparts, made his position unacceptable given the evidence available from Ugarit, Mesopotamia, and South Arabia. The agreement of evidence from Mesopotamia and Ugarit concerning Athtar's astral character and gender binarism were indicators for Dahood that these traits were quite ancient.

Caquot (1956:45-60) noted that Athtar does not occupy the place of prominence afforded Baal, Yamm, and Mot in Ugaritic mythology and that he appears as a lesser figure who enjoys little glory. For him, he is characterized as jealous, pretentious, and incapable, and seems also to disappear immediately after his failure to take Baal's place atop Mt. Ṣapon.

Caquot pondered whether it was possible to reconstruct a complete Athtar myth from Ugaritic and outside data, particularly since Athtar held a position of high regard in other Semitic religions. He also wondered if data from elsewhere in the Near East were reconcilable with the relatively unflattering picture of Athtar presented at Ugarit.[34] He noted that in South Arabian inscriptions Athtar is the great god of the heavens who is mentioned regularly at the head of god lists. Though other gods are given places of greater prominence as protectors of capitals and those who engender

[34] These issues remain central in the debate over Athtar today.

kings, Caquot suspected that there existed a more primitive phase of religious history in which Athtar was the primary deity. By contrast, the information found at Ugarit did not lend itself to such clear interpretation. In his opinion, there appeared to be a gradual debasement of Athtar at Ugarit. Based on his interpretation, Athtar is cast in a most favorable light in the *Hymn to Nikkal and Yariḫ* (KTU 1.24), but in a largely negative one in the recounting of his conflict with Yamm (KTU 1.2) and his failure on Ṣapon (KTU 1.6). He viewed him as an inept replacement for Baal and impotent in his encounter with Yamm. Caquot wondered whether, perhaps, some part of Athtar mythology had been lost at Ugarit in which Athtar was returned to his original stature (1956:49). Caquot's conclusion, based on characteristics described in divine epithets, was that in South Arabia, Athtar was the supreme being of the heavens—a protector and fertility god. The astral characteristics which he accrued in Mesopotamia and at Ugarit were, however, the result of secondary identification with astral phenomena (1956:57). According to Caquot, Athtar was master of life, of the waters which bestow it, and of the heavens which dispense the waters. He was, in effect, similar to Ugaritic Baal in function (1956:58). His degradation at Ugarit seemed, therefore, to be a regional phenomenon (limited to Ugarit) rather than a pan-Near Eastern one. The implication is that at Ugarit, Athtar was eclipsed by a god (Baal) with a role identical to his own, but whose non-astral character made him more acceptable to a non-nomadic population. Caquot also believed that sedentarized Semites would be less likely to pay homage to an astral god than their non-sedentarized counterparts (1956:57-58). Prerogatives belonging to Athtar in a non-urban setting were assigned to Baal at Ugarit which resulted in the astral deity's fall from favor.

Several of the points made by Caquot are credible. First, it is almost certain that the Ugaritic corpus is missing a substantial amount of mythological material relating to Athtar and other gods. This is clear from the abrupt ending we have at KTU 1.2 III 24 and KTU 1.6 I 67. One is unable to say at this point whether such material included any reference to Athtar's return to glory. From what is extant, the picture is a complicated one—so complicated in fact that one is led to reflect on an old form-critical problem—the relationship between literary genre and cultural information. Specifically, how does one construct a profile of a god from information found in genres that have unique (and not always complementary) agenda. Caquot's conclusion that astralization is secondary in the case of Athtar needs further examination as do his generalizations about non-sedentarized peoples, particularly those responsible for producing the epigraphic material in South Arabia.

Gaster (1950:126-127, 196-199) saw Athtar's role being confined to that of artificial irrigation. The episode on Ṣapon illustrated, for him, the inadequacy of irrigation when compared to natural rainfall. For him, Athtar's failure to fill Baal's throne was symbolic of this reality. He saw Athtar as a god of "inferior status" who was unable to assume control of the earth and the waters. He was, therefore, a god whose aspirations far exceeded his qualifications.

With regard to the etymology of the divine name, Athtar, Gaster noted the Arabic cognate *ᶜaθarī* "soil artificially irrigated,"[35] and *ᶜāθūr*,[36] which designates a trench or canal dug for irrigation purposes. He also suggested that Athtar in South Arabia and Ištar in Mesopotamia fulfill these roles within their respective religious systems. Gaster concluded that as a deity associated with artificial irrigation, Athtar's rise to power during Baal's absence was most appropriate since Baal's disappearance corresponds to the dry season in Syria-Palestine. Moreover, Athtar's effectiveness was but a partial substitute for the full range of Baal's power. He was unable to fill his throne on Ṣapon, but was competent enough to provide temporary sustenance for earth until Baal returns. Gaster also believed that the episode at Ṣapon represented the mythologization of the institution of the temporary king (interrex) who rules in place of the actual king during that time when the legitimate ruler is thought to have died or considered to be no longer in power (1950:196).

Gaster's characterization of Athtar as one lacking the qualifications to fulfill his aspirations is somewhat attractive, but troubling. It interprets KTU 1.6 in a manner that is much more negative than the evidence actually suggests. There are also questions about his translation of √*ᶜθr* in Arabic. The meanings he cites are not primary meanings and *ᶜaθarī* refers to land watered by rain or run-off.[37]

---

[35] On this etymology cf. also Smith (1969:99, n. 2).

[36] He recognizes a similar semantic range in Hebrew √*ᶜšr* in Psalm 65:10, where √*šqḥ* denotes the method of providing water from underground water sources (1950:126, n. 35).

[37] J. Huehnergard first pointed this out to me. Cf. also the comments of Smith (1969:99 n. 2.) on *ᶜaθūr* and *ᶜaθarī*. In contrast to Gaster's position, there are others (e.g., Ryckmans in Leidlmair 1962:186-192) who claim that there is no satisfactory etymology for the name Athtar.

Roberts' (1972:37-40) study of the early Semitic pantheon, though dated, is still considered by many to be the standard on the subject. He concluded that the names Athtar and Athtart originally designated Venus as the morning and evening stars—the former being male and the latter female. This gender-based distinction was preserved only in West Semitic. The masculine form assumed dominance in the East where the Semitic population, recalling the old god's androgynous character, did not allow the grammatical gender of the divine name to interfere with Athtar's development as a goddess.

Roberts suspected that Sumerian influence may have played a part in this unusual combination of traits. The personal names *Eštar-laba*, "Eshtar is a lion," *Eštar-pāliq*, "Eshtar is a slayer," and *Eštar-qarrād*, "Eshtar is a warrior," indicated for him that the typing of Athtar as war goddess had taken place by the Old Akkadian period. He also believed that this may have been accompanied by typing as sex goddess. The precise manner by which these aspects were combined is not known, but he proposed that the male persona may have originally been assigned the war aspect while the female was assigned the love aspect. In late tradition, both elements were combined to form the picture of Ištar as beautiful, fickle, and vicious. Roberts also saw these elements combined in Ugaritic Anat and Athtart.

Roberts' analysis of the data is generally acceptable with one exception—the assignation of separate aspects of character to morning and evening manifestations of Venus seems somewhat facile.[38] Athtar and Athtart may have shared a common body of traits which were not necessarily separable along gender based lines.

Further, if one may judge from Roberts' list of Ištar personal names, Athtar clearly has social and astral characteristics, masculine and feminine aspects, and general ambiguity with regard to grammatical gender—at least in Mesopotamia.[39] The names *Eštar-mutī*, "Eshtar is my man," and *Eštar-*

---

[38] There is also a problem with the notion that Athtart was a sex goddess. Evidence in support of this position is lacking. J. Hackett (1989:65-76) has noted the problem inherent in classifying all goddesses, for example, as sex goddesses. For this reason, it seems preferable to think in terms of individual power profiles when discussing gods and goddesses. This allows the uniqueness of each individual deity to be described without the use of categorizations that are artificial or inaccurate (e.g. "sex goddesses").

[39] Personal names containing theophoric elements are helpful in determining what traits people perceive as being characteristic of a god or goddess. As such there is al-

ummī, "Eshtar is my mother," establish that both male and female roles were part of early East-Semitic typology. *Eštar-pāliq*, "Eshtar is a slayer," *Eštar-rabiat* (fem.), "Eshtar is great," *Eštar-imittī*, "Eshtar is my support," *Eštar-laba*, "Eshtar is a lion," *Eštar-ṣil*, "Eshtar is protection," *Eštar-paluḫ* (masc.), "Eshtar is Awe Inspiring," *Eštar-qarrād*, "Eshtar is a warrior," *Eštar-rēṣ*, "Eshtar is my helper," and *Eštar-šadu*, "Eshtar is a mountain," illustrate warlike traits. A possible reference to Eshtar as provider of fertility is found in the name *Eštar-nuḫšī* "Eshtar is my wealth." Evidence of early astralization is found in the name *Eštar-nūrī*, "Eshtar is my light." Surprisingly, an attestation of Eshtar as a god of wisdom is found in the name *Eštar-mūda*. *Eštar-dān* and *Eštar-danat*, "Eshtar is strong," are examples of the ambiguous nature of the grammatical gender of the name, in spite of the preference for the grammatically male name Ištar in Mesopotamia.

This range of characteristics is evidence that Athtar, by the Old Akkadian period, was thought of in social, astral, zoomorphic (?),[40] and warlike terms. The extent to which these characteristics are echoed in the mythological and other materials from Syria-Palestine, Mesopotamia, and elsewhere needs to be examined further.

Heimpel (1982) provided a summary of current knowledge about Near Eastern Venus deities. Among those major manifestations listed in his treatment were: Inanna (also known as Ninsiʾana and Dilbad), Ishtar, Nanay, Aziz and Uzza, Balthi, and Astarte. Also included, though not discussed in great detail, were Ugaritic Athtar, Eblaite Aštar, and south Arabian *ʿθtr* (who bears the epithet *šrqn wǵrbn* "eastern and western one").

---

ways a question as to the locus of authority in making an association between an attribute and a particular deity. For example, the name *Eštar-ummī* may indicate that in popular perception, the goddess Eštar has characteristics which would make her identifiable as a mother figure. It may also reflect the feeling of the name giver; that individual may feel that Eštar has acted toward him/her or the person named as though the goddess were a mother. This perception may or may not be consonant with that of the official cultus or popular perception. It may be conditioned largely by the namer's personal encounter with the goddess in the course of a given set of circumstances. This suggests that personal names must be treated with a degree of caution as there is always a question concerning whether one encounters in them evidence of official theology, popular piety, or personal faith.

[40] The name *Eštar-laba* may (possibly) be so construed. The lion image may be a symbolic reference to the god's strength rather than a zoomorphic reference.

After a brief introductory discussion of the evidence for each god, he concluded that: (1) the Sumerians and other Semitic peoples (for which scholars possess documentation) venerated a Venus deity; (2) the evening and morning appearances of Venus were understood as manifestations of a single planet in prehistoric times; (3) #2 preceded the fusion of planetary and anthropomorphic aspects of Venus in the ancient Near East; (4) while Sumerian Inanna was female, Semitic Venus deities were generally male; (5) Akkadian Ištar—originally male—changed sex under Sumerian influence; (6) north Arabian al-ʿUzza was female and eclipsed north Arabian Aziz in importance; (7) the change in sex from Aziz to al-ʿUzza may have occurred under the influence of Aramean Nanay, Balthi, and Kaukabta (another possibility is to see al-ʿUzza as a south Arabian deity); (8) the theory that Canaanites and north Arabians possessed separate deities for morning and evening stars cannot be substantiated; (9) al-ʿUzza, Aziz, south Arabian ʿθtr, and perhaps also Ugaritic Athtar, Eblaite Aštar, and original Akkadian Ištar (i.e., before being influenced by Sumerian Inanna) were worshipped as the morning star; and (10) the Inanna/Ištar fusion in Mesopotamia produced regional variations of the Venus deity—one being north Babylonian, male, and identified with the morning star, another being south Babylonian, female, and identified with the evening star.

Smith's are the most recent treatments of Athtar (1994, 1995). In them he offers an excellent summary of prior scholarship, a regional classification of primary evidence relating to Athtar (e.g., Syro-Mesopotamian sources from the Third and Second Millennia; sources extant in Moabite, Aramaic, North Arabian, and Phoenician; and Epigraphic sources from South Arabia), an examination of the etymology of the name Athtar, and an assessment of his place in KTU 1.6 I. Among the more important conclusions found in his most recent treatment (1995) are the following: (1) that Athtar is not androgynous; (2) that textual evidence from Emar and Ugarit suggests that Athtar was an astral and martial deity; that Epigraphic South Arabian texts characterize Athtar as an astral god, protector, and occasional water provider; (4) that KTU 1.2 III and 1.6 I 63 indicate that Athtar is a god who is not powerful enough to be king; (5) that there is no clear Semitic etymology for the name Athtar; and (6) that Athtar's weakness as found in Ugaritic sources indicates the demise of his cult and replacement as god of water and war by Baal.

There remains a disconcerting lack of clarity about Athtar, even with the significant gains that have resulted from recent epigraphic discoveries[41] and studies. For example, Heimpel's catalogue resolves some important questions but raises others. It is clear that popular migration and diffusion have taken place in the ancient Near East and account for the spread of religious and other ideas. Unfortunately, the socio-cultural phenomena that precede, instigate, accompany, or result from such processes are not clear.[42]

Smith (1995) offers the most balanced and, with regard to future research on Athtar, useful synthesis of available data. From his findings one can see the potential benefit of contextualizing evidence about Athtar—i.e., treating evidence from particular regions and time periods as independent sources to be examined primarily within their immediate socio-cultural setting. New light might be cast on Athtar and other gods by studies that are more specific—i.e., in terms of the regions and textual genres selected for analysis and in terms of the cultural settings in which Venus deities are venerated. One senses from prior studies an unresolved tension between the "lumpers" and the "splitters." Greater attention should be given to the specific character traits of Venus deities found in Greece, Rome, Syria-Palestine, and Mesopotamia and to the implicit limitations of data mediated through particular literary genres (e.g., personal names, myths, votive inscriptions, etc.). Data-specific interpretive paradigms should be developed and tested in order to extract as much information as possible from the available sources.

One paradigm that is potentially useful in the interpretation of myth and epic involves the examination of divine and human character profiles. This method provides the basis for the reassessment of Athtar in the following section.

---

[41] See for example the seven inscriptions on objects found at Eliachin bearing the divine name *ᶜθtrm* (Deutsch and Heltzer 1994:69-87).

[42] See also Strugnell's treatment (1959) and that of Pope (1965a).

CHAPTER SIX

ATHTAR—A RECONSIDERATION OF UGARITIC DATA

The importance of the mythological and epic literature from Ugarit has long been recognized by linguists, scholars of religion, and others with an interest in the cultural landscape of ancient Greece, Syria-Palestine and Mesopotamia. The major literary texts (the *Baal Cycle* and the epics of *Kirta*, and *Aqhat*) have been mined repeatedly for the wealth of ethnological data they contain—particularly those pertaining to Canaanite language and religion. As a result, our knowledge of these areas has been increased considerably and the body of comparative evidence for biblical research has been augmented extensively.

In spite of the gains made in the aforementioned areas, in no way could one conclude that consensus has been reached regarding many important aspects of Ugarit culture. Debate over the socio-political make-up of the city's population, the place of its language in the Semitic continuum, the nature of its religious institutions and ritual practices, the composition of its pantheon (and the precise roles of its constituent divinities), and the relationship between the content of its myths and socio-cultural realities continues. Of these areas of concern, the latter two are of greatest interest to the author and have provided the inspiration for this brief investigation.

The existence of "god lists" in the corpus of Ugaritic texts enables one to approximate the number of deities that may have been prominent in the religious life of the Ugaritic populace and the order in which they appear in these lists suggests something about their relative importance in the minds of those responsible for the keeping of official records. A survey of secondary literature reveals that the major gods (e.g., El, Baal, and Asherah) have received a considerable amount of attention. This is due, perhaps in part, to the importance of these deities to Hebrew Bible research. However, the roles that many of the minor deities play in the pantheon have not been sufficiently investigated. Of these gods, those categorized by scholars as "astral deities" (i.e., those identifiable with celestial bodies) are deserving of special attention. While planetary deities are found in many of the cultures of the ancient Near East, their profile of responsibilities appears to be a cultural variable rather than a universal. Thus, each astral deity must be examined within a specific context before cross-cultural generalizations can be made. Moreover, the selection of appropriate methodologies for the analysis of textual (and other) data from Ugarit confronts one directly with the problem of the interpretation of ancient folklore and the relationship between myth and other "tangible" aspects of culture. In the case of the *Baal Cycle*, we have the additional problem of determining whether it should be treated as a coherent unit or viewed as an amalgamation of independent stories.

Neal Walls, in his treatment of the goddess Anat in Ugaritic myth (1992:1-11) has called attention to the fact that prior generations of scholars (most of whom were linguists and biblical critics rather than anthropologists, ethnologists, or trained mythographers) have been influenced by theoretical presuppositions about myth and culture that make many of their conclusions about Ugaritic myth untrustworthy. As a corrective measure, he has suggested the use of a pluralistic approach to myth that seeks to avoid the reductionist tendencies of prior interpretive methods. I agree in principle with this kind of approach, with one major qualification. It should always be understood that the researcher is in fact assuming the posture of a "theory-tester"—one who applies hypotheses and paradigms to a body of evidence, draws conclusions, and then compares these with findings produced by other tests. This necessitates that one treat Ugaritic mythology as a literary and artistic product of Ugaritic culture that reflects the mind(s) of its creator(s) and her/his/their life-settings. It is also a repository of ethnological data. Therefore, all methods must be sensitive to the cultural information contained in any given text and its use in the conveyance of meaning.[43] It is in the treatment of ancient myth as artifact and cultural data-base that the way is paved for the testing of *new* theories that may help to shed light on unresolved problems. While it is unrealistic to expect that either a single interpretive model or a grand synthesis of pre-existing ones will emerge from this enterprise, it is not beyond reason to expect that modifications could be made in our knowledge of the pluriformity of function and meaning in ancient myth.[44]

---

[43] The examination of cultural data in literary texts might be termed *ethnological criticism*. The use of *emic* and *etic* devices to discern, classify, and analyze this information is one of the tasks of this method.

[44] It must of course be kept in mind that the ancient myths that we have from Ugarit were probably composed orally and that the object of our study provides us with little more than the written record of a single performance of any given myth (perhaps with secondary additions and corrections after the story assumed a fixed non-oral form).

As noted above, the god Athtar presents some particularly vexing problems relative to his place in the Ugaritic pantheon and the interpretation of the texts that provide our knowledge about him. Scholars have long asserted that he is to be identified with the planet Venus in its aspect as star of the morning. This position has been supported by comparative linguistic and mythological data from Mesopotamia, South Arabia, Israel, and Greece.[45]

With regard to the overall profile of Athtar, information about him is found in four different textual genres—myth (the *Baal Cycle*), ritual (*Nikkal and Yariḫ*), lists of personal names, and god lists[46]—each presenting its own peculiarities and hermeneutical challenges. These individual sources are best treated as independent witnesses. A separate examination of the evidence available from each genre might lead to the formulation of a more specific (and hopefully useful and accurate) profile of the god as he is encountered in each text. Once this is done, a composite profile could be made and the connection between these data and socio-political realities could be explored.[47]

6.1 Athtar in the Baal Cycle—Background

This section will examine information about Athtar found in the *Baal Cycle* (KTU 1.1-1.6) which shall be treated as a continuous and complete literary unit. Its primary goals will be to re-evaluate the nature and importance of this god based on an analysis of a single aspect of the narrative—character development. In so doing, the view of Athtar's status in the myth expressed by Gaster (1950:126) more than four decades ago will be reevaluated:

---

[45] Unfortunately, it is difficult to confirm this identification based on the Ugaritic evidence alone.

[46] From these alone we have learned that the pantheon was large, conflate, and fluid. In excess of one hundred deities—some of which were non-Semitic—were worshipped at Ugarit. One is left with the impression that this number fluctuated in response to socio-political and other changes in Syria-Palestine.

[47] The most prudent research strategy is one that seeks to examine available information on a case by case basis and pays careful attention to the genre, function, and original social location of available sources. It should also discourage synthesis until a thorough understanding of source idiosyncrasy and the range of interpretive options of a particular text are obtained. This is particularly true in the instance of the lesser known divinities like Athtar.

> It is apparent that Ashtar is a god of inferior status who aspires to dominion over both the earth and the waters but who is regarded in each case as not fully qualified to wield it.

This view has continued to enjoy favor among contemporary scholars (cf. Oldenburg 1969:42; Gibson 1976:19; de Moor 1987:85, note 415). Most recently, Smith's (1994:250; 1995:640) assessment of Ugaritic Athtar as a water provider and warrior who is replaced by Baal and too weak to function as king is quite similar to that of Gaster. A secondary goal is to see if there is present within the myth an indigenous model for understanding divine personhood. Such a model would help in understanding Athtar's nature and function in this myth.

This treatment should also be understood as a *test-case* to determine the feasibility of character study as an avenue of inquiry in the overall analysis of Ugaritic literature. This initial foray limits itself, therefore, to the examination of two gods—Baal (the deity around whom the myth revolves) and Athtar (the god designated to take Baal's place atop Mt. Ṣapon when Baal dies and descends to the underworld).

In examining personal information about these gods I am interested in discovering whether there are *substantial* differences in the data employed in divine description and to what extent these should be viewed as significant. These findings will be used in conjunction with a close reading (one sensitive to plot and theme) of the texts that describe Athtar's activities in the *Baal Cycle*. Finally, some tentative observations will be made about the possible connection between the *Baal Cycle* and the culture of Ugarit, and about the appropriateness of the myth's use as ethnological "map." If the conclusions of this *test-case* confirm the appropriateness of the model, then similar character studies can be done of other gods found in this cycle and of other divine and human personages found in other key Ugaritic texts (e.g., *Aqhat* and *Kirta*). The task must, of necessity, be largely descriptive since there exists no speculative work in Ugaritic literature that deals with personhood.

6.1.1 Athtar and Baal—A Comparison of Personal Profiles

The Baal Myth contains much information of a personal nature about the gods that lends itself to categorization. The following charts represent my classification of those data used to describe Athtar and Baal.[48]

Athtar

Epithets				
	Patronymic	-------	-------	
	Military	-------	-------	
	Political	1.2. III 12	d mlk[49]	possessor of kingship
	Zoomorphic	1.2 III 20	lbum[50]	lion
	Intellectual	1.6 I 48	ydᶜ ylḥn	he knows, he understands
	Physical Traits	1.6. I 50	dq anm	(the one who is) minute in strength
		1.6 I 55	ᶜrẓ	terror inspiring; awesome

Possessions	1.2 III 13 (?)	ḥrḥrtm	torches
	1.2 III 13 (?)	išt, išt	fire
	1.2.III 18	[ksa] mlkk	throne of (your) kingship
	1.2 III 18	ḫṭ mθpṭk	scepter of your rule
Domicile	1.2 III 19-20	ank in bt [l]y [km] ilm	there is no house for me like the gods

[48] The chart has been influenced by the system for classifying cultural phenomena in Murdock et al. (1987) and Levenson and O'Leary (1991:xvii-xxi). It is assumed that an individual member of a culture will be socialized so as to function with an awareness of those aspects of culture that will promote her/his survival. While one may not assume that such education will result in total familiarity with every aspect of life, one could state, with few reservations, that a basic understanding of many of life's essential elements—particularly those related to family and immediate social environment—will be conveyed. At the level of narrative, the gods in the Baal myth are partially anthropomorphized members of a family with considerable wealth and influence. Thus, one can assume that each character will assume roles and behave in ways that permit anthropological categorization and analysis.

[49] Here, I follow the suggested reading of Herdner (CTA:10 note 6).

[50] Here I follow the reading of Gordon (UT:196).

		wḥẓr [k bn] [qd]š	nor court like Qudshu's sons
Divine Locus	1.2 III 20 (?)	bnpšny	into our (dual) throat
	1.6 I 57	bṣrrt ṣpn	in the far reaches of Ṣapon
	1.6 I 58-59	lkḥθ aliyn b^{c}l	on the throne of Baal the Conqueror
	1.6 I 65	arṣ	underworld
Marital Status	1.2 III 22-23	in aθt [l]k k[m] [ilm]	you have no wife like the gods
Family and Kin	1.2 III 16, 19	θr il abk	Bull El, your father
		θr il aby	Bull El, my father
	1.6 I 43-46	yṣḥ il lrbt aθrt ym	El cried to Lady Athirat of the Sea
		šm^{c} lrbt aθr[t] ym	Hear O Lady Athirat of the Sea
		tn aḥd b bnk amlkn	Give one of your sons so that I may make him king
Servants	1.2 III 20	kθrm	The Kotharim
Political Role	1.2 III 22	mlkt [w] im l mlkt	I am king, indeed I am king
	1.6 I 55	ymlk ^{c}θtr ^{c}rẓ	Athtar the terrible became king
	1.6 I 57-59	y^{c}l bṣrrt ṣpn	He ascended to the far reaches of Ṣapon
		yθb lkḥθ aliyn b^{c}l	He sat in Baal the Conqueror's throne
	1.6 I 63-64	yrd ^{c}θtr ^{c}rẓ	Athtar the terrible descended
		yrd lkḥθ aliyn b^{c}l	He came down from Baal the Conqueror's throne

		wymlk barṣ il klh	And He became king of the Underworld, god of all of it
Patron/Matron	1.6 I 53-54	w^{c}n rbt aθrt ym	And Lady Athirat of the Sea answered
		blt nmlk ^{c}θtr ^{c}rẓ	Should we not make Athtar the terrible king
Body Parts	1.6 I 59-60	p^{c}nh rišh	his feet his head
Physical Traits	1.6 I 59-61	p^{c}nh ltmǵyn hdm	his feet did not reach the stool
		rišh l ymǵy apsh	his head did not reach its top

Actions[51]

Verbs Used To Describe Activities

KTU 1.2	KTU 1.6	
√ybl	-------	carry
√yrd	√yrd	descend
√^{c}ny	√^{c}ny	answer
√mlk	√mlk	reign, be king
-------	√^{c}ly	ascend
-------	√yθb	sit

Athtar's epithets identify him with zoomorphic phenomena and are also indicative of his political activity, (physical) strength, and intellect ("He knows and He understands). Mention is not made of his lineage in his epithets, though it is referred to elsewhere—he is son of El and Asherah. There

[51] Athtar's actions can be outlined as follows: KTU 1.2 III 12-14—Descends to domicile of Yamm and challenges him(?); KTU 1.2 III 18-22—Complains of not having a house, though he is king; KTU 1.6 I 56-61—Ascends Baal's mountain and sits in Baal's throne; KTU 1.6 I 62—(Voluntarily) abdicates Baal's throne; and KTU 1.6 I 63-65—Descends from Baal's mountain and becomes (by his own power) king of Arṣ (the underworld).

is no reference made to his prowess as a warrior. The inventory of his possessions reveals that while he owns little, that which he owns is indicative of his power (i.e. throne of his kingship and scepter of his authority).[52] He has no permanent place of residence like the other gods (1.2 III 19-20), though he does enjoy freedom of movement that allows him to travel from Baal's home on Mt. Ṣapon to the underworld.[53] He has no wife. It is possible that the *kθrm* mentioned in 1.2 III 20 are his servants. His political role seems clear, regardless of the fact that he has no home (i.e., he is "king"). When last he is encountered, he is king of the Underworld. He has two political benefactors—El and Asherah (also his parents), though the former's understanding of him is based on a negative construct (1.6 I 50-52). As far as his physical appearance is concerned, he is said to be "minute in strength" and "terror inspiring." With regard to anatomy, mention is made of his head and feet. It is also said that he is shorter than Baal (1.6 I 59-61). In surveying the verbs used to describe his range of activities one finds that he answers, carries, ascends, descends, sits, and reigns as king. Even though the available information is terse, it is also telling. Athtar is a mysterious (no home, very little personal property, refuses to retain power given to him by his political patrons) yet active and intelligent cosmic force with power over the underworld.

Baal

Epithets

Patronymic	1.2. I 35	bn dgn	Son of Dagan
Meteorologic	1.2 I V 29	rkb ᶜrpt	Cloud Rider
Military	1.2. IV 28	aliyn b[ᶜl]	Baal the Conquering One
	1.3 III 14	aliy qrdm	Conqueror of Warriors
Political	1.3 I 3-4	zbl bᶜl arṣ	Prince, Lord Earth
Unspecified	1.2 I 46	gmr hd	Haddu, the One Who Completes
	1.2 IV 28	šm	The Name

[52] The significance of the torches and fire is unclear.

[53] See M. Smith's note on divine travel as indicator of divine rank (1984:359). Much remains to be done on this and other aspects of *cosmic culture* as they are reflected in Ugaritic myth. In fact, a full ethnography of cosmic culture might well be a worthwhile undertaking.

	1.4 VII 36	hd	Haddu
	1.4 VII 39	dmrn	Dmrn
Possessions	1.2 I 35	pδh	his gold
	1.2 I 39	mšḫt	slaughtering weapon
	1.2 I 39	mḫṣ	smiting/slaying weapon
	1.2 IV 6	rgm	word
	1.2 IV 6	hwth	his word
	1.2 IV 10	mlk ʿlmk	eternal kingship
	1.2 IV 10	drkt dt drdrk	everlasting dominion
	1.3 I 10	ks	cup
	1.3 I 11	krp[[m]]nm	wine goblets
	1.3.I 12	ridn	jar
	1.3 I 13	ks qdš	holy cup
	1.3.I 15-16	alp kd bḫmr	1000 pitchers of wine
	1.3.I 17	rbt (kd bḫmr ?)	myriad (pitchers of wine)
	1.3 III 29-31	btk ǵry il ṣpn	on my rock/mountain (divine) Ṣapon
		bqdš bǵr nḥlty	in the holy place, on my ancestral mount
		bnʿm bgbʿ tliyt	in the good place, on the hill of my victory
	1.3 IV 26	mdlh	his lightning ?
	1.3 IV 27	[q]rnh	his horn (lightning ?)
	1.3 IV 41	alp, mria	Two sacrificial animals prepared for feasting are listed in this passage—ox and fatling
	1.4 V 6	mṭrh	his rain
	1.4 V 7	θkt b glθ	ship in/on the ?
	1.4 V 9	brqm	lighting
	1.4 VI 36-38	<b>hty bnt dt ksp	I have built my house of silver,
		hkly dtm ḫrṣ	my palace of gold
	1.4 VI 59	ks ḫrṣ	cups of gold
	1.4 VII 9-10	θθ lθθm ʿr	66 cities
		šbʿm šbʿ pdr	77 towns

	1.4 VII 17-19	ḥln, urbt, bdqt	window, window, breach (Gibson)
	1.4 VII 41	arz	cedar
	1.4 VII 44	arṣ drkt	land of (Baal's) dominion
	1.4 VI I 52	hmlt ʾarṣ	Earth's folk, multitude
	1.5 V 7	ʿrptk, rḥk	your clouds, your winds
	1.5 V 22-24	ip[d]	robe
	1.6 V 2-3	ktp	type of weapon
		ṣmd	stick/warclub
	1.6 V 5-6	ksi mlkh	throne of his kingship
		kḥθ drkth	seat/throne of his dominion
Domicile	1.3 V 38-40	in bt lbʿl	There is no house
		km ʾilm	for Baal like the gods
		ḥṣr kb[n] aθrt	nor court like Asherah's sons
		mθb ʾil mδll b[nh]	The dwelling of El is the shelter of his son
Divine Locus	1.2 IV 7	tḥt ksʾi zbl ym	beneath Prince Yamm's throne
	1.3 I 21-22	bṣrrt ṣpn	in the recesses of Ṣapon
	1.3 III 29-31	btk ǵry ʾl ṣpn	on my rock/mountain (divine) Ṣapon
		bqdš bǵr nḥlty	in the holy place, on my ancestral mount
		bnʿm bgbʿ tliyt	in the good place, on the hill of my victory
	1.3 IV 38	mrym ṣpn	heights of Ṣapon

	1.4 V 24	balp šd rbt kmn	1000 fields (away), myriad hectares
	1.5 VI 8-9	npl arṣ	he fell to the underworld
Marital Status	1.3 IV 40	šrḥq aθt lpnnh	He removed his wives from him
Family and Kin			
Progenitor	1.2 I 35	bn dgn	Son of Dagan
	1.3 V 35-36	lyṣḥ θr il abh	Indeed Bull El, his father cried out
		il mlk dyknnh	El the king who established him
Siblings	1.4 VI 44-55	----------------	Among those listed as attendees at Baal's feast are his brothers (aḫh), his kin (aryh), Athirat's seventy sons (šb^{c}m bn aθrt), gods (ilm) and goddesses (ilht)
Spouse(s)	1.3 IV 40	šrḥq aθt lpnnh	He removed his wives from him
Offspring			
Male	1.5 V 22-24	wtldn mθ al[iyn b^{c}]l šlbšn ip[d]	and she bore him a lad, Baal the Conqueror clothed him with a robe
Female	1.3 I 23	bnth	his daughters
	1.3 I 23-24	pdry bt ar	Pidray daughter of light

	3. I 24-25	ṭly b[t] rb	Ṭallay [da]ughter of mist
	1.3 III 7-8	arṣy bt yᶜbdr	Arṣay daughter of yᶜbdr
Servants	1.2. I 35	ᶜnnh	his answerers ?
	1.3 I 2	prdmn	?
	1.3 I 19	nᶜm	charming/lovely one
	1.3 I 20	ǵzr ṭb ql	sweet voiced boy/warrior/hero
	1.3 III 8	ǵlmm	messengers
	1.3 III 36	gpn wugr	Gapn and Ugar
	1.4 VII 45-46	dll, ᶜdd	?; courier, herald[54]
	1.5 V 8-9	šbᶜt ǵlmk	7 messengers
		θmn ḫnzrk	8 swine/squires[55]
Political Role	1.2 IV 32	ym lmt bᶜlm yml[k]	Yamm is dead; let Baal reign (as king)
	1.3 V 32-33	mlkn aliyn bᶜl	Baal the Conqueror is our king
		θpṭn in dᶜlnh	Our judge, there is no one else over us
	1.3 V 35-36	l yṣḥ θr il abh	Indeed Bull El, his father cried out
		il mlk dyknnh	El the king who established him
	1.4 VII 49-50	aḥdy dymlk ᶜl ilm	I am the only one who rules over the gods
	1.4 VII 51	dyšb[ᶜ] hmlt arṣ	who satisfies the earth's multitude
	1.5 I 12	ᶜbdk an wdᶜlmk	I am your servant forever (to Mot)
	1.5 VI 8	npl arṣ	he fell into the underworld

54 See Gibson (1976:154).

55 Cf. Miller (1970) on animal names as titles of nobility.

Political Patron	1.3 V 35-36	l yṣḥ θr il abh	Indeed Bull El, his father cried out
		il mlk dyknnh	El the king who established him
Body Parts	1.2 I 39	yd	hand
	1.2 I 39	ymn	right hand
	1.2 IV 6	ph	his mouth
	1.2 IV 6	špth	his lips
	1.2 IV 6	gh	his voice
	1.2 IV 14	uṣbᶜt	fingers
	1.2 IV 38	rišh	his head
	1.2 IV 40	ᶜnh	his eyes
	1.3 I 11	klat ydh	both of his hands
	1.5 I 6	amtm	elbows
	1.5 V 12	pnk	your face
	1.5 V 25	lirth	to his breast
Physical Traits	1.6 VI 17ff.	bᶜl ᶜṣ	Baal was strong
Sexual Activity	1.5 V 19-21	škb ᶜmnh šbᶜ l šbᶜm	He laid with her 7, indeed 70 times
		tšᶜly θmn lθmnym	She let him mount 8, even 80 times
Knowledge of Social Customs			
Social Deference	1.3 III 8-14	----------	Sequence of commands issued to messengers suggests an established method for delivering a message to a superior
Gift Giving	1.4 I 20-44 1.4 II 27-31	----------	Sequence of events narrated appears to illustrate an established method for gift giving in exchange for a favor or as part of visitation ritual

Hospitality	1.3 IV 40-42	----------	Baal prepares a meal for his sister Anat when she arrives at his mountain
	1.4 VI 44-59	----------	Every indication is given here that Baal prepares a festal meal and invites a huge cadre of gods and goddesses

Emotions

Anger	1.2 I 38	ap anš	anger (he was a companion of anger)
Hatred	1.4 III 17	θn dbḥm šna bᶜl	Baal hates two sacrifices
Joy	1.4 V 36	šmḫ aliyn bᶜl	Baal the Conqueror rejoiced
Fear	1.5 II 6-7	yraun aliyn bᶜl	Baal the Conqueror fears him
		θtᶜnn rkb ᶜrpt	the Cloud Rider is afraid of him
Love	1.5 V 18	yuhb ᶜglt	He loved a heifer

Actions

Commands Issued

KTU 1.2 I		KTU 1.3 VI		KTU 1.4 VIII	
√nšʾ	lift, raise	√[ᶜ]br	cross over	√ytn (pnm)	set (face)
KTU 1.3 III		√mšr	proceed	√yrd	go down
√ᶜrb	enter	√mǵy	reach, arrive	√spr	count
√hbr	bow down	√ytn (pnm)	set face	√nǵr	guard
√qll	fall down	KTU 1.4 I			
√ḫwy	bow down	√skn	take care (Gibson)		
√kbd	honor	KTU 1.4 V			
√rgm	say	√tbᶜ	depart		
√θny	repeat	√bny	build		
√qry	provide ?	√rwm	G—be high, L—raise		
√šyt	place	KTU 1.4 VII			
√nsk	pour	√ptḥ	open		

KTU 1.3 III (Continued)

√ḥwš	hurry
√ᶜṣy[56]	strive, press on
√ᶜbṣ[57]	hasten, hurry
√lsm	run
√wtḥ	hasten
√ʾtw	come, go

Verbs Used To Describe Activities

KTU 1.2 I

√qwm	stand
√gᶜr	rebuke
√ᶜny	answer
√ʾḫd	seize
√rgm	say

KTU 1.2. IV

√ǵwr[58]	sink down
√ytn	(g) give voice
√qθθ	drag
√šyt?	place
√šty?	drink
√kly	destroy
√bθθ?[59]	scatter
√bwθ?	be ashamed

KTU 1.3 III

√byn	know, understand
√bǵy	show

KTU 1.3 IV

√ᶜyn	behold

KTU 1.4 III, IV

√mǵy	reach
√šnʾ	hate
√mgn	beseech (w/gifts)
√ǵzy	entreat (w/gifts)
√šty	drink
√[l]ḥm	eat
√tbʾ	depart

KTU 1.4 V

√šry	flash
√ᶜdn	(ᶜdn) appoint (a season)
√šmḫ	rejoice
√ṣyḥ	shout

KTU 1.4 VI

√ᶜdb	prepare
√ṭbḫ	slaughter
√šql	slay
√pwq	drink, Š—Causative

KTU 1.5 IV

√npᶜ	flourish
√qrb	come near

KTU 1.5 V

√šmᶜ	hear
√ahb	love
√škb	lie down
√lbš	dress

KTU 1.5 VI

√npl	fall
√ḫlq	perish

KTU 1.6 V

√mḫṣ	smite
√mṣḫ	kick, trample

KTU 1.6 VI

√ᶜyn	behold
√ngḥ	gore
√nθk	bite
√qll	fall down
√ᶜzz	be strong

---

[56] See Gibson (1976:154).

[57] See Gibson (1976:153).

[58] See Gibson (1976:155).

[59] See Gibson (1976:144).

KTU 1.3 IV (Continued)			
√rḥq	Š, make distant	KTU 1.4 VII	
		√ʿdr[60]	?
KTU 1.3 V		√θwb	return
√ʾny[61] groan		√ḫd	seize
		√[ʿ]rb	enter
		√ptḥ	open
		√mlk	rule
		√hlk	go
		√yṣʾ	go out
		√mrʾ	command
		√šbʿ	satiate, satisfy

Mortality	1.5 VI 8-10	npl larṣ	He fell to the underworld
		mt aliyn bʿl	Baal the Conqueror has died
		ḫlq zbl bʿl arṣ	Prince, Lord Earth has perished
Resurrection	1.6 III 20-21	kḥy aliyn bʿl	Indeed Baal the Conqueror lives
		kʾiθ zbl bʿl arṣ	Prince, Lord Earth exists

Baal's epithets identify him with meteorological phenomena, establish his lineage (he is Dagan's son), and broadly delimit the nature of his political office (he is Lord of Earth). They are also indicative of his status and prowess as a warrior. Interestingly, no mention is made of his intellect. The inventory of his possessions is substantial. It includes personal wealth (gold—1.2 I 35), weapons of various kinds (slaughtering weapon and smiting weapon—1.2 I 39, lightning—1.3 IV 26, and horns—1.4 V 27,[62] a cedar club—1.4 VII 41, a sword? and a war club—1.6 V 2-3), his word—1.2 IV 6, utensils for festal events (cups, goblets, jars—1.3 I 10-13; 1.4 VI 59), abundant food and drink—1.3 I 15-17; 1.3 IV 41, his kingship and dominion—1.2 IV 10, his throne—1.6 V 5-6, his house (with its window—1.4 VI 36-38; 1.4 VII 17-19), land (i.e., his ancestral mountain—

[60] √*ʿbr* has been suggested as an alternate reading (KTU:20—col. VII, note 4).

[61] See Gibson (1976:141).

[62] Perhaps this is a reference to lightning.

1.3 III 29-31; 1.4 VII 44), various forms of precipitation—1.4 V 6), human beings—1.4 VII 52, and urban centers—1.4 VII 9-10. At one point he lived in the home of El and Asherah but eventually has a lavish home constructed for himself.

His many travails take him to a variety of loci, the most important of which are his mountain in the recesses of Ṣapon (1.3 III 29-31) and the underworld (1.5 VI 8-9). He is not confined to a single locus; he has freedom of movement. Baal has dual lineage—he is son of Dagan and son of El. How this is to be understood is unclear. On one level, all gods are children of El because he is their creator. As a result, Baal has many siblings (1.4 VI 44-45). He has wives[63] (though we are not given their names), three daughters (1.3 I 23-25; 1.3 III 7-8), and one son—conceived and born just before his descent to Death's domain (1.5 V 22-24). He has a corps of servants that includes messengers (1.3 III 8), "answerers" (1.2 I 35), and musicians/singers (1.3 I 20).

With regard to his political position, Baal is king and judge of the gods (1.3 V 32-33). His position has been confirmed by his father and political patron El (1.3 V 35-36) and secured by his own defeat of Yamm (1.2 IV 32). His fight with Death, which ends in a draw, also helps to shore up his authority.

As far as bodily parts are concerned, mention is made of Baal's hands (1.2 I 39; 1.3 I 11), fingers (1.2 IV 14), elbows (1.5 I 6), breast (1.5 V 25), head (1.2 IV 38), face (1.5 V 12), eyes (1.2 IV 40), mouth (1.2 IV 6), lips (1.2 IV 6), and voice (1.2 IV 6). Of his physical traits, we are told simply that he is "strong" (1.6 VI 17ff.). Mention is also made of Baal's sexual activity (1.5 V 19-21) and his fertility.

Baal is also characterized as one who understands three important social conventions: deference to superiors (1.3 III 8-14), gift exchange (1.4 I 20-44; 1.4 II 27-31), and the extension of hospitality (1.3 IV 40-42; 1.4 VI 44-59). He is also said to experience five emotions—love (1.5 V 18), joy (1.4 V 36), fear (1.5 II 6-7), anger (1.2 I 38), and hatred (1.4 III 17).

Baal is a giver of commands (to his servants and to those gods upon whose services and mediation he relies). In surveying the verbs used to describe his range of activities one finds that Baal is active physically (he stands, enters, exits, eats, drinks, shouts, slaughters, prepares, etc.), intellectually (he understands), and emotionally (see above). He is also subject to death and rebirth (1.5 VI 8-10; 1.6 III 20-21). Baal is an active force

---

[63] This assumes that *ʾθt* in 1.3 IV 40 is plural.

whose personal traits characterize him as a wealthy male aristocrat in cosmic society.

It is clear from these charts that the author(s) has/have provided a comprehensive grid for understanding divine personhood, thus yielding important background information about each god. Detail is often spare, but there does seem to be a purposefulness in the selection and presentation of personal data. Physical characteristics are important, but one does not find the kind of physiognomic speculation typical of later Greek handbooks.[64] It is even questionable whether the "physiognomic consciousness"[65] which has been noted in the work of Homer and Hesiod is in evidence here. It is better, perhaps, to speak of the presence of an *ethnological consciousness* in the Baal myth that is sensitive to the importance of personal detail as such is conveyed by a character's possession of certain basic attributes (physical, intellectual, and emotional) and performance of particular actions.[66]

Athtar's character is not as extensively developed as that of Baal. This is to be expected given that Baal is a major actor in the myth.[67] Contrary to the view expressed by Gaster and others, there is no reason to conclude that Athtar is cast in a negative light. His profile is minimal yet effective in establishing his authority, status, and power. At most one is given the impression that there is what might be termed a "crisis of construction" in Ugaritic theology that is expressed in the difference of opinion between El and Asherah about making Athtar king in Baal's absence. Asherah says of him that "he knows" and "understands"—i.e., he is intelligent. El counters

---

[64] Cf. the excellent overview of these materials, and of physiognomy in general, in Evans (1969). I do not dismiss the possibility that there was an interest in physiognomy at Ugarit or, at least, an awareness of the connection between the external appearance and internal state of a person. Spareness of detail can be used in literary artifice. If such interest did exist in Ugaritic literary circles, it is conceivable that the mythic genre, as understood by the author(s) of the *Baal Cycle*, either did not find it to be an appropriate vehicle to convey this information, or were of the opinion that their audience was already so well aware of it that they would supply the missing detailsthemselves.

[65] This is the designation used by Evans (1969:6). Her treatment of physiognomy in Greek Epic is most interesting (pp. 58-66). See especially her very brief sketch of divine physiognomy in the *Iliad* (p. 60).

[66] One might also denote this as cultural awareness.

[67] One would expect a different situation to obtain in a myth about Athtar generated and used in a cult center devoted to him.

that he is "minute in strength." However, it must be remembered that it is Athtar himself who decides to descend to the underworld and make himself king over it. It is also interesting to note that no mention is made of El or Asherah confirming his regency there. He obtains authority without the assistance of a benefactor. Baal is a far more engaging figure than Athtar. He is cast as a socially-oriented figure. He is wealthy, strong, emotionally well-rounded, vigorous, commanding, virile, and intelligent (though the latter attribute is not given great emphasis, except with regard to his familiarity with cosmic cultural customs). As to the significance of Athtar's profile, it must be said that while it is different from that of Baal it in no way suggests that he is pathetic or impotent. The most that can be said is that he is *enigmatic.*

If the profiles of Baal and Athtar may be treated as representative models of male divine personhood, it might be argued that Athtar serves as the cosmic archetype of divine powers whose *numinous* force has yet to be comprehended fully (and *socialized*) while Baal serves as the model for those that are perhaps more familiar, predictable, acceptable, or accessible to the ancient author(s) of the myth and their human audience. The connection between these purported cosmic truths and social realities in Ugaritic culture remains to be seen.

6.1.2 KTU 1.2 III 1-24—An Overview

Leaving aside the question of how best to interpret KTU 1.1-1.6 as a literary unit,[68] it can be said safely that among the interests expressed by the author(s) of these tablets, one of the more important is that concerning the political ambitions and battles of the god Baal. Herdner has suggested that the texts making up the Baal cycle follow the arrangement in her edition (1963:xi) while de Moor (1971:42) prefers the order KTU 1.3, 1.1, 1.2, 1.4, 1.5, 1.6. Gibson has proposed a third possible arrangement (KTU 1.2 III; 1.1 IV; 1.2 I; 1.2 IV; 1.3; 1.4; 1.5; 1.6) (1976:37-81). A fourth arrangement—that of Coogan (1978)—begins with KTU 1.2 I, moves to 1.2 IV, and proceeds sequentially from 1.3 to 1.6. Each of these proposals has merit. I have chosen the order KTU 1.1, 1.2 III, 1.2 I, 1.2 IV, 1.3, 1.4, 1.5, 1.6 for the purposes of this *test- case,* though I feel less than certain about

[68] The hermeneutical debate has yet to be resolved. M. Smith (1986b:313-332) has provided a most helpful overview and categorization of prior interpretive efforts, though I am not convinced by his conclusion that the kingship theme provides the best single interpretive framework for understanding the myth.

the placement of 1.1 and the sequential arrangement of columns in 1.2 (particularly 1.2 II).[69]

6.1.2.1 Analysis[70]

These lines are so poorly preserved that reconstructions and interpretations vary considerably. This has led to great variety in reconstruction and exegesis.[71] It is virtually impossible to determine the setting of lines 1-3. KTU's reconstruction suggests that reference is being made to the homeland of Kothar-wa-Ḫasis and to that of El (lines 3-5). It is possible that the beginning of the text, now lost, told of El's summons to the divine craftsman, whose skills were needed for the construction of Yamm's palace. Once the scene shifts to El's abode (line 4), an unidentified figure does homage to him (lines 5-6). Context suggests that the unnamed figure is Kothar himself. It is to Kothar that El's comments are directed in line 7 and the command to begin construction of a palace for Yamm, which is Kothar's responsibility, occupies all of lines 5-12.

Athtar registers displeasure at this and prepares (apparently) to engage Yamm in conflict (lines 12-14). Šapaš warns against this (lines 15-18) and reminds Athtar of El's probable response to this action. Athtar is undeterred. He proclaims his disdain at having no house like the other gods (lines 18-22). Šapaš, the voice of moderation, replies that he—Athtar—has no wife like the other gods and is, at least by implication, not deserving of this benefit (lines 22-24). Here the text ends abruptly.

The absence of context and the abrupt ending of the text make it virtually impossible to establish where the events narrated here fit in relationship to others described in the Baal Epic. Nonetheless, the major thrust of the text appears to be with the construction of Yamm's palace and the impact that this has upon Athtar. Beyond this, one is limited in what one can say about where to place this episode.

---

[69] KTU 1.101 may have some relationship to the cycle—perhaps at the beginning as de Moor has suggested (1987:1-2).

[70] The KTU edition has been followed unless otherwise indicated. Athtar's role in this text is an important one. Regrettably, its poor state of preservation has made its reconstruction difficult. However, it is better to reconstruct cautiously than to avoid the text altogether.

[71] Cf. for example Gaster (1950:115, 133-134), (de Moor 1971:36-37, 121; 1987:35-38), Pope (1955:102), and Gibson (1976:3-4).

1-3

[ ]ad[ ]n[ ]	
[li-kaptā]ri li-raḥuqi [ʾi]li[-mi ḫakpati]	To Kaphtor, to the remote god of Hakpati
[li-raḥuqi ʾilānīma]	To the distant (one) of the gods
[θinê maθpadêmi[72] taḥta ᶜênāti ʾarṣi]	Two layers beneath the springs of earth,
[θalāθa mat(a)ḫa ǵayarīma[73]]	Three stretches of the swamps

If the KTU reconstruction is accurate, reference is made here to the home of Kothar-wa-Ḫasis, the divine craftsman, whose home is Crete (Kaphtor).[74] He is not a central figure in the exploits of the younger gods in the Ugaritic pantheon, neither does he figure as a contender for Baal's throne. He assists and is subject to the decrees of El. He is (technically) a contract worker for El and Baal. His skills are necessary for the construction of houses (temples) and for success in battle.

The phrase *li-raḥuqi ʾilānīma* is spatially and metaphorically significant. Kothar-wa-Ḫasis's home is removed from the contiguous areas of Syria-Palestine and Mesopotamia and his special skills are possessed by no other god.

4-14

[ʾiddaka] la-yattin pānīma ᶜimma [ʾi]li	Then he set face toward El,
mabbukê na[harêmi qirba ʾappiqê tihāmatêmi]	At the sources of the two rivers, in the midst of the springs of the two deeps.
[yaglû] ðada[75] ʾi[li]	He reaches the tent of El.
wa-yibāʾu [qa]rša malki [ʾabī šanīma]	He enters the tent of the King, the Father of Years.
[li-paᶜnê ʾili yahburu] wa-yaqūlu	At the feet of El he bows and falls.
[ya]štaḥwi[yu] wa-yakabbi[du-nahu]	He bows down and he honors him.

---

[72] "Layer" (Aistleitner 1974:341).

[73] "Ground water "cf. Arabic *ǵawr-* , "ground depression" and *ǵāra*, "to seep out" (water) (Aistleitner 1974:247).

[74] See Gaster (1950:144-145) for a discussion of the role of Kothar-wa-ḫasis in Ugaritic mythology.

[75] Here, I follow the reading suggested in KTU:8, note 3).

[ʾaḫ]ra ya[ʿni θōru ʾilu ʾabū-hu][76]	Afterwards, Bull, El his father answers:
[šamaʿ la]-kôθaru wa-ḫa[sīsu]	"Hear O Kothar wa-Ḫasis
tabaʿ binī bahatī yammi	Depart, build houses (for) Yamm,
[rāmi]ma hêkalla θāpiṭi na[hari]	raise a palace for Judge River.
[na]haru tôki [ ]tabaʿ kôθaru wa-[ḫasīsu]	...River, midst of..., Depart O Kothar wa-Ḫasis.
[ta]bnv̆-nna bahatī-mi zubūli yammi	May you build houses (for) Prince Yamm.
[tarāmi]m[77] hêka[lla li-θāpiṭi] nahari	May you raise a palace for Judge River,
bi-tôki u[pqt yammi]	in the midst of the *Upqt* ? of Yamm.
[ḥuš baha]tīhu tabnv̆[-nna][78]	Hurry, may you build his house/houses.
[ḥu]š tarām[ima-nna[79]	Hurry, may you raise
hêka]ll[ahu ʾalpa šada ʾaḫāda] bêtu]	his palace/palaces.
	May the house encompass a thousand fields,
[ribbata] kumāna hêkallu	ten thousand hectares the palace.
ušbš [yammu bê]tu bi-ǵalmu	(?)...Yamm, house, with a lad
li-šadi mr yammi-mi	at the fields.....Yamm
[Baʿlu]bi-yammi yammu yamut	Baal ...in the seas...May Yamm die...
yʿm[d]n pn ʿaθtaru dū mu[lki][80] [ ]	Then...Athtar the king[81]...

[76] Herdner's proposed restoration for the end of line 6 and the beginning of line 7 has been adopted (CTA:9, note 4).

[77] The reconstruction of Herdner, *[t(?)rm]m* has been adopted (CTA:10).

[78] I have taken this to be a G, 2nd, singular. masc. Energic from √*bny* "to build" (UT:373).

[79] I have treated this as an L, 2nd, singular, jussive, with Energic from √*rwm* "to be high" (UT:483).

[80] I have adopted the reading *d . m[lk]* suggested as a possibility by Herdner (CTA:10, note 6).

[81] This is literally, "the one of (i.e., possessing) kingship."

[ ]ḥv̆rḥv̆rātu-mi[82] wa-dx[x]n [xxx]	
ʾisăti ʾaš[it] h[xxx] ʾišātu	...torches...let me place fire...fire
[ ]y yābilūma-mi ʾub[l xxx] θ[x]xk	...bearers...
yarid[xxx] i[xxxx i]n binu	he descended...son

Kothar sets out toward the home of El, at the base of the cosmic mountain in the far reaches of the north. Upon entering the tent of El, he pays him homage, symbolic of the fact that he is subject to El's authority. Kothar receives his orders. He is to construct a house for Yamm. This sets the stage for his conflict with Baal which takes place later. With a house, Yamm will have an important symbol of kingship before his rival Baal. Later Šapaš will be the voice of moderation which prevents a battle between Yamm and Athtar.

Attention should be paid to the fact that Athtar is the only character called *dū mulki* "possessor of kingship." It should also be noted that he holds this title in spite of the fact that he has neither house nor spouse.
No indication is given, at this point, of how Athtar came to be king. Since he is the sole authority in the distribution of kingship, one might assume that El is responsible for elevating him to this status (1.6 I 55), but it must be remembered that he descends to the underworld and makes himself king (1.6 I 63-66).

It is possible that his title has a specialized meaning. If he is an astral deity, *dū mulki* could be a reference to Athtar's authority over the assembly of celestial gods. Another possibility is that the appellation is a remnant from an earlier stratum in Athtar theology which has been adopted at Ugarit, but retains little of its original meaning. The title is an appropriate one in light of the events described in KTU 1.6 I 63-66.[83] The suggestion that it may have a specialized meaning is also credible. El and Baal are, in effect, co-regents in this myth (El is senior sovereign) though the former is more active than the latter. It is not unreasonable to suppose that El would have similar arrangements (i.e., shared regency) with other minor gods, each having her/his own sphere of authority.

---

[82] I follow Gibson (1976:146) who suggests the meaning "torch, brand" for *ḥrḥrt,* which is derived from √*ḥrr* II "to scorch" (UT:399). I have vocalized it as a *qvtqvt* (reduplicated) feminine plural form with enclitic *-mi* .

[83] The reading *d mlk* is strange and unparalleled in the lore of Ugarit. However, it is precisely its strangeness that commends it as a possible reading here.

15-18a

[ ]nn nīratu ʾilīma šapšu tiššaʾu	...light of the gods, Šapaš
gā-ha wa-ta[ṣīḥu]	lifts her voice and cries out:
[šama]ʿa mʿ[??] [xx yaθ]ʾiru[84]	"Hear!...Bull El your
θôru ʾilu ʾabū-ka	father will exact blood-guilt
li-panī zubūli yammi	before Prince Yamm,
li-panī [θā]piṭi nahari	before Judge River.
[ʾêka ʾa]l yišmaʿu-ka θôru [ʾi]lu ʾabū-ka	How, indeed, shall Bull El your father hear you?
la-yiššaʾu [ʾā]llata[85] θibti-ka	Surely, he will pull up the support of your throne platform.
[la-ya]hpuku [kussiʾa] mulki-ka	Surely, he will upset the throne of your kingship.
la-yaθabbiru ḫaṭṭa maθpaṭi-ka	Surely, he will shatter the scepter of your authority."

Šapaš warns Athtar against resisting El's will. Perhaps the fragmentary remains of lines 13-14 once made explicit reference to Athtar's plan to attack and destroy Yamm and expressed Athtar's feeling that this plot might go unnoticed by El. The sun goddess also warns that resistance to the plan to construct a temple for Yamm will result in the exaction of blood guilt and the overturning of his throne platform (lines 16-17).

18b-22a

wa-yaʿni ʿaθ[ta]ru dū [mul]ki[86] x[ ]	And Athtar the king answered...
[lā-yi]qqaḥu bi-ya θôru ʾilu ʾabī	"Bull El my father will not take ... from me?
ʾanāku ʾêna bêtu [li-]ya [kamā] ʾilīma	As for me, there is no house for me like the gods,
wa-ḥaẓiru [ka-banī qud]ši	or a court like the sons of Holiness.[87]

---

[84] Cf. Arabic *θaʾara* "to engage in a blood feud" (Aistleitner 1974:330).

[85] "A part of a building, strong support, column"; cf. Arabic *ʾālat* "instrument, device, organ" (Aistleitner 1974:23).

[86] I am following the reading *d m[l]k* proposed by Gibson (1976:38).

[87] This is Athirat's title.

labi[ʾ]u-mi[88] < ʾanāku >[89]	I am indeed the Lion.
ʾaridu bi-napšê-nǐyā[90]	I shall descend into the two graves of both of us.
tirḫaṣūna kôθarūma [yaθi]bū	The Kotharim shall wash (me?). Let them sit
bi-[bêti][91] [zubūli] yammi	in the house of Prince Yamm,
bi-hêkalli θāpiṭi naha[ri]	in the palace of Judge River.
yaθʾir θôru ʾilu ʾabū-hu	Let Bull El his father seek blood-guilt
li-[panī zu]būli ya[mmi]	before Prince Yamm,
[li-panī θāpiṭi nahari]	before Judge River.
malaktu [wa-]ʾim[92] la-malaktu	I am king (?) indeed, I am king"

Athtar's complaint is similar to that made to El by Athirat on Baal's behalf (KTU 1.4 IV 50-53).

ʾêna bêtu li-baʿli kamā ʾilīma	There is no house for Baal like the gods,
wa-ḥaṣiru ka-banī ʾaθirati	and no court like the sons of Athirat..
môθabu ʾili maẓlīlu bini-hu	The dwelling of El is the shelter of his son,
môθabu rabbati ʾaθirati yammi	the dwelling of Lady Athirat of the Sea.

This plea does not go unanswered. El grants permission for the construction of the temple and Kothar-wa-Ḫasis is summoned by Baal and given instructions. From what is extant in the text, neither Athtar nor any other spokesperson presents a request to El. Athtar seems to take matters into his

---

[88] I am following the reading of Virolleaud and Gordon cited by Herdner (CTA:10, note 17).

[89] This restoration supposes that the scribe has omitted the 1cs personal pronoun. It (or some other addition) is needed to make sense of this line.

[90] Following Gibson (1976:38 note 5, 153) the reference here is to the domain of Yamm and possibly that of Mot. This extension of meaning does not seem unreasonable given the data cited by Gordon (UT:446). For a different reading of this line, see Caquot, Sznycer, and Herdner (1974:125).

[91] Reading with Herdner (CTA:10 , note 19).

[92] Gordon (UT:360, 391) notes that the reading *ʾm* for "if" is unusual. One expects to find *hm* used instead. I have left the particle untranslated because its exact meaning is difficult to determine in light of the lacunae in this line.

own hands and challenges Yamm. He reminds Šapaš of his position, boasting of his title and defying the powers of Death.

He seems to indicate that he plans to descend into the underworld in pursuit of Yamm.[93] As a sojourner through the underworld he is (theoretically) in regular contact with both Sea and Death.[94] He would have no reason to fear the inhabitants of these regions because he is partially chthonic.

22b-24

wan <taᶜni šapšu >[95]	And Šapaš answered:
ᵓêna ᵓaθθatu [li-]ka ka[mā ᵓilīma]	"There is no wife for you like the gods."
[ ] zubūlu yammu yuθa[θib] θāpiṭu naharu	...Prince Yamm was seated, Judge River...
[ ]yišlaḥūna	....they sent
wa-yaᶜni ᶜaθtaru	and Athtar answered:

It is unfortunate that the text breaks off so abruptly. We know nothing of the resolution of the conflict. It is possible that the conclusion was similar to that in KTU 1.6 VI 30-35 where Mot ceases his battle with Baal after being warned by Šapaš of El's retribution. Perhaps Athtar halted his assault on Yamm. Nothing conclusive can be said about this.

---

[93] If Athtar is the morning star, this may be an important issue in understanding the role that astral deities played in the ancient Near East. It is possible that they are partially independent because they span two realms—the heavens and the underworld. This may be particularly true of the old triad of Sun, Moon, and Venus/Athtar. More needs to be done on the characterization of astral gods in all of the genres of Ugaritidliterature.

[94] I assume here that such a descent, similar to that of Šapaš, is at least hypothetically possible. The sun regularly sets in the west, hence it is quite realistic to suppose that Šapaš enters Yamm's domain at sunset (from the perspective of one living on the coast of the Mediterranean). Such a course could be assumed for other astral deities who are may be seen in the early morning and in the evening (Moon and Venus for example).

[95] Speakers have changed here. Perhaps this is Šapaš speaking. A line marking the change in speakers could have been omitted in the process of transmission.

6.1.2.2 Athtar's Status in KTU 1.2

Conclusions about this text must be modest. If the reconstruction of the events narrated is correct, Athtar is doing nothing different from Yamm or Baal. He makes a request for a permanent home and prepares to do battle with one of the members of the divine family. There is nothing in these lines that suggests that Athtar's stature is any less than that of Yamm or Baal.

This text clearly indicates that Athtar has some measure of authority among his divine peers. Even if the conjectural reading *d mlk* is left out of consideration, the statement *malaktu [wa-]ʾim lā-malaktu* "I am king...indeed, I am king" indicates that he has this status. Line 20 may refer to his descent to the underworld (similar to that mentioned in KTU 1.6 I). In no way does the tone of this descent or any other aspect of this text seem negative with regard to Athtar.

Athtar is characterized as a fully functioning (though homeless and unmarried) administrative deity (king) who is interested in acquiring possessions (house). He also has the freedom of movement and strength to descend to the underworld and challenge his adversaries. Athtar's function in the plot of this episode is not at variance with the holistic overview of his personality presented above.

6.1.3 KTU 1.6 I 43-67—An Overview

After Baal's death a replacement must be named to continue Baal's functions. This text describes the sequence of events that leads to the designation of Athtar as that replacement. The text is well preserved but ends abruptly with a break after line 66. The plot is not a complicated one, but there are two important themes that are woven into the episode: (1) Asherah and El as Athtar's co-benefactors, and (2) voluntary divine abdication.

6.1.3.1 Analysis

43-46

gām[96] yaṣiḥ ʾilu li-rabbati[97] ʾaθirati yammi	EM[98]		El cried aloud to Lady Athirat of the Sea:
šamaʿī li-rabbatu ʾaθira[t]u yammi[99]	13	1	"Hear O Lady Athirat of the Sea,
tinī ʾaḥada bi-banīka ʾamallikannu[100]	14	1	Give one of your sons that I may make him king."

With Baal the conqueror dead, a power vacuum exists in the divine assembly. El mourns, Anat is distraught. All wonder what will become of creation without Baal. With the assistance of Šapaš, Anat recovers Baal's body and buries it atop Ṣapon. After sacrifice for the fallen warrior, she reports his death to El and Asherah. Opportunity exists now for Asherah to name another son to replace Baal as Ṣapon's ruler, and El asks her advice in choosing a successor.

47-54

wa-taʿni rabbatu ʾaθiratu yammi	EM	And Lady Athirat of the Sea answered:

---

[96] BH *gam* in Psalm 137:1, which some translate "loudly" (UT:378), should be compared. BDB cites the Arabic root √*gmm* meaning "to become much or abundant," and translates BH *gam* "also, moreover" (BDB:168). Segert (1984:182) suggests the vocalization *gū/gā/gī* for Ugaritic *gū* meaning "voice." One is led to conclude that the final *mêm* is either enclitic or adverbial. Any of the following vocalizations seems reasonable: *gam, gūm, or gām.*

[97] Compare the root √*rbb* in Hebrew meaning "to be/become many, much" (BDB:912-913), and the Aramaic adj. *rb* "great" (BDB:1112). See also Huehnergard's vocalization (UV:176).

[98] EM = Extra Metrical Line.

[99] Cross has described this as a sentence name from a cultic formula or litany, the divine name (frequently a verbal element) being the first part thereof. These evolve like other hypocoristic names, often leaving only the first verbal element. Other examples of this type of name include *ʾalʾiyu qarrādima > ʾalʾiyānu [once ʾalʾiyu baʿl]* "I prevail over the heroes," *yadiʿ yilḥan,* "he knows, he understands," and *rākib/rakub ʿarapāti,* "cloud rider" (1973:66-67).

[100] Akkadian *malāku,* "to counsel, to advise" (AHw^2:593) could be compared, but lacks the semantic range necessary in this context. Hebrew √*mlk* (*mālāk*) "to be/become king" (BDB:573-574) is more appropriate in this instance.

bal[101] namallika yadiᶜ yilḥan[102]	9	1	"Surely, let us make Yadi Yilḥan king."
wa-yaᶜni luṭpānu[103] ʾilu dū paʾidi[104]	EM		And Luṭpan, El the kindly one, answered

---

[101] In Hebrew poetic and prophetic style, *bal* is equivalent to *lōʾ*. Its root is possibly √*blh* meaning "to waste away." Note also Hebrew *bəlī, bélet (>biltî),* which were originally substantives (GKC:481; BDB:115). In Ugaritic, *bl(t)* is at times positive, but Gordon believes that in such instances the nuance is that of a rhetorical question with negative *bl(t)* (UT:372). He would translate *bal* here with a negative force, and *biltī* in line 54 with a positive force. I translate the first occurrence as a positive (emphatic) particle and the latter as a negative particle introducing a rhetorical question.

[102] Cross translates "he knows, he understands" (1973:66-67). See also Cross (1973:67, note 84) for reference to the use of *ylḥn* in the Amman Citadel Inscription. Aistleitner translates *bl nmlk ydᶜ ylḥnn* "bestellen wir zum König den, der versteht unterwürfig zu sein" (1974:170). Gordon cites Elephantine Aramaic *lḥn* "servitor" and suggests "to serve" as the meaning of the root √*lḥn.* He also notes the Arabic meaning of the root, "to be intelligent." Aufrecht (1989:154, 161) reads *ylnn* rather than *ylḥn* in line 4 of the Amman Citadel Inscription.

[103] This is an El epithet. Aistleitner translates it as "der Gütige" from Arabic *laṭīf,* "gütig, freundlich" (1974:170). Gordon notes the variant reading *lẓpn ʾil ðpʾid* in UT 77:44-45, the use of *lṭpn* alone in UT 49:IV:35, and its combination with *qdš* in UT 125:11 = 125:21-22 (UT:428).

[104] Aistleitner translates *pʾid* as "gemütsvoll" citing Arabic *fuʾād,* "Herz, Sinn." Gordon suggests "mercy" (UT:466). Cross compares a number of epithets including *ðū ṭôbi* "the merciful one" (15th century Proto-Sinaitic Inscription), ʾil *ðū ᶜālami* "El, the ancient one" (Proto-Sinaitic Inscription), and *ðū gitti* "lord of Gath/Lord of the winepress" (Proto-Sinaitic Inscription). Epithets of this type are, in his opinion, a common 15th-century phenomenon. In the Proto-Sinaitic Inscriptions in particular, he sees evidence of the equation of Egyptian and Canaanite gods (Ptaḥ = El, Ḥatḥor = Asherah). He cites survivals in the Hebrew Bible like *zê sīnay* (< *ðū sīnay*) in Judges 5:5, and also notes sporadic usage of *zū* before verbs (*zū qānîtā* "whom you did create" in Exodus 15:16) and believes that this too is common in 15th century Palestine. He also brings in additional evidence from Amorite personal names (*zū ḫatni, zū sumim*) and states that *ðū* in divine epithets is common in Old Canaanite and very frequent in South Arabic (Cross 1973:19-20, notes 37 and 44).

daqqu[105] ᵓānīma[106] lā yarūẓu[107] ᶜimma baᶜli	13	l	"(One so) minute in strength cannot race with Baal.
lā yaᶜdubu[108] murḥa[109] ᶜimma	10	l	He cannot handle the spear with Dagan's Son
kītammassā-mi[110]	5	b	when they test one another."

---

[105] The root √*dqq* is attested in Arabic, Ethiopic, Akkadian, Aramaic, and Biblical Hebrew with the meaning "to crush, pulverize, thresh." Note should be taken also of the additional Arabic and Akkadian nuance "to be/become thin, minute" (BDB:200). In Biblical Hebrew one finds the adjective *daq,* "small, fine, thin" (BDB:201), in Arabic *diqq* which Aistleitner translates "zart, dünn, "and in Ethiopic *daqīq,* "zerstossen, klein" (1974:81). Note also that in the Ugaritic polyglot vocabulary *daqqu* is the equivalent of Akkadian *ṣeḫru* (UV:119).

[106] Compare Biblical Hebrew √*ᵓwn* II, "be at ease, rest, enjoy a life of plenty," and *ᵓôn,* "vigor, wealth; strength" (BDB:20).

[107] KTU reads *yrq* here. I have adopted the reading of Herdner (CTA:39). For the final *ẓ* of *yrẓ,* compare the Biblical Hebrew root √*rwṣ* meaning "to run" (BDB:930).

[108] Gordon proposes the meaning "to prepare, make, set," for the root √*ᶜdb.* The masculine noun *ᶜdb* in UT 2029:19 he translates as "agent (to whom a land grant is assigned for management)," and the feminine noun *ᶜdbt* he thinks might be a general word like "arrangement" which has multiple nuances (UT:454). Hebrew √*ᶜzb* II (BDB:737) should also be compared. In the present context, one should expect a verb detailing what is done with a *murḥu* "spear." Perhaps "to throw" or "to handle" (with a wider meaning reflecting all of the things one might do with a spear—for example warfare, competition, etc.). Here, the idea might be that *Yadiᶜ Yilhan* is not as good a spear handler (in battle or displays of skill) as Baal.

[109] Biblical Hebrew *rōmaḥ* "spear, lance" is to be compared (BDB:942). Gordon cites North Egyptian *mrḥ.* It is generally believed that this form in Egyptian was borrowed from a Northwest-Semitic dialect like Ugaritic and that *mrḥ,* wherever it occurs, is a metathesized form of *rmḥ.* Other reflexes are Arabic *rumḥ*, Ethiopic *ramḥ*, and Coptic *marah* (BDB:942; UT:437-438).

[110] This is a difficult line. Gibson (1976:75) reads *k msm* "when the time is right," in agreement with Caquot, Sznycer, and Herdner. He treats *msm* as a noun (?) meaning "opportune moment" from Arabic *mawsimu* which has the same meaning (1976:151). The major problem with this is that Herdner reads *ktmsm* (CTA 6.1.52). I agree with Mullen's interpretation of *k* in *ktmsm* as adverbial *kī* (1980:37, note 64). I am also in agreement with him that the form should be derived from the root √*mss*, and that the final *m* is to be treated as an enclitic *-mi.* He compares the meaning of this

wa-ᶜanû rabbatu ʾaθiratu yammi	EM		And Lady Athirat of the Sea answered:
baltī namallika ᶜaθtara ᶜarīẓa[111]	7	1	"Should we not make Athtar the terrible king."

Asherah is shrewd, she recommends Athtar as a replacement, but refers to him by his epithet *Yadiʾ Yilḥan.* This might be seen as an appeal to El's ego. Emphasis on Athtar's sagacity might make El look favorably upon the recommendation. El's response is interesting. He *constructs* Athtar differently. He does not question his intelligence and no mention is made of what Athtar "knows" and "understands." Instead, he suggests that Athtar does not possess the competitive skills or acumen as warrior to challenge Baal. The implication here is that if the replacement named could not conceivably defeat Baal in combat, then he is not a suitable replacement for him. Asherah persists and recommends Athtar once again, making reference this time to his epithet "terrible/awesome."

55-61a

yumallak ᶜaθtaru ᶜarīẓu	9	1	Athtar the terrible was made king.
ʾappūnaka ᶜaθtaru ᶜarīẓu	10	1	Then Athtar the terrible
yaᶜli bi-ṣarūrāti ṣapāni[112]	10	1	went up to the far reaches of Ṣapon.

---

verb to Arabic *massa,* "to feel, touch, hit, befall." This reading preserves the imagery of the contest initiated in line 50. I have followed a suggestion made by Cross (personal communication) and vocalized *tmsm* as an N 3rd masc. dual. verb.

[111] I have followed Mullen's suggestion of comparing the epithet *ᶜarīẓu* to Biblical Hebrew *nᶜrṣ* used of Yahweh in Psalm 89:8 (Mullen 1980:36-37, note 63). BH *ᶜārîṣ* (as in Ezekiel 28:7 below) "awe-inspiring, terror-striking" should also be compared (BDB:792).

[112] BH has the root √*ṣrr* I "to bind, tie up, be restricted" (BDB:864). Gordon mentions a personal communication from J. Finkel which identifies *ṣrrt ṣpn* with *ṣrwr ᶜwn ʾprym ṣpwnh ḥṭʾtw* in Hos. 13:12. He also proposes that its original meaning might have been "the recesses of the hiding place." In UT text 1111:9 he notes the noun *mṣrrt* from the same root, the meaning of which suggests some manner of "wrap" (UT:476). Gordon wants one to assume that the noun *ṣrrt* refers to the upper reaches of a mountain, hidden by cloud cover. BH *yarkətê ṣāpôn,* "far reaches of the north/Ṣapon," may be compared here. It is found in Is. 14:13; Ezek. 38:6, 15; 39:2; and Psalm 48:3. In some instances, the meaning of Ṣapon is mythological, referring

yaθib[113] li-kaḫθi[114] ʾalʾiyāni baʿli	10	1	He sat in Aliyan Baal's throne.
paʿnāhu lā-tamǵiyāni[115] huduma[116]	11	1	His feet would not reach the stool.
raʾšuhu lā-yamǵiyu ʾapsahu	10	1	His head would not reach its top.

Athtar ascended to the heights of Ṣapon and took his place on the throne of Baal only to discover that his feet would not reach Baal's footstool and his head would not reach the top of the throne. Interestingly, his size was never criticized by Asherah or Baal. In spite of this apparent deficiency, he is not removed from the throne by El. In fact, one hears nothing in the way of a response by El or Asherah. Athtar descends, voluntarily, to the underworld.

61b-67

wa-yaʿni ʿaθtaru ʿarīẓu	EM		And Athtar the terrible answered:
lā-ʾamluku bi-ṣarūrāti ṣapāni	12	1	"I will not rule from atop Ṣapon."
yarid ʿaθtaru ʿarīẓu	8	1	Athtar the terrible came down,
yarid li-kaḫθi ʾalʾiyāni baʿli	9	1	from the throne of Aliyan Baal he descended.

---

to the location of the cosmic mountain, the place of the divine assembly's meeting (Isaiah 14:13), in others it indicates a geographical location far removed, whence menacing foes originate (Ezek. 38:6, 15; 39:2, the Gog/Magog material), and in one instance (Psalm 48:3) Zion is said to be in the "far reaches of the north." Though there is certainly more than a distant relationship between KTU 1.6 I 43-67 and Isaiah 14:4b-20a, Ugaritic *bi-ṣarūrāti ṣapāni* and BH *yarkətê Ṣāpôn* refer to disparate locales, the former to the summit of Mt. Ṣapon, home of Baal, the latter to the Amanus region, where El's home is located (Cross 1973:38-39).

[113] The second edition of KTU reads *yṯb*—a possible misprint. I have adopted the reading of the first edition of KTU —*yθb*.

[114] Gordon cites the Canaanite Amarna gloss *ka-aḫ-šu*, and Friedrich AfO 14 (1944):329-331, who identifies it with Hurrian *kišḫi*, "chair." (UT:418).

[115] The root *√mǵy*, "to reach, come, arrive," is from the Proto-Semitic root **√mθ̣y*. This is one of several Ugaritic words in which the reflex for Proto-Semitic *θ̣* is written with a sign otherwise used exclusively for the reflex of Proto-Semitic *ǵ*: *ǵr* "mountain," *√ǵmʾ* "to be thirsty," *√nǵr* "to guard/protect," *√yqǵ* "to be alert," and *√mǵy* "to arrive." See Gordon (UT:27-28, par. 5.8).

[116] Mullen (1980:36) and Gibson (1976:76,145) translate "footstool." BH *hdm* (BDB:213) should be compared.

wa-yamluk bi-ʾarṣi ʾilu kulliha[117]	12	1	And he ruled over the Underworld,[118] god of all of it.
[xxx .]tišʾabūna bi-raḥabāti[119]	9	1	They drew water in flagons.
[xxxxx . ti]šʾabūna bi-kakkanāti	9	1	They drew water in jars.

Athtar decides not to reign from atop Ṣapon, but to exercise authority over the underworld where his rule continues. The idea that self-recognition of shortcomings is somehow virtuous may be operative here. If so, Athtar can be understood as an honorable figure because he gave up his position before it was taken from him forcibly. Another alternative is to view Athtar's action as that of a self-possessed entity who chooses to relinquish that claim to authority given to him by his benefactors and makes himself king over a region which they have not designated. I find this latter interpretation compelling because it allows the text's most basic meaning to assume priority.

6.1.3.2 Athtar's Status in KTU 1.6

The trend toward viewing this episode as a failure on Athtar's part results from the general tendency to see all of the characters and events in the epic in light of larger hermeneutical efforts that treat Baal's death and the cosmic crisis that ensues before he is resurrected as critical events.[120] While it is certainly true that Baal's death and return to life are important features of the narrative, Athtar need not be characterized simply as an inferior replacement for Baal—a deity whose impotence is in stark contrast to Baal's superior power. To let go of a coveted political position voluntarily (even if one is not in possession of the requisite skills to fulfill its responsibilities effectively) certainly seems rather unusual. To do so and suffer no adverse consequences seems to be an even more radical departure from the expected norm. Yet his descent to the underworld as king implies that on some level Athtar has placed himself in proximity to or relationship with the only god that Baal proves incapable of defeating (KTU 1.6 VI 16-22). Therefore, his

---

[117] Gibson translates "the earth of El, all of it," and cites *ḥkpt ʾil klh* (KTU 1.3 VI 13-14) "Memphis of El, all of it" or "all of broad Memphis," and *ǵr ʾil ṣpn* (KTU 1.3 III 29) "my rock El Ṣapan," in support of his reading (1976:76, note 2). I take this as a reference to the underworld.

[118] On *ʾarṣ* as "underworld" see Smith (1986a:312).

[119] I follow here the reading of KTU.

[120] It is easy to see how Athtar's status could be interpreted minimally and/or negatively in any one of the interpretive systems cited in Smith's study (1986b:313-323) because all of them are Baal-centered interpretations.

unusual behavior only serves to highlight the mystery surrounding him—his *otherness* when compared to Baal. From a thematic standpoint, Baal's death and Athtar's peculiar behavior receive equal emphasis.

This episode asserts that Athtar is an enigmatic, but powerful, force. This picture is not at variance with that obtained from an éxamination of his personal profile.

6.2 Athtar in the Baal Myth—An Alternate Interpretation

This study has called into question the conclusion of Gaster and others that Athtar has diminished status in the *Baal Cycle.* Both are strong and independent divine personages within the myth. It has also established that there does in fact appear to be an indigenous model for understanding divine personhood which has influenced Ugaritic literature, the components of which are discernible in the descriptions of Baal and Athtar. Although these descriptions are technically *etic* the density and diversity of descriptive material suggest the existence of corresponding *emic* taxonomies and speculation relative to character—divine and human.

Examining the personal characteristics of Baal and Athtar more closely has facilitated a more in-depth comparison of the relationship of these two gods to one another. Thus, the feasibility of character study as an avenue of inquiry in the analysis of Ugaritic literature would appear to be strongly indicated. This initial *test-case* has also found that there are differences in the data employed in divine description and that these are significant. They enable one to delineate the status of a god more explicitly and provide a needed control for expository work which is reliant upon hermeneutical frameworks which assume that the *Baal Cycle* has a single unifying theme. The plot and theme of the two texts examined describing Athtar's activities provide no support for viewing Athtar as inferior to Baal.

Finally, there is almost certainly a connection between the *Baal Cycle* and the culture of Ugarit.[121] Moreover, there seems to be merit in the use of this myth as *ethnological map,* so long as it is understood that a map is an artistic and intellectual construct which reflects reality as seen through the

---

[121] The question of whether the mythological and epic texts found at Ugarit were originally generated there remains unresolved. That the texts contain material whose origin is much earlier is quite likely. Equally perplexing is the degree to which the texts as they now exist have been shaped by the aesthetic, world view, social location, and political exigencies of the bard who dictated them.

mind's eye of its creator(s). The use of the map metaphor in the interpretation of myth enables us to treat it as a window through which to view cultural actualities as perceived and creatively characterized by the mythological map maker. In addition to personal detail, the *Baal Cycle* contains a vast amount of cultural information that is capable of categorization by *emic* and *etic* devices.[122] It also commends itself as a data-base for the testing of theories. Unfortunately, more needs to be known about the material culture of Ugarit and about daily life in its multi-ethnic urban environment before the chasm between the speculative world of myth and the more concrete sphere of socio-cultural *realia* can be bridged.[123] At the very least, this interpretive model provides a control for other long-established interpretive efforts.

As for these wider implications of this particular *test-case*, it confirms the appropriateness of character study as a hermeneutical model, and indicates the need for similar examinations of other gods and mortals in this and the remaining Ugaritic myths (*Kirta* and *Aqhat*). The results of these must be awaited before a more comprehensive understanding of divine and human personhood in Ugaritic literary tradition can be obtained. Nonetheless, it is safe to say that in the masterpiece that is the *Baal Cycle*, Athtar's is one of many descanting personalities in a polysemous cosmic libretto that provides the ethnological underpinnings for Ugaritic society.

6.3 Dawn, Dusk, and the "Resplendent Warrior" in KTU 1.23

The combination of liturgical rubrics, repetitiveness, unusual mythological references, and shifting scenes found in KTU 1.23 has contributed to the long-standing debate about its purpose and meaning. The most convincing interpretive framework involves seeing it as "the libretto to a cultic drama"

---

[122] Among these may be included gods, persons, places, times, implements of war, emotive responses, divine polarities, metals, stones, natural disasters, travel routes, animals, measurements of distance, colors, numbers, abstract principles and concepts, cities, clothing, items used in textile manufacture, cooking and eating implements, items used in the construction of buildings, items used in the conduct of commerce, and ethnic groups.

[123] This is particularly important if we hope to gain any understanding of the place of women in Ugaritic society and of goddesses and female figures in Ugaritic literature. The tendency to make generalizations based on questionable presuppositions has been commented on by Walls (1992:1-11) and Hackett (1989:65-76).

(Cross 1974a:246; Gaster 1950:225).[124] The mythological sections describe El's seduction of his two wives and the birth of his two children Dawn and Dusk. These offspring are variously called, *ilm n*^{c}*mm*, "beautiful gods" (KTU 1.23.1, 23, 58, 60), *agzrym bn ym*, "ravenous[125] sons of the day" (KTU 1.23.23, 58-59, 61), *ynqm bap zd aθrt*, "those who suck on the teats of the Lady's breasts" (KTU 1.23.24, 59, 61), and *bn šrm*, "sons of the shining ones" (KTU 1.23.2, 22). Gray (1949:72-73, 83; 1965:169-174) suggested that the gods Šaḥar and Šalim are hypostases of Athtar, that worship of the god Šalim was centered at Jerusalem at least from the time of the Egyptian *Execration Texts* which give the name of the city as *Urušlmm*, and that during the period of the Israelite monarchy, this god was also worshipped under the names Athtar, Milkom (in Ammon), and Kemoš (in Moab) (1965:171, 173). As mentioned above, he based his findings on the presumed absence of Athtar in Ugaritic offering lists and his minor role in Ugaritic mythology (1969:170).[126] What Gray did not mention is that Athtar appears as a theophoric element in personal names at Ugarit, along with Šaḥar and Šalim.[127] For Gray's thesis to be correct, one would have to allow for the assimilation of Athtar to Šaḥar and Šalim in god lists and hypostatization in onomastica. This seems highly unlikely. Furthermore, Old Akkadian personal names attest the presence of Athtar and Šalim in the earliest Semitic pantheon (Roberts 1972:36, 51, 57). Therefore Athtar, Šaḥar, and Šalim are best treated as independent entities, with the latter two taken as the deification of first light (early morning) and evening (just after the setting of the sun). Evidence does not suggest that they represent the morning and evening stars.

---

[124] The original setting of the festival cannot be determined with specificity. Gaster himself proposed two dates. In an early article he associated this text with the Tammuz rites of the autumnal equinox (1941:294). In a later study, he proposed that the text was the order of service for the Canaanite feast of first fruits held in the spring which was itself the prototype for the Israelite feast of Weeks (1950:227). Internal evidence supports neither contention strongly.

[125] I follow here the translation of Cross (personal communication) who compares KTU 1.23.63 which reads *wndd gzr l<g>zr*, "and they wandered/moved back and forth, bite to bite." He also cites Isaiah 9:19—*ygzr* ^{c}*l ymyn wr*^{c}*b* "He ravens on the right and is hungry," in which *ygzr* is derived from √*gzr* "to cut, divide" (BDB:160).

[126] Attestations of Athtar in Ugaritic god lists are now known to exist.

[127] For Ugaritic onomastic data see Gröndahl (1967:113-114, 192, 193) as well as Gordon 's glossary (UT:508-519).

6.3.1 *Analysis*

Three passages require consideration: lines 8-11 which introduce the travails of the god *mt wšr*, 52-56 announcing both the birth of the gracious gods and preparation for the arrival of Šapaš and the *kbkbm knm* "Fixed Stars," and 61-64 which tell briefly of the characteristics of these newborn gods.

8-11

m(ô/u)tu wa-šarru yaθibu	8	1	Death and Shining One[128] sits—
badi-hu ḫaṭṭu θakāli	8	1	in one hand, the scepter of bereavement
badi-hu ḫaṭṭu ʾulmāni	8	1	in the other, the staff of widowhood.
yazabbirū-na-nnŭ zabarī-mi gapni	12	1	Let them prune him with the prunings of the vine.
yaṣammidū-na-nnŭ ṣamadī-mi gapni	12	1	Let them bind him with the bindings of the vine.
yašqīlū[129] šadīmati-ha[130] kamā gapni	7	1	Let them cast (him) to the terraces like a vine.

The identification of the main character, *mt wšr*, is in question. Gaster (1950:241) translated this line "as lord and master sat he enthroned," identified this figure as a dionysiac spirit,[131] and suggested that the viticultural imagery of lines 8-11 lent itself to sexual interpretation. Therefore, pruning = emasculation, the vine stalk = the *membrum virile*, and the pruned vine = slain god. Gibson suggested the translation "Mot and Šar sat down," and proposed that the ensuing scene should be interpreted as the destruction of the god of death (1976:28, 123). He also cited Driver's proposed reading,

---

[128] Alternately "The Resplendent Warrior." On *mt* as "husband; man, warrior" see CAD[10(II)]:313-314. These meanings are attested in Old Babylonian texts, Amarna correspondence, and later Akkadian literature. Cf. Biblical Hebrew *mat* n.m. "male, man" found only in the plural and in the personal names *mətûšāʾēl* and *mətûšelaḥ* (BDB:607) as well as Ethiopic *mət* (pl. *ʾamtāt*) "husband" (Leslau 1987:371).

[129] This is a Š form of the root √*qyl*.

[130] This may perhaps be vocalized *šadīmati-h*.

[131] Gaster has compared Ugaritic *mt* with Akkadian *mutu*.

"Death and Dissolution,"[132] and that of Tsumura, "Death and Evil"[133] (1976:28, n. 1). Mullen (1980:239-240, esp. n. 208) proposed "Mot and Shining One." He compared Ugaritic *šr* with Akkadian *šarāru* meaning "to shine" and with Arabic *šarrār* meaning "sparkling."[134] Regrettably, this is the only known occurrence of this double name in the corpus of divine names from Ugarit, though other double names are attested.[135]

Miller (1987:58), in his discussion on Ugaritic religion, suggested that originally the process of combining names in the "X and Y" pattern involved linking deities who shared obvious relationships (*bᶜl wdgn; špš wyrḫ; ᶜnt wʾθrt*). However, each god retained its own individuality. Later on in the historical process, particular combinations became more or less fixed so that they came to be treated as single gods (*kθr wḫss; mt wšr; nkl wib; qdš wamrr*). These were capable of being broken up and placed in parallel cola of poetry and the conjunction could be dropped—an indication of the fact that the *wa-* had lost its functional significance. Miller suggested that this resulted in the formation of a single name. He cited Atargatis of late Syro-Phoenician religion as an example in which this process has taken place.

Miller's suggestion that the name *mt wšr* refers to a single deity is certainly credible. Unfortunately little else can be said. The implements which this god is said to be holding indicate that one is dealing with a figure associated with death. The binding and pruning seem to fit the picture presented by Gaster of the ritual reenactment of this god's slaughter.

Mullen's vocalization *mōtu wa šarru* for Ugaritic *mt wšr* has been adopted provisionally along with his translation "Death and Shining One."

---

[132] Driver derived *šr* from √*šry*.

[133] Tsumura compared *šr* with Arabic *šarru*.

[134] On p. 239 n. 208, he credited Cross with first pointing out to him "the concept of Ugaritic *šr* as "Shining One" and its parallels with biblical reflections of unsuccessful revolts against the high god." Note however that the G stem of the root √*šrr* is not productive of finite verb forms in Akkadian. It is reflected in the Akkadian adj. *šarūru* (AHw³:1193-1194; CAD¹⁷⁽ᴵᴵ⁾:140-143). Interestingly, Akkadian *šarūru* "radiance, brilliance" is used of the planet Venus in astronomical texts and of the god Ištar in magical and other contexts (CAD¹⁷⁽ᴵᴵ⁾:141-142).

[135] Gordon cited some eight of these in addition to *mt wšr*, and J.C. de Moor proposed more than thirty of these combinations (UT:521-522; de Moor 1970:187-228). Note the following divine names that include the element *šr* in de Moor's list—*ʾil šr* (#23) and *ᶜd wšr* (#157).

His suggestion that the parallel between *šr* here and *hyll bn šḥr* who is cast into the underworld in Isaiah 14:12 also has merit (1980:241). However, a number of questions remain unresolved. If, as Mullen suggested, the connection between the "Shining One" and Mot is explained, in terms of known mythological references, by the former having been cast into the latter's domain, what now are the characteristics of this new independent god? Of what significance is his ritual slaughter? Is an astral or a chthonic god envisioned here? The god Ešmun, a chthonic deity, is also called *šr* "Shining One" in KAI 14, line 17, further complicating matters.[136] There seems to be some ambiguity, therefore, in determining the character of *mt wšr*.

It is conceivable that the celestial peregrinations of the old triad (Sun, Moon, and Venus) may have contributed to the belief that these deities traversed the underworld. This would make them both astral and chthonic, and hence, fittingly called "Shining Ones" for at least a part of their regular cycle of manifestation.[137] If, as Mullen has suggested (1980:238-239),[138] there

---

[136] This datum was first pointed out to me by Cross (personal communication). On the relationship between *Šaḥar* and *Ešmun* see Albright (1946:79, 196 n. 25).

[137] According to Roberts (1972:57), astral deities occupied an important place in the Old Semitic pantheon as is attested by their popularity as theophoric elements in Mesopotamian personal names prior to Ur III. These included *Šamaš, Suʾen, Eštar, Ay(y)a, Šalim, ūmum, and Ištaran* (perhaps). Of these, *Šamaš, Suʾen, and Eštar* (Sun, Moon, and Venus) compose an important triad in the early Semitic period. This is demonstrated by the fact that each of the three occurs in other Semitic languages and by the fact that they represent three of the four deities (*Ay(y)a,* god of fresh water springs is the fourth) who appear most often as theophoric elements in Old Akkadian personal names. Roberts suggested—in agreement with Jacobsen (1968), Nielsen (1942), and Gray (1949), who have proposed that astral veneration is typical of semi-nomadic herdsmen and shepherds—that astral worship must have been of great importance in the early Semitic period, particularly if a semi-nomadic background is assumed for the early Semites.

[138] Interestingly enough, Mullen never clearly acknowledged belief in the Athtar/*hyll*/*mt wšr* equation. However, by noting the persuasiveness of Grelot's (1956) *hyll* /Venus/Athtar identification, and the parallel between Ugaritic *šr* and BH *hyll*, his tacit approval of the Athtar/*hyll*/*mt wšr* identification is implied. He discussed the likely characteristics of the two individual gods whose names make up part of the double name *mt wšr*, but did not develop a personality profile for the god as an independent entity.

is in fact a connection between *mt wšr*, *hyll bn šḥr*, and Athtar, then an alternative vocalization presents itself which makes the identification of this god with the enigmatic figure from Isaiah 14 and Athtar more apparent, and answers some of the questions raised above.

If one vocalizes *mt* as *mutu*, "man, husband" (UT:439) and supposes here a contextualized meaning similar to that found in Isaiah 3:25,[139] the dual name would then connote one who was an astral combatant. The imagery in lines 8-11 is similar to that found in Isaiah 14:5-6.

šbr yhwh mṭh ršᶜym	Yahweh has broken the staff of the rebels,
šbṭ mšlym	the rod of the rulers,
mkh ᶜmym bᶜbrh	the one who arrogantly cut down peoples,
mkt blty srh	with repeated blows,

An unnamed tyrant, identified only as the king of Babylon (14:4a) is addressed and vss. 5-6 begin the description of his demise—an event that is accompanied by rejoicing in the fabric of the cosmos. His fall is hailed by the cedars and cypresses of Lebanon and causes a stirring of activity in Sheol. Thus, the fall of the king is accompanied by a positive response from the created world. This is not unlike what is found in KTU 1.23. There is also striking similarity between the implements held by *mt wšr* and the *mṭh ršᶜym* and *šbṭ mšlym* in Isaiah 14:4. While the heaviest concentration of mythological material is to be found in 14:12-15, it must be remembered that historical and mythic references have been blended impressionistically so as to form a unified historico-mythological piece extending from vss. 4b-20a. As a result, the *hyll* myth in vss. 12-15 is crucial to understanding the king's crimes in vss. 5-6, and 16-17, the response of nature in 7-8, the tumult in Sheol described in vss. 9-11, and the king's fate in vss. 16-20a. There is an implied relationship between the behavior of *hyll* and that of the king. Therefore, the *mṭh ršᶜym* and *šbṭ mšlym* of Isaiah 14:4 can be understood as symbols of chaos and disorder whose importance is both earthly and cosmic. Their destruction is an act which restores political order and cosmic equilibrium. The symbols of authority held in the hands of *mt wšr* might be similarly identified. That chaos is to be associated with the rule of a divine usurper should not surprise. The granting of divine kingship is a prerogative belonging to El (cf. KTU 1.6 I 45-46). The process of binding, pruning, and throwing *mt wšr* to the ground (lines 8-11)

---

[139] The verse reads *mtyk bḥrb yplw // wgbwrtyk bmlḥmh* "your warriors shall fall by the sword and your mighty men in battle."

could possibly symbolize the wresting of power from his hands and the crushing of his hegemony.

If this reading is adopted, the slaughter of this warrior would juxtapose nicely with the *hieros gamos* and the birth of Dawn and Dusk (lines 30-61). The reenactment of his death would symbolize the restoration of cosmic order and the return of fecundity to the universe through the elimination of the forces of chaos. This would seem to be the case even without vocalizing *mt* as *mūtu*. The location of this scene before El's seduction scene and the birth of his sons suggests that this god's destruction was necessary before Šaḥar and Šalim could be conceived and born. The single drawback to this proposal is the account of Mot's death at Anat's hands in KTU 1.6 II 30-37, which lines 8-11 may echo. If *mt wšr* is Athtar—a datum indicated more from similarities between this text and Isaiah 14 than by those shared by Athtar references in the Baal myth and Isaiah 14—one would then need to establish a reason for his ritualized slaughter.

52-56

rigmu la-ʾili yubala	8	1	A message was carried to El.
ʾaθθa[tā-yyū̆]ʾili yalattā	9	1	El's two wives have given birth.
maha yalattā	5	b	What did they bear?
yaldê-yyū̆ šaḥra wa-šali[ma]	9	1	His two sons, Šaḥar and Šalim.
šaʾū ʿudubū li-šapši rabbati	11	1	Raise up, prepare for Lady Šapš
wa-li-kabkabīma k(ā̆/i)nīma	9	1	and the fixed stars.
yahburu šaptê-humā yaššiqu	10	1	He bows, he kisses their lips.
hinna šaptêhumā matuqatā[-mi]	11	1	Behold, their lips are sweet,
[matuqatāmi ka-lurmāni-mi]	10	1	sweet like a pomegranate.
bimā našāqi wa-harû[140]	9	1	In kissing there was conceiving,
bi-ḫabāqi wa-ḥu[m]ḥumtu	9	1	in embracing, passion

The birth of El's sons is announced and a command is given to prepare for the arrival of Šapaš and the "Fixed Stars." Presumably these are other members of the astral contingent who are to witness the birth of Dawn and Dusk. It is not unreasonable to suppose that some of the astral gods either had their own assembly or were accorded special status.[141] Rummel

[140] See UV:288, n. 93 for this form.

[141] The preponderance of Pre-Sargonic and Sargonic personal names in Mesopotamia which have *Šamaš, Suʾen, and Eštar* as theophoric elements may be an indication of the special status enjoyed by these gods (Roberts 1972:57).

(1981:431-441) cited the following parallel references to assemblies of stars and/or astral gods in Ugaritic and biblical literature:

pḫr kkbm (KTU 1.10 I 4)	*kwkby ʾl* (Isaiah 14:13)[142]
	kwkby bqr (Job 38:7)
	hkkbm ʾl (KAI 277:10-11)
ṣbu špš (KTU 1.41.47)	*ṣbʾ hšmym* (1 Kings 22:19)
	ṣbʾ hmrwm (Isaiah 24:21)
mlk ṣbu špš (KTU 1.41.53)	*śr ṣbʾ hšmym* (Joshua 5:14-15)

These are valid parallels. The nature of the phenomena represented is clear. This is the retinue of El, present to witness the momentous occasion of the nativity of Dawn and Dusk.[143] There is no clear connection in this text between the *kbkbm knm* and *mt wšr*. Šaḥar and Šalim are called *bn šrm* "sons of the Shining Ones" (lines 2 and 22), a designation which seems to indicate their genus (i.e., as astral gods). As for the role of the *kbkbm knm* here, a conservative estimate is that their function is similar to that played by the *kwkby bqr* and *bny ʾlhym* in Job 38:7 who, as members of the divine council, rejoiced during the creation of the cosmos.

61-64

šaptu li-ʾarṣi šaptu li-šamêma	11	l	One lip to earth, the other to heaven,
wa-yaʿrubū bi-pī-humā	8	l	and there entered into their mouths
ʿuṣṣurū šamêma	6	b	the birds of the heavens
wa-daggū bi-yammi	6	b	and the fish of the sea,
wa-nadādu gazru li-<ga>zri	9	l	and they wandered back and forth bite to bite.
yaʿdubā ʾô yamīna ʾô šamʾāla	11	l	They placed both the right and the left (hands?)

[142] Cross (1973:45) has suggested that *kwkby ʾl* is a "frozen, archaic expression" which originated in the mythic language of Canaan, and that the phrase refers to the circumpolar stars of the north. Albright noted that these are the stars which never set (1968:232 n. 69).

[143] On the celestial contingent and its functional importance in Canaan and Israel see particularly Albright (1948:380-381) and Cross (1948:200 n. 13, 201 n. 19; 1953:274 n. 1).

bi-pī-humā wa-lā tišba^cāni	11 1	into their mouths, yet they were not sated.

The newborn gods are described as having enormous mouths and ravenous appetites. Gaster (1950:234, 254-255) interpreted this insatiable hunger as a sign of the divine origin of the newborn gods and made the comparison between their appetites and that of the offspring of the sacred marriage rite in Thracian and Macedonian carnival plays. Gibson (1976:30) suggested that if the interpretation of the end of KTU 1.23 by Caquot, Sznycer, and Herdner (1974:359, 363-365, 377)[144] were adopted, the possibility that Šaḥar and Šalim might have been the first-born (perhaps because they represent the division of day from night) of many gods reported in the text becomes more probable. The implication from the end of the text (lines 64-76) would be that the gods require humanity for sustenance in the form of sacrifice in order to survive, their hunger being unsated by the provision of the created order.[145]

Gaster's suggestion (1950:228) that Dawn and Dusk are the counterpart of the Dioscuri in Classical literature who are themselves identical to the morning and evening star places greater emphasis on the appetites of the young gods than it does on their size. This minimalist interpretation of lines 61-64 encourages one to overlook the gaping orifice created when their lips are stretched—an expanse which encompasses the whole of the horizon. All that the eye can see becomes subject to their feeding frenzy. What better picture could one have of the full expanse of the human field of vision? The cosmos in its entirety is their feeding ground, and though they partake in quantity of its plenty, they remain unsatiated. The poet has conjured a powerful image of infinity (spatial and temporal) and of the limitlessness which one beholds at sunrise and sunset. These gods are the embodiment of the events which mark the initiation and termination of a single day. Hence, both their appetite and their feeding times are without limit. It seems clear

[144] The idea that Šaḥar and Šalim are first-born gods overlooks the fact that El has an amorous liaison with his daughters (who have, of course, been born prior to Dawn and Dusk) making it impossible for Šaḥar and Šalim to be El's first-born.

[145] Caquot , Sznycer, and Herdner (1974:359) say the following regarding the portrayal of the character, appetite, and departure from the steppe of the gracious gods found at the end of this myth—"Elle montre que ce sont des gloutons, que les produits de la nature sauvage ne suffisent pas à les rassasier. Ce n'est qu'en quittant la "steppe" pour le domaine du "gardien de cultures" qu'ils trouvent de quoi satisfaire leur appétit."

that this is not an image of a single celestial body (e.g., Venus) visible in the skies during morning or evening. It is, instead, a picture of a far greater manifestation, that of the heavens themselves, illuminated in the hours of morning and evening.

6.3.2 Summary

Regrettably *mt wšr* is an isolated name in Ugaritic literature. In its present setting, the ritual reenactment of his death is given importance because it precedes the events leading to the birth of Dawn and Dusk. The identification of this god, and his connection to *hyll bn šḥr* of Is. 14:12 is strongly indicated by the semantic correspondence between *hyll* and *šr*. Lines 52-56 indicate that the birth of El's children is to be attended by the sun goddess and other astral deities. The description of the newborn gods in lines 61-64 makes clear that they are not hypostases of the morning and evening star, but represent the deification of first light and early evening.

It is tempting to see in lines 8-11 the ritual binding of a hypostasis of Athtar—a god whose astral traits are not expressly emphasized in the *Baal Cycle*, but whose ascent and descent might certainly have led theologians at Ugarit to ponder his role in the heavens and in the underworld. Unfortunately, the most that one can say from the Ugaritic evidence encountered thus far is that such an identification is suggested by the fact that both Athtar and *mt wšr* are associated with features of the underworld.

6.4 KTU 1.24

This is an extremely difficult text which has produced little in the way of scholarly consensus regarding its genre and meaning.[146] There have also been questions raised about the identification of some of the characters men-

---

[146] Goetze (1941:353-354) suggested that lines 40-50 have no connection with the Nikkal poem and excluded them from his study. Gaster (1938:81-82) proposed a threefold structure for the poem which consists of a Prologue, Mythos, and Epilogue—similar to Homeric Hymns. He set the poem within the ritual context of a secular marriage rite and reasoned that a full set of ritual acts and ceremonial were an integral part of its performance. Gordon characterized the poem as an *hieros gamos*, and suggested that the ceremony reflected within it mirrored actual marital practices (1937:30-31). Gibson characterized the text as a prayer or incantation (1976:31).

tioned in the text.[147] Major studies have included those of Virolleaud (1936), Gordon (1937), Gaster (1938), Ginsberg (1938; 1939), Goetze (1941), Tsevat (1952), and Hermann (1968). Even at this point in time, interpretation must proceed along very conservative lines.

The poem is divided into two parts, these sections being separated by a horizontal line drawn on the tablet. There is also a horizontal line drawn after line 50. The first section of the poem extends from line 1- 39 while the second consists of lines 40-50. The first section is a hymn to *Nkl wib* (*Nikkal wa-ʾibb*)[148] and *Ḫrḫb* (*Ḫarḫab*, *Ḫirḫibi*, or the like). The poem begins with a hymnic salutation (lines 1-3) similar to that in KTU 1.23.1-2, proceeds with a description of the successful consummation of the marriage of *Nkl* and *Yrḫ* (lines 4-5), and moves forward with an announcement to the *kθrt* that a son is to be born to the divine newlyweds (lines 6-14). The text continues with the story of the successful courtship of the goddess Nikkal and the moon-god *Yrḫ* (*Yariḫ*) in which *Ḫrḫb* served as marriage broker (lines 15-37), and concludes with the pronouncement of a blessing in *Yrḫ*'s name on those hearing the poem (lines 38-39).

The second part consists of a hymn to the *kθrt* (lines 40-43) and what seems to be a petition to El, the *kθrt*, or both on behalf of *Prbḫt* (lines 44-50). Gibson suggested that lines 44-50 give away the purpose of the entire composition which is intended as an incantation to secure a blissful marriage, fruitful union, and safe birth—events echoed in lines 1-38 (1976:31).

---

[147] These have included *Nkl wib*, *ḫrḫb*, the *kθrt* , and *prbḫt*. See, for example, Ginsberg's interpretation of the *kθrt* as human female singers (1938:13), Gordon's contention that *Nkl* is a goddess (1937:30), Goetze's refusal to accept Ginsberg's identification of *Nkl wib* as a double-name (1941:354-357), and the difference of opinion between Gaster, who suggested the *ḫrḫb* was a spirit of spring and patron of lovers (1938:83), and Goetze (1941:358-359), who proposed that the name may consist of Hurrian *ḫiriḫi* (a divine name probably identical to Mt. Ḫiriḫi north of Assyria) with suffixed *-bi* (used to form adjectives of appurtenance). He suggested that the name meant "the one of Mt. Ḫiriḫi." For other proposals cf. Margolis (1972a:53-61; 1972b:113-117), and Lichtenstein (1972:97-111).

[148] Tsevat (1952:61-62) demonstrated conclusively that this is the correct reading of the name. He derived the etymology of Ugaritic *ib*, the second element in the double name *nkl wib*, from Akkadian *enbu* , "fruit," an epithet of the Mesopotamian moon god, Sin. This requires taking *ib* as a loanword (against West-Semitic *ʿēnab*). See also Blau (1972:57-82, esp. 74-78).

The structure and content of the composition indicate that he may well be correct.

6.4.1 Analysis

Lines 23-33 contain brief but illuminating information about Athtar.

23-33

wa-yaʿni ḫarḫab malku qêẓi	9	l	And Ḫarḫab king of summer fruit answered:
la-nuʿmānu[149] ʾili-mi	7	l	"O beloved of El,
la-ḫatanu-mi baʿli	7	l	O son-in-law of Baal,
tarriḫa pidrayya bitta [ʾāri]	9	l	pay a bride price for Pidray, daughter of light.
ʾaqarribu-ka ʾabā-ha baʿla	10	l	I will bring you to her father Baal.
yiǵtăr[150] ʿaθtaru	6	b	Let Athtar sink.
tatarriḫa li-ka yv̆bv̆rdv̆mayya[151]	10	l	May you acquire Ybrdmy for yourself,
bitta [ʾa]bī-ha[152]	5	b	(prized?) daughter of her father.

[149] Goetze (1941:368-369) suggested that *lnʿmn* may be an adverbial construction in which nunation has survived, similar in formation to Canaanite **ʾumnam* (in which mimation has survived). He treated *lnʿmn ʾlm lḫtnm* as a syntactic unit meaning "Well! So El himself is to become father-in law." Note should be taken of Goetze's analysis of *lḫtnm,* which he treated as a noun with prefixed *lamedh* functioning as Akkadian *lū* (1941:367). I have taken *lnʿmn* as a noun with a prefixed vocative *lamedh.*

[150] KTU has confirmed the reading *yǵtr,* proposed by Herdner (CTA:103). Gibson (1976:129, 155) adopted this reading and has analyzed the form as the Gt preterite of *√ǵwr,* "to be jealous," and cited Arabic *ǵâra* as cognate. The literal meaning of the Arabic cognate, however, is "to sink, be low."

[151] Vocalization and meaning are uncertain here. It is possible that this is the name of a goddess (Gordon 1965:408).

[152] The proposed reconstruction of KTU has been followed.

labiʾu[153] yuᶜārar[154]	6	b	Let t he Lion' be aroused."
wa-yaᶜni yariḫu nāyiru šamīma	12	1	Then Yariḫ, light of the heavens, answered,
wan-[155]ᶜanā̆ ᶜimmana			
nikkala ḫatanī[156]	9	1	indeed he did answer: "My marriage (will be) with Nikkal."
ʾaḫra nikkala yariḫu yutarriḫ	11	1	Afterwards, Yariḫ paid the bride price for Nikkal.

Gibson's observation that Ḫarḫab's role is that of "marriage broker" (1976:31) is correct. Ḫarḫab tries unsuccessfully to persuade Yariḫ to marry Baal's daughter Pidray—*Ybrdmy* being either an alternate name for her or an epithet—and offers to help negotiate the contract. He is told that Athtar, the "lion" will "sink" and "be roused." The exact meaning of these actions is unclear, but context suggests one of three possible meanings: (1) that they refer to jealousy (Gibson 1976:129,155); (2) that they are a rather banal recounting of the most prominent elements of Athtar's regular cycle of heavenly manifestation; or (3) that the reference is to a reduction in Athtar's status caused by Yariḫ's success in wedding Nikkal. Of these possibilities, the second seems more plausible than the first or third. Yariḫ is unmoved by the prodding and announces that Nikkal is his mate of choice. He proceeds at that point to pay the bride price to secure her.

Athtar's role is a small one. Ḫarḫab comes across as something of a trickster. His plot to wed Pidray and Yariḫ may be aimed at making Athtar envious. One is not told specifically that Athtar has a romantic interest in Pidray. This may be implied from the response which Ḫarḫab expects from Athtar. *Labiʾu* "lion" appears to be an epithet of Athtar. It is possibly attested also in KTU 1.2 III 20. The main point here seems to be that Athtar will not be a major stumbling block because of his movement—a character-

[153] KTU and Gordon (1965:183) read *lbʾu*. Herdner (CTA:103, and n. 13) proposed either *lbʾu* or *lbb*. Of these, *labiʾu*, "lion," makes better sense. While *libbu*, "heart" is possible, the form *lbb,* as Herdner noted (CTA:103 n. 13), is not in keeping with standard orthographic practice found at Ugarit. The expected form is *lb*.

[154] The form has been vocalized as an L passive imperfect of √ᶜ*yr* III, "to arouse" (Gordon 1965:456, 461).

[155] This form has been treated as a *waw* with suffixed *-n*, used for intensification (Gordon 1965:110).

[156] This form has been taken as a masculine noun with 1cs suffix.

istic that prevents him, perhaps, from posing a challenge to a would be suitor.

6.4.2 Summary

This text could be interpreted as biting or sarcastic with Athtar being the object of scorn—a god incapable of maintaining an amorous liaison. On the other hand, it could simply be seen as an astralized interpretation of Athtar's behavior that is used as background for the wedding of two other deities. Of these options, the latter is more appealing.

6.5 Personal Names and God Lists

Personal names are idiosyncratic sources for the reconstruction of social *realia* because of the many factors that contribute to naming practices. All that may be said with confidence is that the personal names *ᶜθtr ab*, *ᶜθtr um*, *ᶜbd ᶜθtr*, *ᶜθtry*, *ᶜθtrn*, *aš-tar-a-bi*, and *bin-aš-tar-mi* indicate that the theophoric element *ᶜθtr/aštar* bore no social stigma in at least some sectors of the Ugaritic populace.[157]

Athtar is present in Ugaritic lists of deities and offerings (de Moor 1970:189ff.). Among the former, his name is found in KTU 1.118 (which is used in the restoration of 1.47) and in Ugaritica V N, nr. 170 (RS 26.142). In KTU 1.118 he appears after such gods as El, Dagan, Baal Ṣapān, and Yariḫ. He appears before Asherah, Anat, Šapaš, Athtart, and Rešep. Therefore, it is reasonable to suppose that his cultus was as active as that of other gods and that he was not understood as a lesser member of the official Ugaritic pantheon. In fact, de Moor suggests that the importance of a god within the Ugaritic pantheon can be measured by that god's presence in at least four of the literary genres extant at Ugarit (1970:217). These include: (A) Alphabetic lists of deities, (B) Syllabic lists of Deities, (C) Offering texts, (D) Myths, (E) Legends, (F) Incantations and Prayers, (G) Rituals, (H) Oracles, and (I) Profane Texts. Athtar appears in five genres—(A), (B), (C), (D), and (F)—a numeric representation just below that of Baal (eight genres), Athtart (eight genres), Anat (seven genres), El (seven genres), Šapaš (seven genres), Dagan (six genres), Yariḫ and Kothar (six genres), and Asherah (six genres).

---

[157] Cf. Gröndahl (1967:83, 113-114) on these personal names.

6.6 *Athtar—The Ugaritic Evidence Reconsidered Holistically*

Keeping in mind the genres in which Athtar appears and the rules of logic and discourse peculiar to each one, comparison of information about any one god is not easily made. These genres convey meaning in different ways—i.e., each selects and employs information about gods in particular ways.

The following can be said of the combined Ugaritic evidence concerning Athtar: (1) in terms of mythology, Athtar is an enemy of neither Baal nor El—at no point is there evidence that he conspired to overthrow either of these gods; (2) he is appointed as a replacement for Baal through the intercession of Asherah, his main political benefactor—El approves his appointment and he assumes authority without conflict; (3) his abdication is voluntary—there are no data to suggest that he was removed forcibly from office; (4) epithets in the *Baal Cycle* indicate that Athtar is wise; (5) Athtar's overall characterization in the *Baal Cycle* indicates that he is a mysterious (no home, very little personal property, refuses to retain power given to him by his political patrons) yet active and intelligent cosmic force with power over the underworld; (6) KTU 1.23 and 1.24 provide possible allusions to Athtar's role as an astral deity, but both of these texts are very difficult to interpret—of these, only the former (KTU 1.23) might suggest that Athtar (if he is identified with *mt wšr*) is debased in any way, though this is by no means conclusive since his ritual sacrifice could be interpreted in a positive manner.[158]

The overall picture of Athtar that obtains from this collective evidence is one that portrays him as a strange but powerful force. His elusiveness as a figure might easily have lent itself to negative interpretation by theologians at Ugarit and elsewhere in Syria-Palestine. It is also possible that other Ugaritic traditions about Athtar existed in which his character and exploits were constructed differently. One is reminded of the multiplicity of responses that humans are capable of having when faced with an enigma. Most fall within a continuum that has acceptance and demonization as its poles. At Ugarit, the choice with regard to all that Athtar embodied seems to have been something akin to acceptance and reverent awe.

---

[158] If the death is a ritualized one that precedes rebirth, then the event is not wholly negative. Also, the death of this figure occurs before the birth of Dawn and Dusk, once again, linking death with birth.

These findings must be taken into consideration when analyzing possible reflexes of Athtar and mythological references concerning his activities outside of the Ugaritic literary corpus.

CHAPTER SEVEN

CR^A REFLEXES IN THE HEBREW BIBLE—AN ANALYSIS

This section contains a close reading of purported biblical reflexes of CR^A. At its conclusion, the value of each text as a reflex of the myth will be reconsidered. In the analysis of Isaiah 14, Albright's claim that Athtar = *hyll* and his proposal that the text is a biblical reflex of a Canaanite myth will be explored.

7.1 Genesis 6:1-4[159]

7.1.1 Overview

Several satisfactory treatments of this text exist, of which Gunkel (1901), Kraeling (1947), Childs (1960), Speiser (1964), Von Rad (1972), Cassuto (1961), Westermann (1974), Petersen (1976), Clines (1976), and Hendel (1987) must be noted. The old correlation of brevity with originality when assessing the age of biblical literature has long been discarded as minimalist and completely at variance with what is known about orally composed literature.[160] At the same time it has also been argued that the Priestly stratum of the Pentateuch is essentially editorial in nature rather than being a narrative source (Cross 1973:324-325).[161] The implications of these two developments and their impact on short, seemingly independent, passages in the Hebrew Bible cannot be underestimated. Genesis 6:1-4 has troubled generations of interpreters precisely because of its length and its suspect relationship to the narrative traditions which it precedes. It is, by all appearances, a "summary-composite," components of at least three myths being found

---

[159] While it is impossible to reconstruct the poetic original (no doubt an oral composition) from the existing prose, in a manner similar to that attempted by Sievers (1904:17, 249-250), it makes sense to try to recover something of the original scope and symmetry of this passage in order to understand its meaning. For this reason the graphic presentation of the reconstructed text is stichometric (i.e., line by line), but this is in no way to be construed as an indication that Genesis 6:1-4 consists of poetry as opposed to prose.

[160] See especially the critique of Gunkel by Cross (1983a:22).

[161] For opposing viewpoints and a summary of recent scholarship on the Pentateuch see Blenkinsopp (1992).

within it. Its author was an editor, probably the Priestly tradent rather than the Yahwist, though the Yahwist and Priestly editor had knowledge of its traditions. As part of the preface to the flood story, it serves to accent the pervasiveness of sin which leads to the destruction of the earth.

7.1.2 Analysis

1-2

ויהי כי־החל האדם לרב על־פני האדמה ובנות ילדו להם:
ויראו בני־[ ]אלהים [ ] בנות [ ]אדם כי טבת הנה ויקחו
להם נשים מכל אשר בחרו:

way-yahī kī hiḥill haʾ-ʾadam la-rubb ʿal panê haʾ-ʾadamā[162]
wa-banōt[163] yulladū la-himm
way-yirʾū[164] banê [ ]ʾilōhīm[165] [ ]banōt [ ]ʾadam[166] kī ṭōbōt hinnā
way-yiqqaḥū la-himm našīm mik-kull ʾašr baḥarū

When mankind began to increase upon earth,
and daughters were born to them,
the gods saw that mortal women were beautiful,
and they took for themselves wives from those they selected.

The *waw consecutive* in *wyhy* is thematically disjunctive. The sequence of converted imperfect forms follows *brʾm* in 5:2. *Wyhy* is then ubiquitous throughout the genealogical section ending at 5:32. In 6:1 and 6:5 *wyhy ky* and *wyrʾ yhwh ky* are found respectively. It cannot be merely coincidental that these come at the beginning of short blocks of material which separate the genealogical material from the beginning of the flood narrative. 6:1-4

---

[162] OG *hēnika ērxanto hoi anthropoi polloi ginesthai epi tēs gēs*, "...at that time when/when men began to be numerous upon the earth." The texts of OG and MT are identical.

[163] OG reads *thygateres*, "daughters."

[164] OG reads *idontes*, "having seen." It does not reflect a reading superior to MT.

[165] The original here may have been *bny ʾlym*, a designation for the members of the divine council similar to that found in Ugaritic lore. Another possibility would be to emend to *bny <ʾl-m>*, "the sons of El himself / the very sons of El," though this is a less attractive alternative.

[166] The definite articles before *ʾlhym*, *bnwt*, and *ʾdm* obscure the intended mythological allusion which juxtaposes the gods and the offspring of mortals. For this reason they have not been included in the reconstruction of the text.

tells of divine-human commingling leading to a reduction of the human life span. 6:5-8 briefly recounts the wickedness leading to Yahweh's decision to eliminate humankind and Noah's favor in Yahweh's eye, the reason for which is not given. 6:9 appears to be a secondary insertion intended to link 6:1-8 with 6:11ff (its function being to explain why Noah found favor with Yahweh). If 6:11ff is rejoined to 5:32 not only does the resulting narrative proceed smoothly, but the sequence of converted imperfects continues without interruption. This leads one to suspect that the construction Converted Imperfect + *ky* is used in this context to mark the intrusion of secondary material. Continuity is maintained, but distinctiveness is indicated. There is a strong possibility that 6:5-8 is an alternate introduction to the flood story while 6:1-4 retains elements of another introductory scenario establishing the reasons for the destruction of humanity (involving the offspring of the divine-human union and the disruption of cosmic harmony) which have been muted. In its present form, 6:1-4 maintains its independent character in spite of some internal discontinuities and visible seams. Ultimately, the Converted Imperfect + *ky* pattern does draw attention away from the flood and directs it toward the gods, mortal women, the "fallen ones," and Noah.

The gods and their copulation with mortal women is a motif attested in Greece. Its origin, like that of most mythological material, is subject to debate. An important issue is the extent to which such union is considered to be a crime elsewhere in the ancient Near East. The editorial hand responsible for the present shape of Gen. 6:1-4 considered it to be a reprehensible act, the penalty for which was to be paid by humans. The change of the penalty in v. 3 (from punishment of the gods?) and the positioning of this passage before the flood narrative reflect the editor's desire to place the onus of cosmic breakdown on human agency.

3-4

ויאמר יהוה לא־ידון רוחי באדם לעלם [ ]
הוא בשׂר והיו ימיו מאה ועשׂרים שׁנה: הנפלים היו בארץ בימים
ההם וגם [ ] יבאו בני [ ]אלהים אל־בנות [ ]אדם וילדו
להם המה [ ]גברים אשר מעולם אנשי השם:

way-yōʾmir yahwe[167]

[167] OG reads *kyrios ho theos*, "the Lord God," possibly reflecting *yhwh ʾlhym*. MT is superior.

lōʾ yadunn rūḥī ba-ʾadam[168] la-ʿōlam [ ][169]
hūʾ baśar[170] wa-hayū yama(y)w[171] miʾā wa-ʿiśrīm šanā[172]
han-napīlīm[173] hayū baʾ-ʾarṣ bay-yamīm hah-him
wa-gam [ ][174] yabōʾū banê [ ]ʾilōhīm ʾil banōt [ ]ʾadam
wa-yaladū la-himm himmā [ ]gibbōrīm[175] ʾašr miʿ-ʿōlam ʾanašê haš-šim[176]

And Yahweh said:
"My spirit will not be strong[177] in mankind forever
He is flesh, and his time span shall be one hundred and twenty years."
The, "fallen ones,"[178] were on earth in those days.

---

[168] OG *en tois anthropois toutois*, "in these men," is an expansionistic reading.

[169] MT *bšgm* is not found in OG and may have been added after the OG was completed. It is also possible that the translator of OG took it to mean, "because," or, "by reason of," and that *dia to* is evidence of this. It seems more likely that a late editor added it in order to explain the cryptic statement from Yahweh which comes before it.

[170] OG reads *dia to einai autous sarkas*, "because they are flesh."

[171] OG reads *hai ēmerai autōn*, "their days," against MT, "his days."

[172] One suspects strongly that the quote attributed to Yahweh was not an original part of the tale describing the commingling of the gods and mortal women. Condemnation of the activity would be more appropriately directed toward the gods and it is likely that originally a statement doing exactly that stood in place of the present one. An editor has shifted the focus of the myth to the earthly realm and the result is an apologia for a human's limited life span.

[173] OG reads *hoi gigantes*, "the giants."

[174] *ʾḥry kn ʾšr* is treated here as a late gloss. I agree, however, with Hendel (1987:21 note 38) that its purpose is to account for the existence of the "fallen ones" after the flood.

[175] OG reads *ekeinoi ēsan hoi gigantes*, "these have been the giants."

[176] Note that OG *hoi anthrōpoi hoi onomastoi*, "men of name," may reflect a Hebrew *Vorlage* that read *hʾnšy hšm* against MT which reads *ʾnšy hšm*.

[177] We follow Hendel's suggestion that the root here is √*dnn*, "to be strong" (1987:15 n. 10).

[178] Or the, "well known/very fallen one," if *napīli-mi* (*qatīl* form with enclitic *mêm* for emphasis) is read. If this suggestion is followed then it must be assumed that *hyw* (3cpl) was altered from original *hyh* (3ms) by a later editor unfamiliar with the use and meaning of the *enclitic mêm*. The plural form has been preferred in this reconstruction.

> And, moreover, the sons of the gods copulated with mortal women,
> and they bore (offspring) for them—these are the ancient heroes, men of renown.

It is disconcerting that punishment is directed against humanity for activity which is initiated by the gods. The relationship of the punishment to the crime is also unclear. No offspring of the union is mentioned in vss. 1-2, so there is no reason to limit the tenure of semi-immortal creatures who could upset the order of nature. Humanity is mentioned (in the generic sense) in the opening verse but without character development relative to the course of events which follows, the major characters being the gods and mortal women. V. 3 introduces a penalty directed at humanity generally. Punishment is leveled against all of humankind because of the liaisons between mortal women and gods.

The question of guilt is unresolved. The penalty is well-defined, the motivation is ambiguous, and an accusatory finger is pointed neither toward the gods nor mortal men. Who is culpable? Is the Yahwist suggesting that women should be blamed. If so, this would not be an unanticipated manipulation of material given the Yahwist's tendency to attribute sin to human free agency and the disruption of paradise to Eve.

7.1.3 Summary

Westermann is on the right track when he isolates two thematic strains here,[179] and takes 6:4a to be an "antiquarian gloss" (1974:368, 378). Another possibility which Westermann rejects is that v. 3 in its present form was intended to be placed after v. 4 (1974:373). This is not as unacceptable a solution as Westermann suggests. If the secondary gloss, "...and afterwards" is removed from v. 4, the plot would remain perfectly clear: (1) humanity increases with resulting increase in female offspring; (2) gods find human offspring favorable and mate with them; (3) liminal offspring are produced (neither fully human nor fully divine); (4) a state of imbalance in cosmic order results; and (5) damage control is instituted—a life span is established for liminal creatures. The "ancient heroes" and "men of renown" are not so much evil as they are disruptive. Their life span must be limited to insure the proper equilibrium between finite and infinite beings. Vs. 3 is not necessarily concerned with "infringement" (Westermann 1974:373). It

---

[179] His designation of these traditions as narratives (1974:368) is not convincing. These are almost certainly poetic and orally transmitted sources.

addresses the consequences of a unique form of life and its ontological impact on the universe.

Liminality is generally handled in one of two ways, either spatially or temporally. In Mesopotamia, Gilgamesh is denied eternal life. The alewife, a liminal figure living at the shores of the sea of Death, reminds Gilgamesh of the dividing line that exists between the earthly and divine worlds. Atraḫasis and his spouse are removed from the world of mortals after surviving the flood which destroyed all creatures. It was not his collusion with Enki that accounted for this. It was, rather, that he had survived the death decree of the gods—an ontological impossibility. Liminality can also be ascribed to gods like Enki (who violates a divine decree in *Atraḫasis* and plays an important role in the creation of mankind) and Canaanite Kothar-wa-Ḫasis (the immortal craftsman and maker of implements of war mentioned in the *Baal Cycle*—he is allied to no one and lives in far off Kaphtor).

Even in the present arrangement of verses, the focus of the plot represented by this outline remains fairly clear, but a blurring of meaning has resulted from a rearrangement of verses (v. 4 being moved from its original position after v. 2), the secondary insertion of *ʾḥry kn ʾšr* in v. 4, the muting of the penalty in v. 3, and the present location of the text just prior to the story of the flood. These suggest that the two traditions which have been brought together here each delineated penalty-bearing actions. The first was sexual misconduct between gods and mortals (carrying a penalty originally directed against the gods). The second was the birth of children resulting from the union of gods and mortals (resulting in the limiting of the life span of these demi-gods). It is in fact possible that these are two parts of an original myth in which the gods and the offspring were punished, but in which the remainder of humanity is left alone. The Priestly writer and/or the Yahwist had knowledge of both of these traditions The Priestly writer also had access to flood traditions from Israel and Mesopotamia. The Mesopotamian material envisioned the flood as a means of birth control, the motivation for which was the "noise" of humankind. The editorial hand that produced the present arrangement of verses and the placement of 6:1-4 as a preface to the flood narrative subsumed all of these themes (penalty against the gods for violation of the human/divine boundary, establishment of parameters for liminal life forms, population control due to noise) and made them serve the larger purpose of describing the sin of humanity and the wrath of Yahweh. 6:4a is more than an "antiquarian gloss" (Westermann 1974:378, following the opinion of Skinner). It is the one element in the tale that gives it spatio-temporal specificity. It is set during the time when the "fallen ones" were on earth. The setting is primordial—from the very distant past when the parameters of discourse between the numinous and the mundane differed from those of the narrative present.

That the "fallen ones" could be used in such a way says something about the degree to which the tradition must have penetrated Israelite folklore. The author must have been able to assume that the audience would be familiar with who these beings were, where they had come from, and what they had done to "fall." None of this information is given, so it must have been part of the projected audience's general knowledge. Subsequent generations of interpreters have not been so fortunate for two reasons: (1) the extension of the basic meaning of *npylym* to include the meaning "giants" (Num. 13:33)[180], and (2) the ubiquity of √*npl* in the Hebrew Bible. The original meaning of the root remains a mystery. Westermann suggests that *npylym* was first used to describe "semi-gods" akin to Gilgamesh and other mythical figures whose ancestry contains a mixture of mortal and immortal elements (1974:378).

The root √*npl* appears frequently in Biblical Hebrew with the basic meaning "to fall, to lie" (BDB:656). In the G stem, it can mean to fall by accident (Ex. 21:33), to fall as a result of a violent death (1 Sam. 4:10), to fall prostrate—in a faint or under supernatural experience (1 Sam. 28:20; Num. 24:4, 16), to fall upon—meaning to attack (Jer. 48:32), to fall into bed (Ex. 21:18), to fall (figuratively) into a deep sleep (Gen. 15:12), or (in 1 Sam. 19:24) to lie/lie prostrate (BDB:656-658).

Of the nouns formed from this root, *npylym/nplym* (BH *nəpīlîm/nəpîlîm*) is the most enigmatic. It is found only in Genesis 6:4 and in Num. 13:33 (twice). BDB suggests the meaning "giants" (658) based on the Old Greek translation (*gigantes*) of *npylym* in Gen. 6:4. The OG may have been influenced by Greek folklore; it does not reflect the lexical meaning of the Hebrew root.

---

[180] Westermann points to scholars like Cassuto, Kraeling, Humbert, Delitzsch, Nahor and others, who attempted to deal with the meaning of √*npl* in Ezekiel 32:20, 22, 23, 24, and 27 (1974:378). This should certainly be augmented by an examination of each occurrence of the root in literature with considerable mythological content. Nominal forms should come under heavy scrutiny. It is possible that the revocalization of participial and infinitival forms may reveal clues to the original meaning of *npyl* and *npylym*.

Grammatically, *npylym* can be vocalized as a masculine plural *qāṭîl* form[181] (as in BDB), or a masculine singular *qāṭîl* form with enclitic *mêm* attached for emphasis. Either could be the case here, though we suspect that the masculine plural form is more easily defensible. The presence of enclitic *mêm* is somewhat dubious in this text (cf. comments above) and the form takes a plural verb in 6:4 (*hyw*), though this could be the result of a later correction. Since 6:4 is little more than a gloss intended to give a concrete historical reference to the story of the sexual exploits of the gods with mortal women, nothing is said of who these beings are. The author has assumed that the *npylym* are so well known that elaboration is not required. Given this set of circumstances, the most acceptable translation is one based on the meaning of the root, hence, "the fallen ones." From a literary-critical standpoint, it is not insignificant that the story for which it is a referent begins with a crossing of the boundary between the abode of the gods and that of humans (possibly a descent from a higher realm—the heavens—if these are gods of the upper region rather than chthonic deities) and mentions the demise (or "fall" if the resulting decrease in life span is treated allegorically) of humanity as a result of this activity. Beyond lexical (based on the meaning of the root), morphological (established by an assessment of the noun pattern), and contextual (determined by immediate usage) evidence, there is little upon which to base a more substantial conclusion.

In Num. 13:33, the *npylym* are said to be occupying the land of Canaan. The statement *bny ᶜnq mn hnpylym* is either a parenthetical remark or secondary addition intended to define who the *npylym* were and to distinguish between the mythical *npylym* (in Gen. 6:4) and those occupying the land of Canaan. An examination of the story of the spies reveals that the actual identification of the *npylym* is not one of the focal points of the plot. The *npylym* serve as one of many "excuses" cited for not proceeding with the conquest of Canaan. The episode highlights Caleb's (of Judah) moderating influence in the debate over whether to invade Canaan, and reinforces the place of the tribe of Judah as a leader in the program of conquest; it is its representative who is able to see beyond the unfounded fears of the spies and the congregation. After being named (13:4-16) and dispatched (13:17), the spies return with a mixed report (13:25-29, 31-33). The land was good, but occupied by the Anaqim (13:28), Amalekites, Hittites, Jebusites, Amorites, and Canaanites (13:29). Caleb, also one of

---

[181] For more on the meaning of this and other nominal patterns see Waltke and O'Connor (1990:83-94).

the spies, reports that there is no obstacle to successful conquest (13:30). Those who accompanied him disagreed, this time claiming that the land "devoured its people" (13:32), that those who lived there were of huge stature, and that the *npylym* (identified as offspring of the Anaqim, who were descendants of the *npylym*) were in the land. Those assembled in the wilderness are said to have been swayed by the negative report of the majority of spies and to have supported a return to Egypt (14:4). The wrath of Yahweh is kindled (14:11-12) and all except Caleb and Joshua (14:24, 30, 38) are fated never to enter Canaan. A plague claims the lives of all the spies except Joshua and Caleb (14:38) and an attempt to conquer the land from the hill country, which Moses advised against, leads to a resounding defeat (14:43-45). Caleb's voice is one of practicality as well as one expressing loyalty to Yahweh (running counter to the "murmuring" of the people). The report itself is arranged in a cyclical fashion from 13:28-32 (beginning and ending with references to the stature of the land's inhabitants), with polar opposites used as its introduction and conclusion. In 13:27 the spies report that the land is good. In 13:33 they report that the *npylym* are there. Within this arrangement, the spies' response uses a progression of excuses.

The Land is Good	13:27
Strong People	13:28
Fortified Cities	13:28
The Anaqim	13:29
Amalekites, Hittites, Jebusites, Amorites, Canaanites	13:29
The Land Devours its People	13:32
People are Monumental in Size	13:32
The *npylym* are there	13:33

The spies report that compared to the *npylym*, they are like grasshoppers (13:33). The operational motif here is that the land is forbidding, its cities unconquerable, and its inhabitants strong. Nothing is said of the *npylym* except that they of greater stature than the spies. Should this be understood literally, figuratively, or in both manners? The third option seems most sensible given the emphasis of the story. Who the *npylym* are is left a mystery, except for the parenthetic/explicating gloss in 13:33, which in light of the above is a secondary addition to the original narrative. The purpose of the gloss was to clear up some of the ambiguity. It seems that 13:33b ("...and we seemed like grasshoppers and so we seemed to them") is also a secondary addition which helps to clarify further who these beings are for a later audience. Originally, the account probably concluded with a reference to the *npylym* and their existence in the land, the purpose being to provide the most compelling in a series of reasons not to occupy the land. The author's intention was to muster images of a land which was itself openly hostile ("it devours/consumes its inhabitants") where mythical creatures dwell (the *npylym*). The effect is that Canaan is perceived as a land where primordial chaos reigns. *Npylym* thus retains its mythological force. No extension of meaning has taken place. The basic meaning "fallen ones" (here certainly a plural form) is retained. 13:33b attempts to impose a layer of different tradition to identify who the *npylym* were. The original narrative needed no such additional embellishment; the identification of the "fallen ones" with primordial reality (perhaps indicating that the immediate audience had knowledge of a *npylym* tradition) being sufficient to create powerful images of dread and death.

Unlike Gen. 6:1-4, which uses the "fallen ones" as a temporal referent, Num. 13-14 uses them as a mythological referent in anti-Canaanite propaganda. In both cases nothing conclusive may be said about who they are or where they come from. References to their stature are of suspect originality in Numbers. In the end, the most that can be said is that they have "fallen" (literally?/figuratively?), they belong among the cast of primordial characters in Israelite folk tradition (predating or of comparable antiquity to the events in Gen 6:1-4), and they are archetypal representations of fear and chaos (Num. 13:33).

Can a case be made for identifying the *npylym* with *mt wšr* of KTU 1.23? Is there indication that the *npylym* share any similarities with Athtar as he is reflected in Ugaritic literature? The lack of explicit astral imagery in Genesis 6:1-4 and the brevity of the text make such an identification problematic. However, it is certainly possible that the observance of the planet Venus in the early morning and/or evening might have conjured images of deposed or "fallen" gods that gave rise to various traditions about the ascending and descending deitiy represented by that planet in Syria-Palestine.[182] The most striking element of the Israelite reflex of that tradi-

---

[182] For a brief explanation of the celestial movement and manifestation of Venus, see Moore (1956:26-31). Heimpel also refers to a study by Hostetter that offers an astronomical interpretation of the Sumerian story of the descent of Inanna to the underworld (1982:59 note 2). A closer look needs to be taken at the relationship between the synodic period of Venus and the mythology of Inanna, Ištar, Athtar, and other known Venus deities.

tion seen thus far—if such is embodied in Genesis 6:1-4—is that it is constructed negatively. The *npylym* do not represent creative and life-giving powers.

A connection between the *npylym* and Athtar is, therefore, not implausible if one allows for regional variation in the conceptualization of the behavior of Venus. Of the available Ugaritic evidence, the data in Genesis 6:1-4 are more reminiscent of the travails of *mt wšr* in KTU 1.23 than they are of Athtar's voluntary descent from Ṣapon in KTU 1.6—an event that is clearly not understood as a "fall." In light of the available information, these modest conclusions seem most prudent.

7.2 Isaiah 14:4b-20

7.2.1 Overview

Driver (1914:229) cites 14:4b-20 as one of several sections in Is. 1-39 which are not from the prophet's hand (others are 13:1-14:4a; 14:21-23; Chs. 24-27, and 34-35). Expositors have attempted to delimit further those passages which are later additions to the corpus, but as of yet consensus has not been reached (Blenkinsopp 1983:107-108).

The poem has generated much debate and rather than offering a patchwork of secondary opinions regarding date, setting, authorship, and purpose, new readings have been presented and an interpretation given that attempts a new synthesis in light of the mythological allusions which the text contains.

7.2.2 Analysis

4-5

איך שבת נגש שבתה מ<ר>הבה:
שבר יהוה מטה רשעים שבט משלים:

ᵓayk šabat[183] nōgēś	5	b	Ah, how the tyrant has ceased,
šabatā[184] ma<r>hibā[185]	6	1	the fury calmed.

---

[183] In 1QIsa^{a} *šb[t]* (restore *taw* where there is stitching in the scroll) is found, the long form *ᵓykh* is used, and *ngś* is preceded by a conjunction. The short form *ᵓyk* and the reading *ngś* of MT have been adopted.

[184] OG inserts a conjunction before this line which has not been adopted. Though it is not unusual to find a conjunction in the second colon of a bicolon such as this,

šabar yahwe maṭṭe rašaʿīm	8	l	Yahweh has broken the staff of the rebels,
šibṭ mōšilīm	4	b	the rod of the rulers,

Verse Type: Quatrain
Meter: b:l::l:b

The poem begins after the manner of other laments, with the interrogative adverb *ʾyk* (2 Sam. 1:19) or *ʾykh* (Lam. 1:1; 2:1; 4:1; Isa. 1:21; Jer. 48:17). The tyrant and his fury are said to have ceased. *Ngś* is also found in Isa. 3:12 referring to youth(s) as rulers in Judah and Jerusalem, in 9:3 as possible reference to a foreign tyrant, and in 60:17 pertaining to righteousness as ruler in Zion's future state. His dominion has been broken. There may be an intentional echo of *ʾdmh lʿlywn* in v. 14 if one is to understand in v. 5 √*mšl* III, "to rule" (BDB:605), and √*mšl* I, "to represent, be like" (BDB:605). The rod, a representation of royal authority, would then be understood not only as the symbol of the one who ruled, but also the one which presumed to make itself like that of Elyon. One senses here the beginning of a polemic against government that seeks to supply all human need, in essence supplanting the god(s) as rulers of the humanity.

6

מכה עמים בעברה מכת בלתי סרה
רדה באף גוים מרדף בלי חשך׃

---

the readings of MT and 1QIs^a along with the idiosyncratic nature of the OG translation of Isaiah caution against its inclusion as an original reading.

[185] 1QIsa^a reads *mrhbh* against MT *mdhbh*. Confusion between *dālet* and *rêš* is not uncommon in the history of textual transmission (on the similarity between these two consonants in the Aramaic script of the late Persian Empire, and third and fourth century formal Jewish scripts, see Cross 1961:142,147) therefore the reading of 1QIsa^a has been preferred. Either *mrhbh* or *mdhbh* would be a difficult reading. In this instance, however, *mrhbh* is a more sensible reading given that in 3:5 *rhb* and *ngś* stand in semantic and grammatical relationship in parallel cola. Both of these forms are finite verbs in verse initial position. The general range of meaning within that context has to do with arrogant behavior and human oppression—though these roots may by no means be construed as synonymous. The translator of OG saw *mrhbh* as being in the same semantic range as *ngś* and there is no reason to suppose some other Hebrew equivalent for OG *epispoudastēs* "one who presses on a work" (LSJ:658).

makke ᶜammīm ba- ᶜibrā	7	l	the one who arrogantly cut down peoples,
makkat biltī sarā[186]	6	b	with repeated blows,
rōde ba- ᵓapp gōyīm	6	b	the one who ruled nations angrily—
muraddip balī ḥaśāk[187]	7	l	an unrelenting persecutor.

---

[186] 1QIsaᵃ presents no major variants. OG reads singular *ethnos* for both *ᶜmym* and *gwym* of MT, though two manuscripts (26, 410) read *ethē*. *Thymos* appears forty-five times in the Greek of Isaiah, twice for *ᶜbrh* and twelve times for *ᵓp*. *Plēgē* is found eleven times in the OG of Isaiah, four times it renders *makkā* "blow, wound" (BDB:646). OG *plēgē* as a translation of MT *makkat* is acceptable. The Hebrew equivalent of *plēgēn thymou*, however, is questionable. *Aniatos* occurs twice in the OG of Isaiah, once representing *ᵓk zry* and here as a translation of *blty srh*. The Hebrew equivalent of *paiōn* is problematic. In twenty of its twenty-five occurrences in Isaiah it translates the verbal root √*nkh*. The root √*rdh* is infrequently used in Isaiah (three times) and it is understandable that the translator would have difficulty finding a Greek counterpart for it. It is reasonable to suppose that OG *pataxas ethnos thymō plēgē aniatō* represents MT *mkh ᶜmym bᶜbrh mkt blty srh*.

[187] OG reads *paiōn ethnos plēgēn thymou*. It is possible that *plēgēn* is an explicating plus intended to differentiate *thymos* used in this instance from its earlier appearance. Another solution involves supposing that OG had the following as its *Vorlage*:

[mkh] bngp ᵓp gwym
[rdh]

In Isaiah 9:12 *plēgē* translates the root √*ngp* "to strike" (BDB:619). *Thymos* would then be translating *ᵓp* as it does on eleven other occasions. *Bngp* should be vocalized as a Qal infinitive absolute. *Mkh* and *rdh* are understood as alternative readings. *Bngp* could have been lost by parablepsis, the trigger being the *pē* which concludes both morphemes. The major problem with this solution is that this phrase is not found elsewhere in Isaiah or in the biblical corpus. An alternate suggestion is to see the OG *Vorlage* as:

rdh gwym bᵓp mrdp bly ḥśk

In this case, *thymou* would need to be understood as the Greek equivalent of *mrdp*, and *plēgē* would need to be treated as the equivalent of *ᵓp*. The major problem with this solution is that *plēgē* never translates *ᵓp* in Isaiah. Nevertheless this is about the only way to avoid having no Greek equivalent for *mrdp*. My vocalization of *mrdp* as a Piel participle adds more symmetry to the second bicolon than does the mascu-

Verse Type: Quatrain
Meter: l:b::b:l

That which smites the peoples is the dominion of the tyrant identified in v. 5. It is relentless. It rules with anger and pursues without restraint. *ᶜbrh* is used of proud Moab in Is. 16:6, and is best translated "arrogance." (BDB:720) In Is. 9:18; 10:6; 13:9, 13; it means "fury/rage" (BDB:720) and always refers to Yahweh's wrath. This may represent an usurpation of divine prerogative, the expression of *ᶜbrh* belonging in divine rule over humanity rather than in the mechanisms of government established by humanity. Thus far, the poet has been less than specific about the object of his ridicule, yet clues have been given regarding the nature of the tyrant's crime. The dual sense of *šbṭ mšlym* ("the rod which dominates"/"the rod which imitates") does not become clear until v. 14, but *ᶜbrh* gives a more direct indication of the tyrant's character. His rule is disproportionate, his behavior not in keeping with the norms established by Yahweh for earthly kings.

7-8

נחה שקטה [ ][ ]ארץ < פצחה > רנה:
גם־ברושים שמחו לך ארזי לבנון
מאז שכבת לא־יעלה [ ]כרת עלינו:

---

line singular noun, translated simply "persecution." Thomas suggested reading *bl yḥśk* (BHS:695). The root √*ḥśk* occurs three times in Isaiah (14:6; 54:2; and 58:1). If the MT reading is accepted, one must contend with the rare usage of *bly* with a finite verb (BDB:115). If Thomas' reading is adopted, then the prefixed form of the verb must be explained. It would be the first encountered in the text to this point. As an alternative, he suggests vocalizing *ḥśk* as an imperative or as an infinitive construct. If it is the latter, then one might suppose that a nominal usage is intended. Hence, *mkt blty srh* and *mrdp bly ḥśk* would be parallel epithets similar to Akkadian *qabal la maḫār* used of Ḫuwawa in the Old Babylonian version of the *Gilgameš Epic* (see col. iii, lines 19-24 of the Yale Tablet in YOSR IV 3:87-101):

pīšu girrāma	His mouth is fire,
napīssu mūtum	his breath is death.
ammīnim taḫsiḫ	Why do you desire
anniam epēšam	to do this?
qabal la maḫār	A battle not to be faced
šupat ḫuwawa	is the onslaught of Ḫuwawa.

naḥā šaqaṭā [ ] [ ]ʾarṣ[188]	6	l	Earth is at rest, quiet.
<paṣaḥā>[189] rinnā	5	b	She breaks forth with a shout.
gam burōšīm śamaḥū lakā	9	l	Even the junipers rejoice at you,
ʾarazê libanōn	6	b	the cedars of Lebanon—
meʾʾaz šakabtā lōʾ yaʿle	8	l	"Since you've lain down, there ascends not,
[ ]kōrit[190] ʿalaynū	5	b	a cutter against us."

Verse Type: Sestet
Meter: l:b::l:b::b:l

The scene has changed dramatically. Ancient Earth is pictured at rest and quiet. Cosmic harmony is envisioned. The Qal of √*šqṭ* meaning "to be quiet, undisturbed" (BDB:1052) is found in Is. 18:4 and 62:1, both times referring to Yahweh. In these instances a sense of divine inactivity is conveyed and such seems to be the case here. The image of a quiet Earth may be an indication that the author believed this to be the normative state of affairs for this olden god, no longer an active member of the pantheon.[191] Her arousal is precipitated, however, by this great event. A joyful shout ensues. The root √*pṣḥ* "to cause to burst forth" (BDB:822), is found a single time

---

[188] 1QIsa^a shows no major textual variants with the exception of *hlbnwn* for MT *lbnwn*, and *š[k]bth wlwʾ* for MT *škbt lʾ*. OG seems to read *šqṭh* as a Qal, passive participle, feminine, singular. It also reads *kl hʾrṣ as* the subject of *pṣḥw*. The definite article has been removed from *ʾrṣ*. 1QIsa^a and OG retain the article here and before *lbnwn*. OG *pasa hē gē* could reflect *kl ʾrṣ* or *kl hʾrṣ* just as *hē kedros tou libanou* could stand for *ʾrzy lbnwn*, *ʾrzy hlbnwn*, or *hʾrzy hlbnwn*. The article retained before *lbnwn* in 1QIsa^a suggests that in at least some instances, the definite article has been added in the process of transmission. *Kl* has been treated as a late addition to the text that resulted when Earth was no longer understood as an active deity. An editor made this insertion and changed *pṣḥh* to *pṣḥw* in order to focus attention on the human inhabitants of earth as those who rejoice.

[189] The emendation of MT *pṣḥw* to *pṣḥh* is based on the belief that originally the old god Earth was pictured here as the subject of the sentence.

[190] The definite article before *krt* has also been eliminated from this reconstruction. While it is retained in 1QIsa^a and OG, it is believed that this is one of many instances in which scribes have leveled through usage of the article in either OG, MT, or 1QIsa^a.

[191] See Cross (1976:331, 333) for a description of the olden gods and their place in creation myths of the ancient Near East..

in Isaiah 1-39, but five times in Deutero-Isaiah. In four of these instances (44:13; 49:23 [*Qərê*]; 54:1; and 55:12) the verb appears together with *rnh* "ringing cry" (BDB:943). In 44:23 the mountains are commanded to burst forth with a ringing cry after the olden gods Earth and Heaven are commanded to sing for joy and shout aloud. A similar context is encountered in 49:13. The noun *rnh* is found in 14:7 and seven times in Deutero-Isaiah (35:10; 44:23; 48:20; 49:13; 51:11; 54:11; 55:12). If one translates *ʾmrt blbbk hšmym ʾʿlh* (14:13) "you said in your heart 'O Heavens I will ascend,'" then one has the olden gods Earth and Heaven paired in this text. Hence, it may be suggested that the offense of the tyrant is that he acted against Yahweh and the olden gods were present to witness his boast and downfall (in much the same way that they function as treaty and covenantal witnesses in Israel and elsewhere in the ancient Near East). The cedars of Lebanon rejoice, and even say (in what may or may not be a taunting tone) that since the tyrant's demise, no one ascends to fell them.[192] Yet the crime's implications extend beyond the mundane realm of human experience; it assumes cosmic importance. Its impact is manifest in the fabric of reality just as violation of treaty or covenant is assumed to have a deleterious effect on the created order. Since kingship on earth requires prior approval by the council of the gods (in Mesopotamia and Canaan) or by Yahweh (in Israel), to exercise it improperly could only engender a forceful response from the gods. Political and natural order are restored when the tyrant is brought low. As a result, this re-establishment of harmony leads Earth herself to rejoice and empowers Lebanon's cedars to comment upon their powerless oppressor.

The noun *brwš* appears twice in Isaiah (14:8; 37:24), two times in Deutero-Isaiah (41:19; 55:13), and once in Trito-Isaiah (60:13). *ʾrz* is found three other times in Isaiah: 2:13; 9:9; 37:24 (the latter resembles closely vss. 13-15 of this poem), and twice in Deutero-Isaiah (41:19; 44:14). *ʾrz* and *brwš* are used as a word pair in parallel cola in 37:24 and 41:19.

9

שׁאול מתחת רגזה לך לקראת בואך
עורר לך רפאים כל־עתודי ארץ

---

[192] It is well known that cedars were valued as a building material in Mesopotamia and Israel. It is unclear whether the cedars should be understood as lamenting a decline in their own importance as a result of the fall of a monarch who is not able to cut them down as he should, or as taunting one whose normal practice was to ravage them.

הקים מכסאותם כל מלכי גוים׃

šaʾōl[193] mittaḥt ragazā lakā	9	l	Sheol below stirs before you,
la-qiraʾt bōʾkā	5	b	to meet your arrival,
ʿōrir lakā rapaʾīm	7	l	rousing the Rephaim before you,
kull ʿattūdê ʾarṣ	5	b	all the he-goats of the Earth.
haqēm[194] mik-kissiʾōtam	7	l	She raises from their thrones,
kull malakê gōyīm	6	b	all the kings of the nations.

Verse Type:	Sestet
Meter:	l:b::l:b::l:b

Sheol, here pictured as the master of the underworld, is agitated at the tyrant's arrival. She rouses the shades (in this instance, the former rulers of earth) from their thrones to meet him. Here, *rpʾym* refers to the chthonic deities who form the council of the underworld, and *ʿtdy ʾrṣ* seems to be an epithet of theirs. These are roused along with the former kings of earthly nations—enjoying their retirement in the land of heroes.

Sheol seems less the monstrous lord of this domain and more the royal page.[195] This is the only instance in Isaiah in which *ʿtwd* is used figuratively of leaders (cf. 1:11 and 34:6).[196] The *rpʾym* appear elsewhere in Isaiah only in the Isaiah Apocalypse (26:14, 19). The Hiphil perfect, 3rd., masc., sg. form *hqym* is impossible since Sheol is the subject (and is feminine in gender). It is vocalized here as an infinitive absolute.[197] At least two understandings of √*rgz* are attractive. Sheol may have been "roused" (in other words, Sheol may have roused herself) at the arrival of the tyrant (a usage similar to that in 28:21 of Yahweh), or Sheol may have "quaked" in terror at his arrival (similar to the usage in 32:10, 11). Either seems possible. The latter would be most appropriate if an ironic or sarcastic tone is intended (Sheol cowering upon the arrival of a deposed and powerless tyrant in her

[193] The vocalization here is uncertain. A second possibility is *šəʾōl*.

[194] I have vocalized this as an infinitive absolute and rejected both MT and 1QIsa[a].

[195] Cross (1983c:160) addressed the problem posed by the mixing of images of the realm of the dead, particular reference being given to the Psalm of Jonah.

[196] The names of male animals were used in Old Hebrew and Ugaritic to apply to important individuals (heroes, etc.) (Cross 1973:4, note 6).

[197] On the use of the infinitive absolute as a substitute for the finite verb see GKC:Par. 113y, gg. The context may fit what Gesenius called a "hurried or otherwise excited style" (GKC:Par. 113y).

own realm). The scene conjured thereby would be of a terrified Sheol running about notifying her fellow gods and heroes of the presence of a new arrival. The purpose of such a device would be to mock a ruler who was less than terrifying in his own lifetime, or to underscore the condemnation, by the kings at least, of one who did not make the grade as a ruler. The kings do not, as a result, direct their brother to the nearest throne. Instead, the *rpʾym* and the kings point him to a seat less treasured. The impression left is that the crime of this individual is somehow worse than that of his counterparts and will be reflected in his status as inhabitant of the underworld. The impact of his crimes haunts him beyond death's veil; even in the domain of Death he will be dishonored. Such punishment suggests an earthly offense of great magnitude. The tyrant's fall results in the jubilant exultation of nature, but in the underworld, the activity is a prelude to the monarch's eternal dishonor.

10-11

כלם יענו ויאמרו אליך
גם־אתה חלית כמונו אלינו נמשלת:
הורד שאול גאונך המית נבל<ת>ך
תחתיך יצע רמה ומכסיך תולעה:

kullām yaʿnū wa-yōʾmirū ʾilaykā	EM		All of them answer and say to you,
gam ʾattā ḥullaytā kamōnū	9	l	"Yea, you are become weak like us,
ʾilaynū nimšaltā	6	b	you have become similar to us."
hūrad šaʾōl[198] gaʾōnkā	8	l	Your arrogance was brought down to Sheol,
himyat nabala<ta>kā	7	b	the din of your folly.
taḥtaykā yuṣṣaʿ rimmā	7	b	Beneath you is spread the maggot,
wa-mukassaykā tōliʿā	8	l	your covering is the worm.

Verse Type: Sestet
Meter: l:b::l:b::b:l

The *rpʾym* and the former kings condemn the fallen tyrant. They tell him that he has been made weak like they are and is now in a state similar to theirs. The root √*ḥlh* "to be weak, sick" (BDB:317) is used of physical in-

[198] An alternate vocalization is *šəʾōl*.

firmity (with moral depravity given a causal connection) in Isaiah 33:24, and of Hezekiah's illness in 38:1, 9; 39:1. In 57:10 it seems to connote weariness due to physical and emotional exhaustion. The Niphal form of √*mšl* occurs at no other point in Isaiah. In Pss. 28:1 and 143:7 it refers to the poet's being "made like" one who goes down to the pit. In Ps. 49:13, 21 its use is in connection with those who trust in themselves and those having riches but no faculty for comprehension. These are said to be "like the beasts of the field." It is interesting that in each of these cases, reference is made to the deterioration of the psychological and physical well-being of humanity. Hence, the tyrant is something other than he used to be. He is weakened, made of similar essence to the *rpʾym* and his previously fallen brethren.

His "exultation/majesty" has accompanied him. In Is. 2:10, 19, 21 majesty is attributed to Yahweh, and in 4:2 to the *ṣmḥ yhwh* "branch of Yahweh." In 13:19 Babylon is called the "glory of the Chaldeans." In 13:11 and 16:6 the connotation is negative (it stands parallel to *gʾwt* and is best translated "arrogance"). In 23:9 (the lament against Tyre) Yahweh plans, through the humiliation of Tyre, to humble the *gʾwn kl ʾrṣ* "the exalted of all the earth" (which stands parallel to *kl nkbdy ʾrṣ* "all the honored of the land").

Hebrew *hmyh* is a *hapax legomenon* meaning "sound, music" (BDB:242). This definition is conditioned by the reading of *nbl* as "musical instrument" (BDB:614). The root √*hmh* can mean "to murmur, growl, roar" (BDB:242) and therefore *hmyh* might be rendered "din, roar." Following 1QIsa[a], *nbltk*—which could be rendered "your folly" (though 1QIs[a] seems to treat it as "your carcass")—might be read instead of MT *nblyk*. No such form appears in MT and the noun *nblh* "senselessness" always appears in the absolute state and never with a pronominal suffix. Nonetheless, reading "your majesty was brought down to Sheol // the din (roar) of your folly," is not an unreasonable proposal. The reference would be to the behavior of the king described in vss. 13-14. In the lament over Abner (2 Sam. 3:33), the agonizing question is posed, "should Abner die the death of a fool (*nbl*)?" Having been victimized through the deceit of Joab, this fate was unbefitting a warrior, yet the same might not be said of the tyrant, whose grand scheme was brought to naught.[199] Here one is given the message that folly, when exercised by kings, has cosmic repercussions.

For his offense, the tyrant is directed to a place appropriate for criminals. Worms are spread for him. His garment (taking *mksyk* as an allusion to that which he will wear) will also be worms.[200] He is, then, not like his brother kings. Even in Sheol he is without honor.

12

איך נפלת משמים הילל בן־שחר
< איך > נגדעת לארץ חולש על־גוים:

ʾayk napaltā[201] miš-šamaym	7	l	How you have fallen from the heavens,
hêlil[202] bin šaḥr	5	b	Helel son of Šaḥar.
<ayk>[203] nigdaʿtā[204] la-ʾarṣ	6	l	How you are crushed to the ground,
ḥōliš ʿal gōyīm	5	b	Weakling over the Nations.

Verse Type: Quatrain
Meter: l:b::l:b

Hyll bn šḥr has fallen.[205] This statement begins that section of the poem most heavily influenced by Canaanite mythology. Albright (1968:232)

[199] This interpretation has been preferred over that proposed by Cheyne and Delitzsch for example, who want to see *nblyk* as a reference to musical instruments. Cheyne translates "cymbals" (1984:90) and Delitzsch translates "harps" (1890:309).

[200] It has this meaning in Isaiah 23:18 (BDB:492).

[201] OG reads 3rd. singular *exepesen.*

[202] OG reads *ho heōsphoros. Hyll* is a divine name whose actual meaning is "shining one" (BDB:237). An alternate vocalization is proposed by Koehler-Baumgartner (HALAT:235, 238) for *hyll* (*hêlāl* "Mondsichel") based on comparative evidence from Arabic (*hilāl* "Neumondsichel") and Ethiopic (*həlāl* "new moon," cf. Leslau 1987:217).

[203] *ʾyk* has been restored here for metrical purposes.

[204] OG reads 3rd. singular *synetribē.*

[205] The meaning "to shine" has been adopted for the root √*hll* proposed by Brown, Driver, and Briggs (BDB:237). Note should also be taken of the meaning "am Horizont erscheinen" proposed by Koehler-Baumgartner (HALAT:238) based on comparative evidence from Arabic (*halla* "begin to shine") and Ethiopic (*halala* "shine, be bright," a denominative verb according to Leslau 1987:217). In my

called this a Canaanite mythological dirge. Gowan (1975:50-67) cited parallels to Mesopotamian folklore, Oldenburg (1970:206-208) drew on South Arabian parallels, and McKay (1970:455, 463) contrasted this text with the Greek Phaeton myth. Gunkel (1895:132-134) proposed a nature myth as its origin, and Childs (1960:69) reconstructed an outline of the myth based on evidence within the poem itself.

Though vss. 4-11a speak of earthly events accompanied by manifestations in the cosmic realm, the focus is on an earthly hegemon whose fall has an impact on the universe. By contrast, the frame of reference shifts in vss. 11bff., the focus continuing to be a dual one, but with greater emphasis being placed on the divine being whose fall is compared to that of the earthly monarch. The result is that in the poem's literary fabric, cyclical and linear time coalesce and the historical and mythological are held in creative tension. The poet has accomplished this by allowing the mythological tradition which he mediates to convey its message without substantial authorial interference. The poet edits very little. Only by way of the rubric in v. 4a does one know who the *mšl* is directed toward. From content alone, one knows only of a foolish king and a cosmic usurper whose failures are woven into the poem in such a way that their identities are virtually indistinguishable from one another.

A political event has been mythologized and a mythological event has been politicized. One possible solution to the problem of the poem's origin was proposed by Childs (1960:69-70). He suggested that the poet drew on a familiar pattern in mythologizing a political happening. Thus, concern over factual events associated with any given king are irrelevant—the poem being the product of the poet's imaginative thinking. Alternately, the poet might have made use of mythological material that described cosmic warfare. This tradition might have seemed particularly appropriate to the author of Is. 14 as primordial justification for the anti-monarchical position that the poem, in its final form, expresses.

The poet allowed the name *hyll bn šḥr* to be perceived as an allusion to the despot whose fall is recounted in vss. 4b-11a. The name retained its force in the minds of the poet's audience as either a divine name or epithet for the god who was said to have behaved similarly in the divine council. As an illustrative allusion to the excesses of an unnamed despot, *hyll bn*

---

opinion, evidence from Arabic and Ethiopic supports the reading of BDB rather than that of HALAT. I suspect that the root √*hll* is primary in Semitic and has the meaning "to shine."

šḥr and his fall contribute to the formation of a scenario that depicts a ruler with grandiose dreams. The tyrant's delusions are, therefore, a reflection of *hyll bn šḥr* and his hunger for cosmic kingship.

13-15

[ ]אתה אמרת בלבבך השמים אעלה
ממעל לכוכבי־אל ארים כסאי

[ ]ʾattā[206] ʾamartā ba-libabakā	10	l	You said in your heart,
haš-šamaym ʾaʿle	5	b	"I will ascend O Heavens,
mim-maʿl la-kôkabê ʾil	7	l	above El's stars,
ʾarīm kissiʾī	5	b	I will establish my throne,

Verse Type: Quatrain
Meter: l:b::l:b

ואשב בהר־מועד בירכתי צפון:
אעלה על־במתי עב אדמה לעליון:
אך אל־שאול תורד אל־ירכתי־בור:

wa-ʾišib ba-harr-mōʿid	7	l	and I will sit on the Assembly Mount,
ba-yarkatê ṣapōn[207]	6	b	in the far reaches of the north.
ʾaʿle ʿal bamōtê ʿab	7	l	I will mount the backs of clouds,
ʾiddamme la-ʿilyōn	6	b	I will make myself like Elyon."
ʾak ʾil šaʾōl tūrad	6	l	But you are brought down to Sheol,
ʾil yarkatê bōr	5	b	to the far reaches of the Pit.

Verse Type: Sestet
Meter: l:b::l:b::l:b

Helel announces to the heavens that he will ascend to the holy mount where Elyon sits and place his throne above the circumpolar stars. These may in fact be similar to the *kwkby šmym* in 13:10 who will not give forth their

---

[206] The conjunction has been omitted here as a late addition in the transmission process.

[207] OG reads *kathiō en orei hypsēlō epi ta orē ta hypsēla ta pros borran.* There is no reason to suppose that OG has a *Vorlage* different from the reading of MT. This is simply an example of translational eccentricity or interpolation triggered by *mwʿd* (which the translator has rendered as *sōteriōn* in 33:20 and *heortē* in 1:14).

light on the day when cosmic upheaval accompanies the destruction of Babylon. Further, he has said that he will sit on the mountain where the divine council meets—in the far reaches of the north. Psalm 48:3 can be compared in which Zion is said to be the holy mount located in the far reaches of the north. The image is of El's abode in the Amanus (Cross 1973:38-39).

ʾʿlh ʿl bmty ʿb is best taken as a reference to Helel's intention to assume a position similar to that of Baal. One can see in this an allusion to the Baal epithet *rkb ʿrpt* "cloud rider." The inclusion of this boast suggests strongly that one is dealing with a fusion of two separate events: (1) an attack against Baal and (2) an attack against El. The author's intention appears to have been to develop a unified primordial archetype of cosmic failure.

The rebel says that he will make himself like Elyon; the only way to accomplish this would be to remove the present holder of that title—El himself.[208] A systematic and cohesive plan is in evidence. ʿlywn is positioned climactically as the final element of the rebel's speech. After his boast to the Heavens he reveals his scheme to ascend above the circumpolar stars (perhaps, astral deities over whom he would also exercise dominion), announces his intention to sit atop the mount of assembly in the far north, makes known his plan to challenge Baal—the cloud rider, and concludes by boasting of his eventual assault against El. The picture created is that of a deranged mind, free associating and contemplating ever higher degrees of power.

16-17

ראיך אליך ישגיחו אליך יתבוננו
הזה האיש מרגיז [ ]ארץ מרעיש ממלכות:
שׂם תבל כמדבר ועריו הרס [ ]

rōʾaykā ʾilaykā yašgīḥū	9	l	Those who see you gaze at you;
ʾilaykā yitbōnanū	7	b	they consider you intently.
ha-ze haʾ-ʾīš margīz [ ]ʾarṣ[209]	7	l	Is this the one who makes Earth quake,
marʿīš mamlakōt	5	b	he who rocks kingdoms,
śam têbil ka-madbar	6	l	who made Earth a desert,

[208] On Elyon as a Yahweh epithet see Cross (1973:71).

[209] In 1QIsa[a] the definite article is supralineal. It has been excluded from this reconstruction as a secondary editorial addition.

wa-ᶜaraw[210] haras	5	b	tore down his own[211] cities,
[ ][212]			

Verse Type:	Sestet
Meter:	l:b::l:b::l:b

The discourse of the *rpᵓym* having ended, the poet resumes the narration. Those who see Helel (in the immediate context—those in Sheol) gaze at him intently and consider him carefully.[213] The root √*šgḥ* "to gaze" (BDB:993) occurs a single time in Isaiah. In Psalm 33:14 it is used of Yahweh watching humankind from the heavens and in the Song of Songs 2:9 it refers to the lover's act of peering from afar (at his beloved?). The Hitpolel of √*byn* "to consider diligently, show oneself attentive" (BDB:106-107) is found in Isa. 1:3 paralleling √*ydᶜ* concerning Israel's failure to know Yahweh. In 43:18 it is used in conjunction with √*zkr* regarding the imperative not to call to mind former things in light of Yahweh's new actions and in 52:18 it augments √*rᵓh* in a passage addressing the recognition of the suffering servant by nations and kings. Here, those watching look at first from afar, then closely. They ask if this is the one who makes earth quake, rocks kingdoms, made the world a desert, and "tore down" (BDB:294) his cities. The root √*rᶜš* is used of the shaking of the earth in Isa. 13:13 and 24:18 (i.e., that shaking which is initiated by Yahweh). In Isa. 22:19 √*hrs*

---

[210] On the vocalization of the 3rd masculine singular suffix on plural nouns as -*aw*, see Cross (EHO:46-47, 54-55, 68-69).

[211] Brown, Driver, and Briggs (BDB:385) note that in this instance *tbl* is apparently masculine. One suspects that understanding the referent of *ᶜryw* as *tbl* influenced this conclusion. *Tbl*, like *ᵓrṣ*, was probably originally a feminine noun whose gender later shifted to masculine. However, according to the translation proposed here, its gender need not be understood as masculine. The referent is the tyrant. One of the reasons that he is despised is precisely because he tore down "his own cities." This could be interpreted as symbolic of disastrous foreign and domestic policy, squandering of public funds, or the neglect of responsibilities which resulted in a decline in the quality of life of those governed.

[212] *ᵓsryw lᵓ ptḥ bytw* has been omitted as an ancient variant for the preceding line which OG, MT, and 1QIsa^a have preserved. Vss. 20ff. have suffered corruption in the transmission process. The proposed reconstruction seeks to restore the integrity of the sestet as a literary unit..

[213] Kissane viewed these individuals as the people who saw the earthly tyrant in his days of glory (1941:173).

refers to what Yahweh will do to the steward Shebna, and in 49:17 (Piel usage) it refers to those who laid Zion waste. *ʾsyryw lʾ ptḥ* has been taken as a variant of *wʿryw hrs.*

This latter part of the poem (vss, 17-20a) has suffered corruption in transmission. As a result, any reconstruction is difficult. *ʿryw* may indicate that we have shifted focus from the primordial to the earthly venue. It may refer to the earthly tyrant's enslavement or oppression of the general populace (particularly since the despot is accused of tearing down his own cities, ruining his land, and slaying people). An alternative would be to treat this as a reference to Helel's having neglected his responsibilities as tutelary deity of a league, city, region, or nation. This abandonment could have been seen as the factor contributing to natural or political catastrophe. Not releasing prisoners could refer to his failure to secure freedom for his faithful in their time of need. The picture which obtained from this reading is of a god who has done the opposite of what is expected of a clan or national deity. This would be an excellent primordial reflex for a story that told of a human monarch who did likewise.

What causes those in Sheol to stare in disbelief? Is it Helel's condition after his fall? Is it his general appearance? Is he far different from what they expected? Van Leeuwen (1980:183), who finds several similarities between Isa. 14 and the *Gilgamesh Epic*, suggests that in Tablet 11.5-7 Utnapishtim is in a weakened state (similar to that of those in Sheol described in Isa. 14:12) when Gilgamesh encounters him. These lines can be understood somewhat differently. Gilgamesh appears to be expressing amazement at the stature of Utnapishtim, given what he knows of his fame. He is, after all, the only human to survive the great flood—the only mortal to have escaped a divinely ordained cataclysm. Nonetheless, in stature, Utnapishtim is neither greater, nor more awe-inspiring, than he is. After the king of Uruk's extensive peregrinations this is a great disappointment.

gummurka libbī ana epēš tuqunti
[x(x)]x aḫi nadattā elu ṣērīka
[qibâ iyâši] kī tazzazma ina puḫur ilāni
balāṭa tašû

My heart conceived you perfect for doing battle
...side. You are cast down upon your back.[214]

---

[214] This appears to be a posture of leisure rather than one of sickness or infirmity.

Tell me, how did you stand here in the midst of the gods?
How did you find life?

Can a similar claim be made of Isa. 14:16-17? After what Helel has said and done, are those who see him amazed at his stature? He is clearly not awe-inspiring. His boasts seem, therefore, to have been ludicrous and his aspirations unbefitting his true genus.

18-20a

[ ] מלכי גוים
[ ] שכבו בכבוד איש בביתו:
ואתה השלכת מקברך כנצר נתעב

[ ]malakê[215]gōyīm			
[ ] šakabū ba-kabōd	11	l	The kings of the nations sleep[216] in glory,
ʾīš ba-bêtō	4	b	each in his house.
wa-ʾattā hušlaktā miq-qibrakā	10	l	But you are cast from your grave,
ka-niṣr nitʿab	4	b	like an abhorred sprout,

Verse Type: Quatrain
Meter: l:b::l:b

לבוש הרגים מטעני חרב
יורדי אל־אבני־בור כפגר מובס:
לא־תחד אתם בקבורה
כי־ארצך שחת עמך הרגת

lubūš harūgīm mutuʿʿanê ḥarb	10	l	clothed with the slain, those pierced by the sword,
yōridê ʾil ʾabanê bōr	8	b	the ones who go down to the stones of the pit,
ka-pagr mūbas	4	b	like a trampled corpse.

[215] It is difficult to establish the original text of vss. 17-18 with certainty. MT is clearly corrupt. *Klm* in vs. 18 is absent from OG. This reconstruction is based on the belief that neither *kl* nor *klm* were original readings.

[216] On the semantic range of √*škb* see BDB:1011-1012.

lōʾ tiḥad ʾittam ba-qubūrā[217]	9	l	You will not be joined with them in the grave,
kī ʾarṣakā[218] šiḥḥattā	7	l	For you ruined your land,
ʿammakā[219] haragtā	6	b	your own people you slew.

Verse Type: Sestet
Meter: l:b::b:l::l:b

At the conclusion of the poem cyclical and linear foci are recombined. Both the earthly tyrant whose exploits are highlighted in vss. 1-11 and Helel, the divine rebel, whose crimes have been described from v. 12 to this point, have now coalesced.[220] In vs. 18 reference is made to divine and human kings. In vss. 19ff., while attention is shifted to the fate of the earthly tyrant, one suspects that the poet intended that a comparable fate be imagined for Helel. Two groups of individuals are mentioned in addition to Helel and the Tyrant—kings (foreign presumably) and those slain in battle. A juxtaposition has been created between the former and the latter. The purpose is to contrast the fates of those who act honorably and those who do not. The poet establishes the implications of this theme for the divine rebel and his human counterpart.

Helel will be relegated to a status below that of other gods. *Mlky gwym* has a dual meaning here. It refers on the one hand to actual earthly rulers and on the other to the gods who decree the fates and guide the destinies of the nations (cf. Dt. 32:8-9). Unlike other gods who are established firmly in their temples ("houses"), Helel is to be cast from his.[221] He is to suffer dishonor because he has abandoned those who put their trust in him. The

[217] OG adds *hon tropon himation en aimati pephyrmenon ouk estai katharon, outos oude suesē katharos.* Its origin is a mystery.

[218] OG reads *tēn gēn mou* "my land."

[219] OG reads *kai ton laon mou* "and my people."

[220] It is also *remotely* possible that the focus remains on *hyll* and that what is described is the destruction of the image associated with his cult. This would shift the attention of the audience to historical time to witness the desecration of a physical representation of the god, an act which mirrored mythological events.

[221] The poet has mixed imagery in the first quatrain by allowing *bytw* "his house" to parallel *qbrk* "your grave." The effect is dramatic. One begins with an image of *hyll* being expelled from his temple (either an actual occurrence or an allusion to his being deposed) and shifts to that of the tyrant being deprived of an honorable burial.

tyrant is denied an honorable end. He is cast from his place of burial and will be treated like common victims of battle whose corpses are walked upon and receive no special handling after death. He suffers this fate because he has brought his land to ruin and caused the demise of his subjects.

One suspects that from the poet's perspective, the tyrant is dead, but his grave has been or is presently being disturbed. This desecration of the tyrant's grave demonstrates the hatred that those who suffered as a result of his hubris had for him. It might also serve as a ritual reenactment of Helel's defeat and disempowerment. The fall of unworthy monarchs was, for the poet, symbolic of the fall of Helel—the rebel who sought power comparable to that of El. Like him, those who sought similar status on earth would suffer an ignominious fate. Just as Helel was cast from his place of authority they too would lose their power. They would also be denied the privileges accorded to warriors and other notable persons at death. They would be denied honor in the eternal place where heroes dwell.

7.2.3 Summary

This text addresses the quest for power and its implications. Van Leeuwen, who compared Isa. 14 and the *Gilgamesh Epic*, stated that in Gilgamesh the "quest for divinity is a subsidiary motif correlate to the basic theme of the pursuit of life in both the intensive and extensive senses of the word" (1980:181). Such is not an exclusive concern of people of privilege. It is a general human concern. Citing Amos 5 as an example, Eissfeldt spoke of how the prophet himself is shattered by the terror of seeing fallen Israel in spite of viewing merely a victory for Israel's god (1965:96). In the case of foreign entities, he saw the prophet as having no sympathy or terror, "only the bitterest scorn and satisfaction" (1965:96). Certainly, emotional release comes from the alleviation of suffering, yet Eissfeldt's description disallows any feeling of remorse over the decline of foreign cities and kings.

Israelite opinion regarding Babylon and its institutions (particularly kingship) was far from monolithic and there must certainly have been those who lamented the city's subjugation by the Persians. The fact that kings, gods, and cities—foreign and domestic—inspire verse with high emotive content implies a more complex and creative process than that allowed for by Eissfeldt. Isa. 47 taunts Babylon but the images used to describe its fall engender sorrow for the once great city left alone without suitors. After suffering the loss of her/his own city or king (e.g., Jerusalem—assuming that the poet either experienced personally or was well-versed in the traditions surrounding its destruction), could an Israelite poet contemplate that of another without having this experience strike a common chord?

It seems, therefore, that this poem describes not just the fall of a rebel god and a human tyrant. It also illustrates the tragedy of government gone mad. At the same time it makes the consequences of the human quest for divinity clear by relating the myth of the fall of an ancient cosmic rebel who thought himself to be Elyon. The moral is that divine and human excess is punished by the ineffable force that rules the universe—Yahweh.

The most likely candidate for the historical personage alluded to here is Nabonidus, the last of the Babylonian monarchs from the Sealand dynasty. This identification is not crucial to the interpretation offered above, because the demise of Helel and the tyrant—whoever he may have been—is symbolic of the decline of kingship as an institution. The criminal activity of the corrupt leader has ceased, his dominion has declined. To this the cosmos responds. Ancient Earth rejoices, the firs and cedars celebrate. They taunt his failure to ascend the mountain regions to cut them. Sheol rouses itself at his arrival. Kings and the *rpʾym* greet him. They rise from their seats and announce that though he is like them, he will enjoy diminished status. They occupy thrones. He is directed to a bed of worms. The tale of Helel, the rebel who would be king, is recounted; it is a fitting symbol of the tyrant's fall. He wanted to occupy El's place in the far reaches of the north. Moreover, he desired to be like the "cloud rider" himself, mighty Baal. He fails and is cast to the pit also. Neither will be held in esteem. Helel will be expelled from his house, and the despot from his grave. Both have failed to discharge their responsibilities; both have allowed their hubris to lead them to excess.

The fall of Babylon, its gods, and its kings was a necessary precursor to the second exodus. The fall of the city and its institutions is an event of major importance to this author and to the glossator who included 13:1-22; 14:1-20a, 22-23; 21:1-10; and 33:1-24 as a part of the Isaianic corpus of chapters 1 to 39. In Isa. 13 the fall of the city is accompanied by cosmic chaos. In Isa. 14 the taunt against the king is placed on the lips of an Israel freed from hard service and in 21:9 the fall of the city is reprised and the announcement made that her gods have been shattered. Isa. 33:18 may contain a reference to Babylonian dominion which is contrasted to vss. 17 and 20 with the messianic (?) king and restored Zion. This may be compared to the fall of Babylon's gods in Isa. 46, the reference to Cyrus as "Bird of Prey" in 46:11, the desperation and abandonment of the city by her diviners in Isa. 47, and the command to escape from Chaldea in 48:20. In Deutero-

Isaiah and Isaiah 1-39 the fall of Babylon signals freedom for Israel. It is within the structure of the larger redacted work of Isaiah 1-66 that Isa. 14:4-20 finds its significance. In its present position it reinforces the doom of Babylon mentioned in ch. 13 and leads the reader forward to chs. 21 and 33. The taunt against Sennacherib (37:22b-29) and most references to Assyria are made subsidiary to the broader theme of the eventual destruction of the archetype of evil cities and the destruction of its king. It is a literary reenactment of what has already transpired and an affirmation of the political freedom desired by the poet and those who share his views. The redactor who placed Isa. 14 in its present place recognized that it was an edifying piece for those who were well acquainted with the eccentricities of Babylonian, Assyrian, Egyptian, and Israelite monarchs and could see in the poem universal allusions to the rule of every king.[222]

Can a case be made for linking Helel with the *npylym* of Genesis 6:1-4. In this text, Helel is cast as a usurper. He desires to take for himself rights and privileges belonging to Baal and El but his plan ends in failure and exile to Sheol. To the extent that this activity threatens the balance of power in the universe and threatens chaos and confusion, Helel and the *npylym* represent similar forces in the universe—those that destabilize cosmic equilibrium (see Mullen 1980:240). In KTU 1.6, where one finds what at first appears to be an almost perfect parallel, Athtar is made king by El. However, he assumes this office legally and relinquishes power voluntarily. He then assumes kingship over the underworld. In Isaiah 14, Helel descends to Sheol with neither power nor honor. None of the remaining Ugaritic data is helpful.

Is there indication that Helel shares any similarities with Athtar as he is reflected in Ugaritic literature? Can a linkage be made between Athtar, *mt wšr*, and *hyll bn šḥr*? The strongest indicatior of a relationship between Athtar, *mt wšr*, and *hyll bn šḥr* is that *šr* and *hyll* have the same general semantic range (cf., the translation of *hyll* in Greek—*heosphoros,* and Latin—*Lucifer*). On this basis, Athtar, *hyll bn šḥr*, and *mt wšr* appear to be related entities. The fact that there is no Ugaritic evidence of a revolt by Athtar against El is a troublesome, though not devastating, datum. The mythological allusions in the poem are of Canaanite origin. It could well be

[222] It is possible that the original author represented a school which saw temple and Davidic kingship as less desirable than a decentralized form of government modeled after the old Israelite league with its shrine, conciliar government, and conditional leadership.

that Isaiah 14 is: (1) a fuller development of the tradition whose fragmentary remains are found in KTU 1.23 (related to *mt wšr*); (2) reflective of a tradition whose Canaanite prototype has yet to be discovered; or (3) an Israelite inversion of the Athtar tradition found in KTU 1.6 whose purpose was to debase Athtar and other astral gods.

7.3 Ezekiel 28:1-10[223]

7.3.1 Overview

Of the previous studies of Ezekiel 28:1-10 and 28:11-19, those of Cooke (1936), Zimmerli (1979), and Eichrodt (1970) should be mentioned. Zimmerli described vss. 1-10 as a "fairly succinct basic text" which "has been secondarily enriched and had its content expanded by the motif of the wisdom of the king of Tyre" (1979:76). By contrast, the present study treats this text as an oracle directed to an unnamed prince of Tyre that draws upon allusions to the god El and his wisdom in illustrating the hubris of an upstart noble. There is no single datum that can be used in determining the time and place of authorship. Mythological material and stereotypical characteristics[224] have been woven into the fabric of the oracle so adroitly that its temporal focus is non-specific. In addition to analyzing the meaning and function of the oracle, particular attention has been directed to the mythological background of the grandiose claims made by the prince, his taking of divine prerogatives, and his punishment.

7.3.2 Analysis

1-2

ויהי דבר־יהוה אלי לאמר: בן־אדם אמר לנגיד צר
כה־אמר [ ] יהוה יען גבה לבך ותאמר אל אני
מושב אלהים ישבתי
בלב ימים ואתה אדם ולא־אל ותתן לבך כלב < אלם >:

[223] A metrical scansion of this text has not been provided. Zimmerli's observation that it is difficult to discern a regular metrical form is correct (1979:76). For this reason, only the reconstruction and vocalization of the text have been given. Line division is intended to approximate, as closely as possible, meaningful sense-units.

[224] Zimmerli notes that the king is not given individual characteristics by the author, but is cast with typical ones (1979:76).

way-yahī dabār yahwe ʾilayy la-ʾumōr	And Yahweh's word came to me saying:
[225]bin-ʾadam ʾumur la-nagīd ṣurr	"Son of man, say to the Prince of Tyre
kō ʾamar [ ][226] yahwe	Thus says Yahweh:
yaʿn gabōh libb-kā	Because you are haughty
wa-tō(ʾ)mir ʾēl ʾanī	and say, ' I am El,
môšab[227] ʾilōhīm yašabtī[228]	I live in the divine habitation
ba-libb yammīm[229]	in the midst of the seas,'
wa-ʾattā ʾadām wa-lōʾ ʾēl	yet you are Adam and not El—
wa-tittin libba-kā ka-libb <ʾil-im>[230]	although you made you heart like that of El.

While it is clear from the introductory formula in vs. 1 that this oracle is directed against the prince of Tyre, it is equally clear from vss. 2ff. that one is dealing with material influenced heavily by older mythological tradition. The poet has allowed free reign to this tradition and permitted the prince's presumption to be expressed unambiguously. He claims identification with El.

It is also important to note that the oracle is not directed against the king of Tyre. This has every appearance of being intentional on the poet's part. This is not an oracle against a hegemon; it is, by contrast, against an individual who desires to be one.[231] The Tyrian king would, to a limited extent, be correct in equating himself with Canaanite El, his right to rule having been decreed by El and the council of gods. As king, his authority in matters temporal was comparable to that of El in matters cosmic. If the imagery of the divine council is extended to earthly government, then one who is a prince (i.e., a member of the royal household whose authority extends to areas delimited by the monarch) may have responsibilities ranging from care

[225] OG adds *kai sou,* "and you."

[226] *ʾdny* is missing from OG.

[227] OG reads *katoikian,* "habitation."

[228] OG reads *katōkēka,* "I have inhabited."

[229] OG reads *thalassēs,* "sea," (gen., sing., masc.) against MT.

[230] I believe that MT *ʾlhym* is an emendation intended to assist in the muting of the mythological imagery prevalent throughout the oracle.

[231] I disagree with Zimmerli (1979:76-77) and Eichrodt (1970:390) who treat *ngyd* in this instance in a manner similar to that in older Israelite contexts (e.g. 1 Sam. 9:16; 10:1).

of mundane matters of state to actual coregency. As such, he would be akin to Baal or one of the other younger gods in the divine assembly (Yamm, Athtar, Mot, etc.). On a cosmic scale, for any of these gods to assume El's prerogatives would be highly irregular. The same may be said of political protocol on earth. However successful or popular a coregent or heir might be, assumption of the kingly prerogatives would be tantamount to usurpation.

It is, therefore, not a king's crime which is described, but that of an ambitious member of the royal cadre whose wisdom, popularity, and political acumen have inspired him to lay claim to the lordship of Tyre. The poet gives the crime a cosmic dimension by incorporating elements from Canaanite myth. The *mwšb ʾlhym* echoes El's abode at the foot of the cosmic mountain. Tyre's actual geographical location could be described as *blb ymym*, "in the heart of the seas."[232] The mythological allusion to El's home at the source of the two rivers, in the heart of the double deep, is also transparent (cf. Kapelrud 1962:721-723).

The boast of the prince is particularly interesting. The translation "I am El" for *ʾl ʾny* has been preferred against the usual "I am a god" (RSV and NRSV). His wisdom, riches, strength, and power, as they are described in vss. 3-5, lead one to suspect that the prince would lay claim to far more than identification as a god (i.e., one of the members of the divine council). By simple equation with the known structure of the local pantheon, this would be nothing unusual. He would, in fact, be the earthly counterpart to one of the children of El.[233] The context suggests that the prince takes himself to be Canaanite El, chief god of the pantheon. This boast is similar to that found in Isaiah 14:12ff and is the crucial feature around which the remainder of vss. 1-10 is constructed. The overstepping of bounds is the dominant theme here, as it is in Isaiah 14. It finds full expression in the statement "I am El."

The background against which this more concrete reference to the Tyrian prince is to be understood must revolve around El and a challenge to his authority, home, and prestige by a divine rebel.[234] The reader is left with the

---

[232] We are in agreement with Cross that *blb ymym* can apply also to a promontory or peninsula (oral communication).

[233] Contrast the comments of Cross (1971:259-279).

[234] My sense of the use of *ʾl* in the Hebrew Bible is somewhat different from that of Cross (1974a:253). I think that there are occasions when *ʾl* is used as the proper

job of identifying the god capable of and inclined toward mounting such opposition against him. The poet's original audience no doubt found this task to be less problematic than modern interpreters. An important clue about his identity is contained in the powers which are ascribed to the god in vss. 3-5.

3-5

הנה חכם אתה מדנאל כל־סתום לא עממוך: בחכמתך
ובתבונתך עשית לך חיל ותעש זהב וכסף באוצרותיך: ברב
חכמתך ברכלתך הרבית חילך ויגבה לבבך בחילך:

hinne ḥakām ʾattā[235] mid-danʾēl	You are indeed wiser than Danel.
kull satūm lōʾ ʿamamū-kā[236]	All that is hidden is not concealed from you.
[237]ba-ḥukmat-kā wa-ba-tabūnat-kā[238]	With your wisdom and understanding,
ʿaśītā la-kā ḥayl	you made yourself strong.
wat-taʿś[239] zahāb wa-kasp ba-ʾōṣarōtay-kā	You made gold and silver for your storehouses.
[240]ba-rabb ḥukmata-kā[241] ba-rakullata-kā	By means of your great wisdom and commerce,
hirbītā ḥêla-kā	you increased your strength,
wa-[242]yigbah libab-kā ba-ḥêla-kā	and you have become haughty with your power.

The prince is said to be wiser than the Danel of Canaanite lore.[243] He is strong, wealthy, and powerful. Reference to wealth, as it related to Tyre and

name of the Canaanite god El in a manner that recognizes the distinction between El and Yahweh.

235 OG reads *mē sophōteros ei sou,* "are you not wiser."

236 OG reads *ē sophoi ouk epaideusan se te epistēmē autōn*, "or did the wise ones not teach you their skill." It is likely that this is an "educated guess" on the translator's part, based on the preceding half of the verse.

237 OG reads *mē ēn* (Hebrew *wbḥkmtk*).

238 OG reads *phronēsei,* "purpose, intention."

239 OG does not translate Hebrew *wtʿš.*

240 OG adds *ē.*

241 OG adds *kai..*

242 This conjunction is missing from OG.

243 See Eichrodt (1969:391).

its prince is best taken literally. Strength and power are characteristic of most gods in the Canaanite pantheon. Wisdom, by contrast, is usually ascribed to El. The combination of wisdom and hubris, however, does create something of a problem. There is no record in Ugaritic myth of a wise and proud contender actively vying for El's throne. In Isaiah 14, the usurper is called *hyll bn šḥr*, suggesting that he was an astral god. By contrast, emphasis is placed here on the usurper's wisdom—a personal trait that has led to corruption.

6-8

לכן כה אמר [ ] יהוה יען תתך [ ]
לבבך כלב < אלם >: לכן
הנני מביא עליך זרים עריצי גוים והריקו חרבותם
על־יפי חכמתך וחללו יפעתך:
לשחת יורדוך ומתה ממותי חלל בלב ימים:

lakēn kō ʾamar [ ][244] yahwe	Therefore thus says Yahweh:
yaʿn titta-kā [ ][245] libab-kā ka-libb <ʾēl-mi>[246]	Because you made your heart like that of El,
lakēn hinninī mibīʾ ʿalay-kā zarīm	therefore observe me now bringing strangers upon you,
ʿarīṣê gōyīm[247]	the terror of nations.
wa-hirīqū ḥarabōtām ʿal yapī ḥukmata-kā[248]	And they will draw their swords against the beauty of your wisdom,

---

[244] ʾ*dny* is a late addition and, therefore, not an original part of the text.

[245] It has been assumed that the marker for the direct object was absent in the earliest form of the oracle.

[246] OG reads *theos*. MT reads ʾ*lhym*. There is evidence suggesting that the text has undergone editorial revision of the kind represented by the addition of ʾ*dny* here and in vss. 2 and 10. One is led to believe, therefore, that (with the possible exception of 28:1) ʾ*lhym* has been leveled through the text by one or more editors seeking to alter the mythological content of the oracle.

[247] OG reads *allotrious loimous apo ethnon*, "foreign plagues from the nations."

[248] OG reads *epi se kai epi to kallos*, "upon you and upon the beauty...,"— an expansionist addition.

wa-ḥillilū yipʿata-kā[249]	and they will despoil your beauty.
laš-šaḥt[250] yôrīdū-kā	They will bring you down to the Pit,
wa-mattā mamôtê ḥalāl[251]	and you will die the death of the slain,
ba-libb yammīm	in the midst of the seas.

The beauty, power, and wisdom of the prince are to be brought to an end in the same way that those of the mythological usurper were halted. Both shall die at the locus of the power they desired. In addition, they shall be brought to the pit (*šḥt*), a reference to Sheol (Dahood 1968:39). In Isaiah 14, Helel is said to have been brought to Sheol. The spoiling of beauty, the bringing low of one who acknowledged no peer, and the defeat of one who supposed that his power was supreme, illustrate that the reversal of fates for those stricken with excessive pride is woven into the fabric of the cosmos; its effects are felt in linear and cyclic time.

9-10

האמר תאמר < אלם > אני לפני הרגך ואתה אדם ולא־אל
ב[ ]מות[ ] ערלים תמות ביד־זרים כי אני דברתי
נאם [ ] יהוה:

ha-ʾamōr tōʾmar <ʾēl-mi> ʾanī la-panê hōriga-kā	Will you continue to say, 'I am El,' before your slayer?
wa-ʾattā ʾadām wa-lōʾ ʾēl	You are, indeed, Adam, and not El.
ba-[252][ ] môt[ ] ʿarilīm tamūt	You will die the death of the uncircumcised,
ba-yad zarīm[253]	by the hand of foreigners,

---

[249] OG reads *kai trōsousi to kallos sou eis apoleian kai katabibasousi se*, "and they will wound your beauty to (the point of) destruction and bring you down."

[250] This is missing from OG.

[251] OG *kai apothanē thanatō traumatiōn,* "and let him die the death of the slain ones."

[252] The preposition here is attested in OG (*en*).

[253] OG and MT contain ancient variants for vs. 10a. They are as follows:

(a) *byd mḥllyk<tmwt>*	MT 9b
(b) *mwt[ ]ʿrlym tmwt*	MT 10a

kī ᵓanī dibbartī	for I have spoken,
naᵓūm [ ] yahwe	Oracle of Yahweh."

The prince and the divine usurper are to die inglorious deaths. They are judged to be finite (*wᵓth ᵓdm wlᵓᵓl*) rather than infinite. For the prince this clearly means death. For his divine counterpart, the meaning could well be the same.

7.3.3 Summary

The tale of a vainglorious god and his presumption to be El is the background for understanding this oracle against the prince of Tyre. Commerce, a trademark of Tyre, and the increased status brought by wealth derived from economic success have led the prince to presume supreme authority likened only to that of El. The transgression of established bounds results in his eventual fall. Memory of a heavenly courtier who challenged El enlivens the oracle. The myth speaks for itself, the slogan "I am El" capturing the essence of human and divine hubris. The result is the same, failure and death.

Within the current Israelite interpretive context, Yahweh, rather than El, is the one against whom the earthly and cosmic crimes have been committed. His proclamation against the prince and the usurper-god issues the timeless reminder that challenges against divine supremacy are dealt with severely. In spite of the complexity of life observable in the universe, the underlying organizational principle is simple; there exist those who are mortal (*ᵓdm*), and those who are gods (*ᵓlym*). Of the gods, only one rules, Yahweh. None may challenge him. The poet believes, obviously, that the council of gods exists, and that it is Yahweh who presides in this council rather than El. The poet transforms this Canaanite myth with only the slightest of interference. For him, it is Yahweh who brought the cosmic rebel low, and who reduces the presumptuous prince. It is Yahweh who calls to mind the finite nature of all who oppose his absolute power.

(c) *en plēthei aperitmētōn* OG 10a

Option (b) has been taken as the original reading. MT *mwty* has been corrected to read the expected singular construct form. It is certainly more reasonable to assume that the *Vorlage* of OG was damaged than to suppose that MT and OG represent different textual traditions. This solution would account for the absence of *byd mḥllyk*. *En plēthei* would then have to be treated as the translator's reconstruction for the damaged area.

For the Yahwistic poet who adapted this older tradition, there was no implicit theological threat in allowing the original source to convey its message, especially when it reinforced the importance of submission to divine rule. The poet simply introduced and concluded the oracle with Yahwistic references. At the beginning one is told that these words are uttered by the prophet against the prince of Tyre. At the conclusion it is Yahweh who pronounces judgment, reminding the prince that he is Adam (literally and metaphorically) not El.

The major problem comes in attempting to identify this divine usurper. The hubris of the usurper is similar to that found in Isaiah 14. The boasts made by the usurper in Ezek. 28:2 (beginning with *ʾl ʾny*) are not unlike the series of claims made in Isaiah 14:13-16 which culminates with *ʾdmh lʿlywn*. The major departure in Ezekiel is that the usurper has been stripped of astral characteristics and has been described as a god whose wisdom has corrupted him. The imagery is anthropomorphic. It is possible that the poet was attempting to establish a wisdom hierarchy in which El/Yahweh was without peer.

Can a case be made for linking the rebel in this text with the *npylym* of Genesis 6:1-4? Again, insofar as rebellion threatens cosmic stasis, the events narrated in Ezekiel 28:1-10 and the *npylym* of Genesis 6:1-4 are symbolic of forces that destabilize the universe (see Mullen 1980:240).

Is there indication that the cosmic rebel described here shares any similarities with Athtar as he is reflected in Ugaritic literature? Can a linkage be made between Athtar, *mt wšr, hyll bn šḥr,* and this unnamed being? Again, there is no Ugaritic tradition that identifies Athtar as rebel. There is, however, an indication from the *Baal Cycle* that he was perceived as a wise god (cf. the epithet *yadiʿ yilḥan*). This would match the tradition of the rebel's wisdom in Ezekiel 28:1-10.

Once again, the fact that there is no Ugaritic evidence of a revolt by a wise god—Athtar or any other deity—against El poses a minor problem. Nonetheless, the mythological allusions in this poem are clearly of Canaanite origin. It could well be that Ezekiel 28:1-10 is: (1) reflective of a tradition whose Canaanite prototype has yet to be discovered or (2) an Israelite inversion of the Athtar tradition found in KTU 1.6 the purpose of which was to debase Canaanite deities whose purported intellectual attributes made them potential rivals of Yahweh.

7.4 Ezekiel 28:11-19[254]

7.4.1 Overview

Zimmerli argued that references to wisdom as they relate to the king of Tyre are secondary additions here and in 28:1-10 (1979:75, 80, 82, 87). It was stated above that these references appear to be an original part of the oracle. The same is true of vss. 11-19. With regard to the date of this text, Zimmerli concluded, based on a comparison of vss. 11-19 with Ch. 27, that Ezekiel's "subdued judgment" indicates that the prophet is still awaiting the fall of the city (1979:89).

In general, caution must be exercised in positing a more specific date for the text because the poet has woven mythological material carefully into the lament. The basic interpretive dilemma is, thus, not unlike that encountered in vss. 1-10 above. The poet's intention was to elevate the king of Tyre and his failures to the status of universal exemplar of the folly of hubris and the reversal of fates which await those who are excessively proud.[255] As a result, the poem has, to a certain extent, a non-specific temporal focus because of the broad applicability of its message. In addition to the meaning and function of the text, particular attention is given to the myth upon which the poet has drawn and to the identity of the figure with whom the king of Tyre is compared.

7.4.2 Analysis

11-13

ויהי דבר־יהוה אלי לאמר: בן־אדם שׂא קינה על־מלך
צור ואמרת לו כה אמר [ ] יהוה אתה חותם תכנית
[ ] וכליל יפי: בעדן גן־אלהים היית כל־אבן יקרה מסכתך
אדם פטדה ויהלם תרשׁישׁ שׁהם וישפה ספיר נפך וברקת וזהב
מלאכת תפיך ונקביך [ ] ביום הבראך [ ]:

---

[254] Once again metrical scansion has proved difficult because of textual corruption and because, as Zimmerli has expressed, its form conveys "a metrically very obscure impression" (1979:87).

[255] Eichrodt's interpretation emphasizes the importance of the change in the king's fate as it is related to the economic prosperity of Tyre and the injustice and violence which unscrupulous commercial policy has caused. The king, who once enjoyed great wealth and the admiration of his peers, is cast to earth where he is now an object of scorn (1970:394-395).

way-yahī dabār yahwe ʾilayy laʾumōr	And the word of Yahweh came to me saying:
bin ʾadām śa qīnā ʿal malk ṣurr	"Son of Man, raise a lament against the king of Tyre,
wa-ʾamartā lō kō ʾamar [ ][256] yahwe	and say to him thus says Yahweh:
ʾattā ḥōtim tuknīt[257]	You are the symbol of proportionality[258]
[ ][259] wa-kalīl[260] yōpī	and perfect in beauty.
ba-ʿidēn[261] gann ʾilōhīm hayītā	You were in Eden, El's garden.[262]
kull ʾabn yaqarā masūkata-kā[263]	Every stone of value was your adornment—[264]
ʾudm piṭdā wa-yahlōm taršīš	carnelian, chrysolite and topaz, jasper,[265]

[256] Following OG, MT *ʾdny* is taken as a secondary editorial gloss.

[257] OG *su aposphragisma homoiōseōs*, "you are the seal of a likeness/pattern," reflects the reading *ʾth ḥtm tbnyt*. Graphic confusion between *bêt* and *kap* could have resulted in the reading of OG. MT *tknyt* is the more difficult reading and has been adopted.

[258] Literally, "you are the seal of proportion." Perhaps one might also translate, "you are the sum total of perfection."

[259] *Mlʾ ḥkmh* "full of wisdom" is missing from OG. It has been taken as a late addition to the Hebrew text. The OG reading has been preferred.

[260] OG reads *stephanos,* "crown."

[261] OG interprets this as a simple substantive rather than as a place name. It reads *tryphē* "softness, luxuriousness."

[262] One suspects a euphemism or metaphor here for the divine council. The accent is on El's ownership and the favored status of the being in question. I suggest that *gn ʾlhym* originally read *gn ʾlm,* "the garden of El himself."

[263] OG reads *endedesai,* "you have put on for yourself."

[264] I do not see a priestly allusion here. Instead I see an allusion to astral deities (Zimmerli 1979:93). That the precious stones are his adornment means that they surround him, hence they are his coterie, his supporters, his subjects.

[265] Brown, Driver, and Briggs (BDB:1076) list Dn 10:6 and Ct 5:14 as instances when *tršyš* is used as a simile of a resplendent body.

šuhm wa-yašpe sappīr nupk wa-barqāt[266]	onyx and jasper(?), sapphire, ruby and emerald;

[266] MT lists nine of the twelve stones found in the first description of the priestly ephod in Ex. 28:17-20. OG mentions twelve stones in its list, adding "and gold and silver" (*argyrion kai chrysion*). This reading is marked with the *obelus* in Mss. O of the Origenic Recension and is missing from several other early Christian witnesses to the Greek text. Taking note of the stones as they are found in Ex. 28:17-20 and in the MT of Ezekiel 28:13, the order has been changed so as to form an inclusio marking the list itself as a self contained unit. The stones are arranged in four groups of three in Exodus:

Arrangement		Stones	
A B C	*ʾdm*	*pṭdh*	*w-brqt*
D E F	*npk*	*spyr*	*w-yhlm*
G H I	*lšm*	*šbw*	*w-ʾḥlmh*
J K L	*tršš*	*w-šhm*	*w-yšph*

In Ezekiel the Stones of the first, second, and fourth tiers in the Exodus list are found arranged as follows:

Arrangement		Stones	
A B F	*ʾdm*	*pṭdh*	*w-yhlm*
J K L	*tršš*	*šhm*	*w-yšph*
E D C	*spyr*	*npk*	*w-brqt*

The fourth tier has been placed between the first and second, but the order of its three stones has remained the same. The order of the stones in tiers one and two has been changed, the third stone in tier one being moved to the third position in tier two, and the third stone in tier four being moved to the third position in tier one. The first and second stones in tier four have been reversed so that the order of the entire row is reversed, creating a chiastic inclusio which seals the list as a three-line, nine-stone unit. The list as it exists in MT of Ezekiel either existed in its present form as a written unit or oral formula before being added to MT, or was reworked by an editor from the list in MT of Exodus specifically for use in this setting. What, then, should be made of the list in OG? Its *Vorlage* probably contained a list of stones. Whether it was one similar to Ezek. 28:13 or Ex. 28:17-20 cannot be known for certain. It is most unlikely that the list in Ezek. 28:13 is a completely foreign addition to the lament in its present form. It is improbable that both the translator of OG and a late editor of MT Ezekiel saw fit independently to insert lists of precious stones to enhance the composition. It is

wa-zahab malʾakt tuppaykā	and (in) gold work (were) your settings
wa-nvqabaykā [ ][267]	
ba-yôm hibbariʾakā [ ][268]	and your anchorings[269] on the day you were created.

One is told specifically that this lament is to be raised over the king of Tyre, in contrast to the prince of Tyre to whom the previous oracle is directed.[270] Interestingly enough, the same myth is used as an artistic device to illustrate the crimes of which the king has been accused. The poem begins in mythological reality rather than in actual time. Once again the poet has exercised considerable restraint in editing and has allowed the myth to convey its message directly. Its main characters are Yahweh and one of his throne guardians. The original characters may have been El and a member of his cadre of gods. Apparently, the author trusted his urbane and literate audience enough to allow them to make the connection between the old Canaanite myth and the historical personage in question.

An entity without flaw is described, perfect in proportion and visage. One sees in him the ultimate manifestation of the creative genius of El/Yahweh. He represents the zenith of the creative process. He is part of the divine court, a member of the council of gods. One also suspects that he is envisioned as one of the stars or deified heavenly bodies which were

---

more likely the case that a list, either the one in Ezekiel 28:13 or some other list with less than the full complement of twelve stones, was the reading which the OG translator had before him. It is also possible that some part of the text was damaged. Desiring either to restore the list to its original form or to embellish it for his current audience, the translator inserted a translation of the list found in Ex. 28 or corrected a list in his *Vorlage* according to that contained in Exodus 28. It would appear that a list of stones of some kind is an integral part of the lament.

267 OG *kai chrysiou eneplēsas tou thēsaurous sou kai tas apothēkas sou en soi*, is not superior to MT. Both attest the reading *bkh* which seems to be secondary and superfluous. It has been eliminated from my reconstruction on these grounds.

268 I have adopted the reading of OG, from which a Greek equivalent for *kōnanū* is missing. It has been treated as a late addition to the text.

269 Hebrew *nqb* is a technical term of uncertain meaning. A cavity or hole could be implied (BDB:666). The value of the vowel in the first syllable is unknown.

270 There is nothing in vss. 1-10 or 11-19 which could be used in making a positive identification of the king or prince mentioned in these two texts.

themselves a part of the governing forces of the cosmos.[271] Of these, he is the most perfect and all other celestial bodies are his personal coterie; they accent his beauty by being comparable in species but inferior in appearance. These were established as his assembly on the day of his creation.

14-15

את־כרוב [ ] [ ]נתתיך בהר קדש [ ]
היית בתוך אבני־אש [ ]
תמים אתה בדרכיך מיום הבראך עד־נמצא עולתה בך:

ʾattā[272] karūb [ ][273]	As for you, O Cherub,
[ ]natattīkā[274] ba-harr qudš [ ][275]	I set you on the holy mount.
hayītā ba-tōk ʾabanê ʾēš [ ][276]	You were in the midst of the fiery stones.

---

[271] I would not go so far as to adopt Zimmerli's alternate suggestion that these *ʾbny ʾš* be treated as those who produce lightning flashes, though I do agree with him that the assembly mount is the setting for what is described in the text (1979:93).

[272] This form has been vocalized as the 2nd., masc., sing., personal pronoun.

[273] MT *mmšḥ hswkk* has been omitted in agreement with OG.

[274] The conjunction preceding *nttyk* has been omitted in agreement with OG.

[275] OG *en orei hagiō theou*, "on the holy mountain of god," is in agreement with MT. Both are, however, corrupt. The heaping on of epithets and descriptives is common during the process of textual transmission. *Gn ʾlhym* in v. 13 and *hr ʾlhym* in v. 17 lead one to believe *hr ʾlhym* improbable here. Equally unsatisfactory is the extended *hr qdš ʾlhym*. Therefore, the preferred reading here is *hr qdš*..

[276] For a sense of the translation of OG one has to begin in the preceding verse, and continue through the first two lines of this section. The full reading is *aph ēs hēmeras ektisthes su, meta tou cheroub ethēka se en orei ayiō theou*, "from the day you were created, you were with the Cherub on the holy mountain of God." Both MT and OG are corrupt and some reconstructive work must be done. OG appears to have leveled some of the parallelism found in the original composition favoring a narrative description of events (note the absence of *wnttyk* in OG), while MT has attracted editorial activity that has redefined the sequence of events making the Tyrian king the recipient of all actions. He is said to have been placed with an anointed Cherub guardian (*nttyk*), to have been present on the mountain of god (*hyyt*), and to have walked about (*hthlkt*) in the midst of stones of fire. I propose that the Cherub was the original focus, and that two actions were featured. The first was his being placed on the holy mount and the second involved his being in the company of the stones of fire. I have treated *hthlkth*, an equivalent for which is also missing from OG,

tamīm ᵓattā ba-darakaykā	You were innocent[277] in your ways,
miy-yôm hibbariᵓakā	from the day you were created,
ᶜad nimṣaᵓ ᶜawlatā bakā	until iniquity was found in you.

There are three possible interpretations of *krwb*: (1) a divine name; (2) an epithet of a Canaanite, Mesopotamian, or Israelite god; (3) a title or classification of beings with a functional significance. The king is being identified with one of the mythological Cherubim (hence, option three).[278] The

---

as a secondary editorial addition not original to the text. The reconstruction of these first three lines represents, in my estimation, the author's original reading. The major problem with any reconstruction is reconciling the sequence of events in OG with those in MT. If vss. 14-15 of OG are retroverted, one has the following Hebrew *Vorlage*:

ᵓth ᵓt krwb	You were with the Cherub
nttyk bhr qdš ᵓlhym	I set you on the holy mount
ᵓ th btwk ᵓbny ᵓš	You were in the midst of fiery stones

My reconstructed reading commends itself for two reasons: (1) its asymmetry (verbless clause followed by two cola—each having its own finite verb form) makes it a more difficult reading, and (2) the second and third cola follow the reading of OG (with the exception of my elimination of *ᵓlhym* at the end of the second colon).

277 The semantic range of *tmym* includes completeness as it is related to truth (BDB:1070-1071).

278 Cherubim are part of the iconographic repertoire of Canaan, Mesopotamia, and Egypt (cf. ANEP plates 332, 386, 393, 456-459, 586, 646-650, 662, 666, and 765). Gaster (1962:128-134) noted that several strands of tradition concerning the Cherubim have been woven into the tapestry of biblical literature. These include the following:

1. The Cherub as guardian of the tree of life (counterpart of sentinel dragons and winged colossi at palace entrances in Babylon and Assyria)

2. The Cherub as throne supporter and ark guardian (comparable to winged figures flanking Hiram of Byblos' throne, the draconic *zōa* who draw chariots and thrones of emperors in Sassanian and Byzantine iconography, and the winged steeds of Yahweh who are the personification of the winds)

implication here is that he was a member of the divine assembly which met at the holy mount, cosmic meeting place of the gods. This must certainly have been the meaning behind the Cherub's having been "set" (i.e., stationed in a position of responsibility or authority) on the holy mount of god.

Hyyth btwk ʾbny ʾš is very mysterious, and one cannot identify its meaning with any measure of certainty. As noted above, it is possible that the "fiery stones" are, in actuality, stars, and that the Cherub being addressed was an astral god. These too would, conceivably, be gathered at the meeting place of the divine assembly. The designation "stones of fire" is not a wholly inappropriate mythological, literary, or poetic image for celestial bodies, particularly stars. The cherub's "innocence" (*tmym*) is established in contradistinction to the "iniquity" (*ʾwlth*) later found in him. It also helps to establish his initial status as a figure of some importance and honor. Context suggests that this is one of El's/Yahweh's trusted counselors or personal guardians who has fallen from favor.

16-17a

[ ] <מלאתה> תוכך חמס ותחטא ואחללך מהר
אלהים <ואאבדך> כרוב [ ] מתוך אבני־אש:
גבה לבך ביפיך
שחת חכמתך על־יפעתך

[ ][279]<millaʾtā>[280]tôkakā[281]ḥamās

Gaster also noted the similarity between the biblical Cherubim and the Mesopotamian *kāribu* (or *kurību*) "intercessor," and listed the following well-known biblical attestations of the Cherubim—2 Sam. 22:11; Psalm 18:11; Ezekiel 1:4-28; 10:3-22; Genesis 3:24; Psalm 80:1; and 99:1.

279 *Brb rkltk* has been taken as a secondary expansionistic addition intended to focus increased attention on the activity of the Tyrian economy as source of the king's sin. See vss. 5 and 18 where *rb* and *rklh* appear in close proximity (and one suspects are original to the text) accenting the king's economic activity. In this single instance, it is interpreted as needlessly repetitious and distracting from the overall emphasis of this section which is on the violence and pride that have corrupted the ruler.

280 The text has been emended in partial agreement with OG.

281 OG *ta tamieia sou*, "your storehouses," is an expansionistic translation of *twkk*.

wa-tiḥṭaʾ	You filled your midst with violence and you sinned,
wa-ʾuḥallilkā[282] mih-harr ʾilōhīm	so I threw you as a profaned thing from the holy mount,
wa-<ʾuʾabbidkā>[283] karūb [ ][284] mit-tôk ʾabanê ʾēš	and I removed you, O Cherub, from the midst of the stones of fire.
gabōh libbakā ba-yupīkā	Because of your beauty, your heart was proud.
šiḥḥattā ḥukmatakā[285] ʿal yipʿatakā[286]	You corrupted your wisdom because of your splendor.

The nature of the offense is absent, though one is told that the Cherub's wisdom was corrupted because of his splendor and that his beauty contributed to his pride. It is almost certainly a crime or offense involving actual or potential harm to Yahweh/El. It resulted in his expulsion from the holy mount and his apparent demotion from the status of astral deity.

17b-18a

על־ארץ השלכתיך לפני מלכים נתתיך לראוה בך:

---

282 OG *etraumatisthēs,* "you were wounded," is either a theologically motivated emendation whose intention was to remove reference to Yahweh's profaning/wounding of the Tyrian ruler, or an attempt to make sense of the unusual syntax of the Hebrew in v. 16—√*ḥll* followed by *mn* being a difficult grammatical construction. OG represents a superior reading.

283 OG *kai ēgage se* "and he (the Cherub) led" is either a circumlocution intended to deal with √*ʾbd* with which the translator may not have been familiar, or a meaning which the translator projected for the construction √*ʾbd* followed by *mn*. The removal has the sense of finality stemming from an act that results in destruction. This fits the semantic range of the root √*ʾbd* in the D stem—"perish, destroy; cause to vanish, blot out" (BDB:1-2). The proposed reconstruction takes *krwb* as a vocative and eliminates the conjunction before the preceding verb (vocalized as a 1st, common, singular, imperfect form).

284 The reading of OG has been followed.

285 OG reads *diephtharē hē epistēmen* "your wisdom was corrupted." This presumes the existence of a D form of √*šḥt* in the *Vorlage* of OG. An active form is preferable.

286 OG reads ...*meta tou kallous sous* "...with your beauty."

מרב עוניך בעול רכלתך חללת מקדשיך

[287]ʿal ʾarṣ hišliktīkā	I threw you to Earth.
la-panê malakīm natattīkā	I put you on display before kings,
la-raʾwā bakā	to behold you.
mir-rubb ʿawōnaykā ba-ʿawl rakullatakā	In the greatness of your iniquity, in the unrighteousness of your trade,
ḥillilta[288] maqdašaykā	you profaned your holy places.

Focus returns to the king of Tyre, emphasis now being placed on commerce as the force which corrupted him. The author intends for an equation to be drawn between the cherub, whose perfection was ruined by violence, and this king. The profanation of temples ("holy places") may be a stock accusation made of all monarchs who have met with popular disfavor or an actual reference to the plundering of temples to produce revenues. One suspects that the former is true in this case.

18b-19

ואוצא־אש מתוכך היא אכלתך ואתנך לאפר על־הארץ לעיני
כל־ראיך: כל־יודעיך בעמים שממו עליך בלהות היית ואינך
עד־עולם:

waʾ-ʾôṣīʾ ʾēš mit-tôkakā hīʾ ʾakalatkā	Therefore, I brought fire from your midst and it consumed you,
waʾ-ʾittinkā la-ʾipr ʿal haʾ-ʾarṣ[289]	and I turned you to ash on the earth,
la-ʿênê kull rōʾaykā	in the eyes of all who beheld you.
kull yōdiʿaykā baʿ-ʿammīm	
šamimū ʿalaykā	All who know you among the peoples are appalled at you.
ballahōt hayītā	You were dreadful,
wa-ʾênakā ʿad ʿôlām	but you will be no longer."

Zimmerli proposed that the intention of vs. 19 was to convey the idea that fire issues forth from the place of sin (the sanctuary) and destroys the sinner (1979:94). However, it is also possible that the poet intended to convey a dual image. Like the cherub, the human king will be made like an astral de-

---

[287] OG adds *dia plēthos hamartiōn sou* "because of the magnitude of your sins." This is an expansionistc reading. The shorter reading of MT has been adopted.

[288] OG, *ebebēlōsa* "I profaned" is not superior to the reading of MT.

[289] OG reads *epi tēs gēs sou* "upon your land."

ity, but with one exception. The flame which is characteristic of the former will consume the latter, reducing him to ash. This will be his end. Like his mythological counterpart, he too will die.

7.4.3 Summary

Yahweh's/El's trusted associate, who was without equal in the created order, is compared to the king of Tyre. Both are fated for destruction because of their pride and their vanity. Corruption has resulted in their being deprived of that which makes them what they are. For the cherub, this involves being expelled from the assembly mount and having his "fire" extinguished metaphorically (i.e., by being deposed as an astral deity). The king is to be exiled from the holy mount (i.e., denied his kingly functions as head of state and chief patron of the cultus). An all consuming fire is to come forth from him, reducing him to ash. Mythological and contemporary metaphors are mixed—the astral god is deposed like an earthly king; the earthly king is consumed by a fire similar to that which causes the stars of heaven, and the cherub, to shine.

Cooke (1936:315), Zimmerli (1979:94ff.), and Eichrodt (1970:392-395) have noted that vss. 11-19 draw on an old Semitic myth. It would appear to have had the following basic outline: (1) Yahweh/El creates a perfect being, divine in nature, incomparable in beauty and wisdom; (2) he is present in Eden (at the Holy Mount) and is placed among the ranks of celestial gods where he enjoys favored status; (3) he is surrounded by other beings of light (astral gods); (4) he is considered blameless until he is found to be filled with violence.—he was corrupted by his beauty and wisdom; and (5) he is driven from the Holy Mount, removed from the ranks of the astral gods, and cast down to earth.

Can a case be made for linking the rebel in this text with the *npylym* of Genesis 6:1-4. As stated in connection with Isaiah 14 and Ezekiel 28:1-10, insofar as rebellion threatens cosmic order, the events narrated in Ezekiel 28:11-19 and the *npylym* of Genesis 6:1-4 are symbolic of forces that threaten harmony in the universe (see Mullen 1980:240).

Is there indication that the cosmic rebel described in Ezekiel 28:11-19 shares any similarities with Athtar as he is reflected in Ugaritic literature? Can a linkage be made between Athtar, *mt wšr, hyll bn šḥr*, the unnamed cosmic rebel in Ezekiel 28:1-10, and the Cherub of vss. 11-19? Once again, there is no Ugaritic tradition that identifies Athtar as rebel. The allusion to the Cherub's wisdom in this text calls to mind the Athtar epithet *yadiᶜ yilhan* known from the *Baal Cycle*. The reference to the Cherub's place with reference to the *ʾbny ʾš* brings to mind *mt wšr* and *hyll bn šḥr.* The Cherub's beauty and perfection are in sharp contrast to the personal attributes of Athtar described in the Baal myth (e.g., he is terror inspiring/awesome and short).

Once again, the fact that there is no Ugaritic evidence of a revolt by either an astral god or a wise god against El is perplexing. However, the mythological allusions in this poem—as is the case with Isaiah 14 and Ezekiel 28:1-10—are clearly of Canaanite origin. It could be that Ezekiel 28:11-19 is: (1) reflective of a tradition whose Canaanite prototype has yet to be discovered or (2) an Israelite inversion of the Athtar tradition found in KTU 1.6 similar in purpose to Isaiah 14 and Ezekiel 28:1-10—to debase Athtar and other Canaanite gods whose characteristics (e.g., astralization, wisdom, beauty, violence, etc.) made them potential rivals of Yahweh.

7.5 Psalm 82

7.5.1 Overview

Several satisfactory treatments of this psalm exist of which those by Briggs and Briggs (1907), Morgenstern (1949), Weiser (1962), Ackerman (1966), and Mullen (1980) should be noted. Its authorship, date, and life-setting are matters of considerable debate. Two of the most plausible solutions to these problems were been made by Ackerman and Morgenstern. Ackerman suggested that it was composed before the united monarchy and was made a part of the liturgy in the Jerusalem temple at some point during the reigns of David and Josiah. He also associated it with the Passover festival celebrated at Shiloh during the period of the tribal league (1966:455, 457). Morgenstern proposed that the original form of the psalm was authored by a Galilean poet who was influenced by both the North Semitic culture of his neighbors in Phoenicia and the universalistic tendencies of the sixth-century B.C.E. He also suggested that it was brought to Jerusalem by festival pilgrims from Galilee in the late 6th century and was incorporated into the official liturgy after systematic revision (1939:80 n. 88, 121-122).

The mythological elements in the psalm make isolating its date and point of origin particularly difficult. For the purpose of interpretation, Ackerman's pre-monarchical date has been adopted. Internal evidence has not suggested a clear point of origin, so one has not been proposed. In addition to the psalm's meaning, particular interest has been expressed in the delimitation of those events transpiring in the divine council according to this psalm and in the exploration of the possible relationship between those events and the sentence issued in vss. 6-8.

7.5.2 Analysis

1

מזמור לאסף
<יהוה> נצב בעדת־אל< ים > בקרב אלהים ישפט:

mizmōr la-ʾasap	EM		A mizmor of Asaph
<yahwe>[290] niṣṣab ba-ʿidat ʾil<īm>[291]	8	1	Yahweh stands in the divine council.
ba-qirb ʾilōhīm yišpuṭ	7	1	He judges in the midst of the gods.

Verse Type:	Bicolon
Meter:	1:1

The scene is the assembly of the gods with Yahweh holding the chief administrative position. Its current provenance is Israelite. El has been supplanted as ruling god in this august gathering by Yahweh. The council motif, originally drawn from Canaan, remains operational. The head of the pantheon is surrounded by a cadre of lesser gods. Yahweh does not appear to be standing as a lesser god in the assembly of El. In this reconstruction of the text, he is pictured as the governing force in the assembly.

2-4

עד־מתי תשפטו־עול ופני רשעים תשאו־סלה:
שפטו[ ] יתום <ו>עני <ענו> ורש הצדיקו:

---

[290] OG reads *ho theos.* This reconstruction agrees with that of Ackerman (1966:278). MT *ʾlhym* has been treated as an Elohistic emendation.

[291] OG reads *synagōgē theōn.* The reading *bʿdt ʾl<ym>* has been adopted in agreement with Ackerman (1966:279-284). He suggested that two Hebrew versions of this verse existed. The first version, *bʿdt ʾlym,* was of Egyptian provenance. The second version, *bʿdt ʾl,* was at home in Palestine. The former became the basis of the reading found in OG. The latter became the reading of MT. Ackerman argued that the reading *bʿdt ʾlym* is the original reading based on parallel designations of the divine council in Ugaritic literature, Syro-Palestinian inscriptional evidence, biblical references to Yahweh's assembly, and the general tendency toward demythologization current within Judaism and early Christianity (which makes it unlikely that the translator of OG would translate *bʿdt ʾl* as *synagōgē theōn*).

פלטו־דל ואביון מיד רשעים הצילו׃

ᶜad matay yišpuṭū ᶜawl	7	1	"How long will you judge unjustly,
wa-panê rašaᶜīm tiśśaʾū silā	9	1	and lift up the faces of the guilty?
šipṭū [ ] yatum <wa->ᶜanī	7	1	Judge the orphan and the weak,
<ᶜanaw> wa-raš haṣdīqū[292]	7	1	give justice to the humble and destitute.
palliṭū dall wa-ʾibyōn	7	1	Deliver the weak and poor;
miy-yad rašaᶜīm haṣṣīlū	8	1	rescue (them) from the hand of the guilty."

Verse Type: Sestet
Meter: 1:1::1:1::1:1

As cosmic rulers, the gods were charged with maintaining the equilibrium of the universe. Broadly conceived, their responsibilities included decreeing the fates of humankind, providing for human sustenance, answering requests of a personal or corporate nature, and dispensing justice. There was also an expectation that they would care for marginalized elements of society. Their duties mirrored those of earthly kings. Administrative responsibilities on earth and among the gods, therefore, included establishing order and ensuring the safety and care of the disenfranchised. Failure to do so was considered a grave offense. One of the most poignant examples of the condemnation of a god for failure to dispense his duties properly is found in the Mesopotamian flood story. In tablet XI of the *Gilgamesh Epic,* Enlil is charged with instituting the flood to escape humanity's noise without taking into consideration the counsel of the other gods. Nothing out of the ordinary is encountered, therefore, in this scenario. Yahweh's condemnation which follows later is roughly equivalent to that of the gods in the council who condemn Enlil for his rashness in the destruction of humanity.

---

[292] OG reads *krinate orphanon kai ptōchon, papeinon kai penēta dikaiōsate.* Ackerman followed a suggestion given to him (in an oral communication) by Cross that treats the current composition of vs. 3 as the result of two forms of textual corruption. The first of these involved a vertical dittography caused by the similarity of endings in *pltw* and *šptw.* This resulted in the placement of *dl* in vs. 3. The second involved the loss of *ᶜnw* from 3b by haplography. This was caused by the proximity of *ᶜnw* to *ᶜny.* Ackerman's reconstruction of the original form of vs. 3 has been adopted (1966:285-287).

The reference here to the lifting of the head of the *ršʿym* concerns the rendering of judgment in a legal case in favor of the incorrect party. There might also be a cosmic dimension involved in their activity (i.e., they could be treated as deities who committed crimes in the cosmos). Such does not seem to be the case here. The poet does not seem concerned with destabilizing activity within the divine council. The question being asked concerns how long these gods intend to pursue a course of action in the cosmos counter to that which is natural for them and in accordance with their place in the divine hierarchy. From a Yahwistic perspective, the condemnation of the gods is based on their failure to live up to contractual obligations sanctioned by Yahweh between themselves and their respective nations. Violation of these covenantal agreements would be just cause for their removal from office.

5

לא ידעו ולא יבינו בחשכה יתהלכו ימוטו כל־מוסדי ארץ:

lōʾ yadaʿū wa-lōʾ yabīnū	9	1	They do not know, they comprehend not.
ba-ḥašikā yithallikū	8	1	They walk around in darkness,
yimmōtū kull môsadê ʾarṣ	8	1	The foundations of the earth totter.

Verse Type:	Tricolon
Meter:	1:1:1

Yahweh's dialogue is interrupted, and the poet inserts a parenthetical remark to describe the character defects of the gods who are, in a sense, on trial. The gods, counter to what one would expect, are said to be without understanding and devoid of comprehension. They are also said to wander in darkness. As a result, the foundations of earth, here symbolic of the harmony of the cosmos and the order inherent in creation, are shaken. The poet has employed a reversal of roles to make clear the serious nature of cosmic affairs. One would expect the gods to provide the qualities which "illumine" humankind. Taken allegorically this could symbolize the gods and their ability to distribute justice effectively. The implication here is that the universe is dark (i.e., without justice) because the gods themselves are corrupt. One senses as well an allusion that could be astral (i.e., astral gods devoid of light who are unable to provide illumination—actual and metaphorical—for those entrusted to their care).

6-7

אני־אמרתי אלהים אתם ובני עליון כלכם:
אכן כאדם תמותון וכ[ ]שׂרים תפלו:

ᵓanī ᵓamartī ᵓilōhīm ᵓattimm	10	1	"I said that you are gods,
wa-banê ᶜilyōn kullikimm	9	1	indeed sons of Elyon all of you,
ᵓakin[293] ka-ᵓadam tamūtūn	8	1	but you will die like Adam,
wa-ka-[ ]śarr-im[294] tippōlū	7	1	what's more, fall like the Shining One."

Verse Type:	Quatrain
Meter:	1:1::1:1

The sentence is pronounced; those who were once gods, offspring of Elyon, will now die like the first human, and fall like the "Shining One," whose identity shall be discussed below.[295] The unique element here is the death sentence pronounced against the gods. Two prominent examples of gods dying by means of execution are found in Mesopotamia. In *Enūma Eliš,* the commander of Tiamat's forces is slain and from his essence the first human is fashioned. A similar sequence of events is found in the account describing the creation of humankind in *Atraḫasis* where the god Geštu-e,[296] leader of the uprising against Enlil, is sacrificed. From his flesh the first mortal is formed. As a result of this, the message being conveyed is that the demise of a god is a matter of considerable weight, even when the god has been accused of criminal activity. In both of these cases, such a death accompanies a marvelous *creative* event. In the *Atraḫasis* account, the god to be slain is even told that the beating of the human heart will be an everlasting reminder of his sacrifice. The circumstances in Psalm 82 are different. The death of the gods mentioned here accompanies Yahweh's exaltation to the

---

[293] I agree with Ackerman that *hymeis de* may have been used by the translator to convey the emphasis intended by MT *ᵓkn* (1966:287).

[294] This is vocalized as the noun *śr* with enclitic *mêm* for emphasis meaning "shining one." The Proto-Semitic root √*śrr* "to shine" is the source of Ugaritic *šr,* Akkadian *šarūru,* and Arabic *šarrār* "sparkling." The consonantal reflex of Proto-Semitic **s* would be Hebrew *ś,* Ugaritic š, and Arabic *š* (cf. Mullen 1980:35-39, 227-245; Huehnergard 1990:56).

[295] Here I disagree with Mullen's reading of pl. *šarīm* "Shining Ones" (1980:229,244).

[296] This divine name was formerly read We-ila (Dalley:15, 36 n. 11, 322).

position of sole authority in the pantheon. There is nothing to ennoble their fall. As irresponsible gods, their death marks the restoration of order to the cosmos and the elimination of disharmony in the pantheon.

8

קומה <יהוה> שפטה הארץ כי־אתה תנחל בכל־הגוים׃

qūmā <yahwi>[297] šupṭā haʾ-ʾarṣ	9	1	Arise O Yahweh, judge the earth,
kī ʾattā tinḥal ba-kull hag-gōyīm	10	1	for you shall inherit all the nations.

Verse Type: Bicolon
Meter: 1:1

Yahweh has become the sole cosmic administrator and is now called to assume the responsibilities of the gods who have been deposed. He has effectively eliminated the divine council. Harmony has been restored to the cosmos by the elimination of ineffective divine rulers and the rise to power of a single governing force.

7.5.3 Summary

In vs. 7 the gods who are condemned by Yahweh are informed that they will fall like the *śrym*, "Shining One." There is no mention of a "Shining One" falling in the Hebrew texts encountered thus far. The closest parallel is that found in KTU 1.23.8-11, where *mt wšr* is bound, pruned, and cast to the ground. There is, however, the fall of *hyll bn šḥr* in Isaiah 14 and the demise of the Cherub in Ezekiel 28:11-19.

Can a case be made for linking the "Shining One" in this text with the *npylym* of Genesis 6:1-4. The being referred to in Psalm 82 is compared with the first human rebel. Both represent threats to cosmic order. The same is, of course, true of the *npylym* in Genesis 6:1-4. They are symbols of the forces that threaten cosmic harmony (see Mullen 1980:240).

Is there indication that the "Shining One" in Psalm 82 shares any similarities with Athtar as he is reflected in Ugaritic literature? Can a linkage be made between Athtar, *mt wšr, hyll bn šḥr*, the unnamed cosmic rebel in Ezekiel 28:1-10, the Cherub and *ʾbny ʾš* of Ezekiel 28:11-19, and this "Shining One?" There is no Ugaritic tradition that identifies Athtar as rebel. An intriguing datum is that the gods in Psalm 82:5 are said neither to

[297] I have treated MT *ʾlhym* as a secondary Elohistic emendation.

"know" nor "comprehend" (*l*ʾ *yd*ᶜ*w wl*ʾ *ybynw*). One is reminded of the Athtar epithet in KTU 1.6 that portrays him in completely antithetic terms—"he knows and understands" (*yadi*ᶜ *yilḥan*).

Once again, the fact that there is no Ugaritic evidence of a revolt by an astral god against El is vexatious. Nevertheless, the mythological allusions in this poem—as is the case with Isaiah 14, Ezekiel 28:1-10, and Ezekiel 28:1-19—are clearly of Canaanite origin. It could be that Psalm 82 is: (1) reflective of a tradition whose Canaanite prototype has yet to be discovered or (2) an Israelite inversion of the Athtar tradition found in KTU 1.6 the goal of which was to debase Athtar and other astral gods by stressing their impotence and their failure to supply human need—flaws of character and essence that made them inferior in strength and power to Yahweh.

In conclusion, Psalm 82 describes Yahweh's assumption of supremacy over the cosmos and elimination of his host. For its author, Yahweh now governs the cosmos without the assistance of a royal coterie. This may reflect an intermediate stage preceding the development of primitive angelology, or it could represent a separate body of tradition which maintained that Yahweh was sole ruler of the universe. The death of primordial man and the fall of the "Shining One" are juxtaposed with the demise of unjust and irresponsible gods.

7.6 Job 38:1-38

7.6.1 Overview

Attitudes about the transmission history, authorship, and purpose of the book of Job have had a profound influence on the translation of many of its more problematic passages (cf., Driver and Gray 1921, Driver 1956, Pope 1965b, Guillaume 1968, Gordis 1978, and Jantzen 1985). The goal of balanced presentation notwithstanding, one of the most valuable aspects of an integrative commentary lies in the synthesis of data and its incorporation into an organizational framework which makes sense of the text.

Unfortunately, even the most balanced of approaches could not hope to overcome some of the more notorious difficulties presented by the text, language, and mythological references in Job. The impossibility of escape from perspectival relativism is clearly illustrated in scholarship on Job. Pope's recent attempt to unlock the book's remaining mysteries, particularly those involving its stock of ancient Near Eastern motifs, represents one of several approaches to the book.

To date, most translations of the more troublesome sections of Job have been conservative. This has tended to obscure the meaning of the theogonic and cosmogonic references contained in the Yahweh Speeches, particularly 38:1-38. There is a decided preference for interpreting this text as little more than a litany of meteorological and/or astronomical phenomena in the commentaries. This makes its meaning and function more obscure than they should be. The translation offered here attempts to clarify some of this ambiguity by making the mythological references more transparent. The sixth-century date of authorship for Job proposed by Cross has also been adopted (1973:343-345).

7.6.2 Analysis

1-3

ויען־יהוה [ ]איוב מנ [ ]סערה ויאמר׃
מי זה מחשיך עצה במלין בלי־דעת׃
אזר־נא כגבר חלציך ואשאלך והודיעני׃

way- yaᶜn[298] yahwe [ ] ʾiyyōb min[ ]saᶜarā[299]	EM	And Yahweh answered Job from the cloud

[298] OG reads *meta de to pausasthai Elioun tēs lexeōs eipen ho kyrios.* I have taken this as an explicating expansion that the translator has inserted (perhaps as an artistic device) to end the Elihu speeches and introduce the Yahweh speeches.

[299] OG reads *dia lailapos kai nephōn,* a problematic reading. *Lailaps* appears for BH *swph* in 27:20, while it has no Hebrew equivalent here. By comparison, the reading for BH *sᶜrh* in 40:6 is *nephous.* The matter is complicated further by the use of *nephos* to translate:

ᶜānān	38:9; 37:11, 16; 26:8, 9; 7:9
ᶜāb	38:34; 30:15; 22:14; 20:6
šaḥaq	38:37; 37:21(Greek equivalent uncertain); 36:28; 35:5

One is left with the choice of either taking *swph* as an ancient variant (marginal or otherwise) in the *Vorlage* of OG, that has somehow dropped out of MT, and emending it to the text, or treating *lailaps* as an addition of the Greek translator (included perhaps for increased clarity or as a literary device). The translator seems at times unconcerned with precision. In 40:1, for example, *yhwh* is translated *kyrios ho theos* (the Greek translation that one would expect for *yhwh ʾlhym*—a divine designation not used in Job). By comparison, for *yhwh* in 42:9 OG has *ho kyrios.* Emendations based on OG readings must therefore be made with great caution. I

way-yaʾmur			and said:
mī ze maḥšīk[300] ʿīṣā	6	b	"Who is this cloaking sound counsel
ba- millīn balī daʿt[301]	6	b	with senseless words?
ʾizur-naʾ ka-gabr ḥalaṣaykā	9	l	Gird your loins as a warrior,
wa- ʾišʾalkā wa- hôdīʿēnī	9	l	so that I may ask you; furthermore tell me:

Verse Type: Quatrain
Meter: b:b::l:l

Job is asked to prepare himself. He is held accountable for earlier charges (cf. 3:1-26; 6:1-7:21; 9:1-10:22; 12:1-14:22; 16:1-17:16; 19:1-29; 21:1-34; 23:1-24:17; 26:1-4 (5-14??); 27:1-12; 29:1-31:40). Confronted by the deity, he is commanded to prepare for conflict. Here, it takes the shape of a catechetical exercise. One gets the sense that the author believes the protagonist to have behaved inappropriately, even unwisely. This should be considered an important part of the overall response which the poet has constructed in the following verses.

4-7

איפה היית ביסדי־ארץ הגד אם־ידעת בינה:
מי־שׂם ממדיה כי תדע או מי־נטה עליה קו:

---

have treated *lailaps* as a Greek addition (taking *nephos* here and in 40:6 as the equivalent of BH *sʿrh*). I have also omitted the definite article before it in agreement with MT 40:6 and (with less certainty) on the strength of the Greek which records no definite article before *lailapos* or *nephōn* .

300 OG reads *ho kryptōn* (retaining the definite article), and inserts *me* before the Greek equivalent of MT *ʿṣh*.There is no compelling reason to prefer either of these readings over MT.

301 Little help is provided by OG. *Ho synechōn* was inserted, perhaps, for added clarity; there may have been some confusion as to the meaning and syntactical function of MT *mḥšyk*. *En kardia* is no doubt an explicating plus, and *bly dʿt* may have seemed to the translator a reference to some activity attempted with Yahweh being unaware (hence, without *his* knowledge), *eme de oietai kryptein,* "...and tries to conceal (it) from me" conveying the translator's general sense of this idea. Masculine plural forms of *mlh* ending in *-īm* (10 times) and *-īn* (Aramaic masculine plural form, 13 times) are found only in Job (see BDB:576).

ʾêpō hayītā ba-yusdī ʾarṣ	9	1	Where were you when I founded Earth?
haggid[302] ʾim yadaʿtā bīnā	8	1	Speak (of it) if you know the story!
mī śam mimaddayhā kī tidaʿ	9	1	Who set her measurements, if you know,
ʾô mī naṭā ʿalayhā qaww[303]	8	1	or who extended the line over her?

Verse Type: Quatrain
Meter: 1:1::1:1

על־מה אדניה הטבעו או מי־ירה אבן פנתה׃
ברן־יחד כוכבי בקר ויריעו כל־בני אלהים׃

ʿal mā ʾadanayhā[304] huṭbaʿū[305]	9	1	How were her foundations sunk,
ʾô mī yarā ʾabn pinnatāh[306]	8	1	or who established her cornerstone,
ba-runn[307] yaḥd kôkabê buqr[308]	7	1	when the Stars of Dawn rejoiced together,
way-yarīʿū kull banê ʾilōhīm[309]	10	1	and all the divine council shouted joyfully?

Verse Type: Quatrain
Meter: 1:1::1:1

---

302 OG, reflecting the text of LXX^{S}, reads *apaggeilon de*, "and report!" LXX^{A} and LXX^{V} have *anaggeilon*, "announce!" I am not convinced that the OG reflects an original Hebrew reading.

303 OG reads *spartion*, "small cord."

304 OG reads *krikoi;* LXX^{A,V} read *styloi*, "columns."

305 OG reads *pepēgasin*, "have been fixed."

306 OG reads *lithon gōnaion*, "mill stone."

307 OG reads *egenēthēsan*, "(they) were created." LXX^{A} reads *egenēthē*, "(it) was created."

308 OG *astra*, "stars," is an interpretive translation.

309 OG reads *ēnesan me phōnē megalē pantes aggeloi mou*, "all my angels praised me with a loud voice." LXX^{A,V} read *ēnesan me en phōnē megalē pantes aggeloi mou kai ymnēsan*, "all my angels praised me with a loud voice and they sang hymns."

Pope's interpretation of vss. 4-6 suggests that the author had in mind a conception of earth as a building set on foundations and constructed according to a fixed design (1965b:250). The language used here unquestionably casts the creator-god as architect. However in v. 13, Earth is brought to life as one who has given shelter to evildoers. The poet has mixed images of earth as the product of divine engineering and Earth as olden god, for artistic effect.

The tone of the events in vss. 4-6 is reminiscent of that found in *Enūma Eliš* (Tablet IV.130ff.).[310] Once Tiamat had been slain, attention shifted to the marvels that Marduk was to work with her corpse. As the artist/creator who fashioned the cosmos, his acumen received greater attention than the medium (Tiamat's body) through which he expressed his genius. Both texts focus attention on the power of the creator rather than on that which is created. That Marduk was working with the body of a slain god had been established before his creative activities began. In Job 38:4-6, the creator-god's skill is also highlighted, but the poet makes no mention of the characteristics or prior history of what is being created, though the author of Job 38 certainly realized that the earth which was created was imbued with life. However, in v. 13 the personification of Earth suggests that reference is being made to the old god Earth. The poet has chosen to draw attention to the force operational in the creation of Earth in the former, and on the culpability of the old god in the latter. The overall purpose of the poet here and elsewhere in the text has been to establish the identity of the god addressing Job. The implied answer is that this is the god who creates the living habitat for humanity and has the power to stand in judgment against even the olden gods.

Though the opening rubric states that it is Yahweh answering Job from the whirlwind, the use of divine names poses a vexing problem in the criticism of the book. In the Prologue and Epilogue, the name *Yhwh* appears frequently; otherwise it occurs only in 12:9 as a possible quotation from Isaiah 41:20 (Gordis 1978:442), and in the Yahweh Speeches (38:1, 40:1, 40:6). It is missing from the interchange between Job and his friends, and from the speeches of Elihu. *ʾdny* is found in 28:28 only (and here too its use is suspect), while *ʾlhym* appears in 5:8, 20:29, and 28:23. Far more frequent are the names *šdy* and *ʾl* which together occur more than ninety

[310] See especially the translations of these lines by Speiser (ANET:67ff.) and Heidel (1951:42ff.). Speiser's numeration of the poem's lines follows that of Labat (1935) (ANET:60).

times. This is not without significance. It has been suggested that the preference for these names is a result of a shift in the character of Yahwism (Cross 1973:59-60).[311] In the sixth century Yahweh is seen less as national deity and more as cosmic creator and controller. Old prophetic forms of discourse are transformed and given new meaning. A new movement is born (which may be designated as proto-Apocalyptic rather than a late prophetic movement) in which the language and symbolic system of an earlier period in Israel's life resurface and are given new meaning.

As an example of the transformation of forms, one may cite Deutero-Isaiah, in which Yahweh becomes the eschatological divine warrior whose battles will result in a restored Israel (e.g. Is. 34-35 for example). It is he who inspires Cyrus (Is. 45), brings down the gods of Babylon (Is. 46) and the city itself (Is. 47), and leads the captives in a new Exodus. In Deutero-Isaiah, Trito-Isaiah, and Ezekiel, the Canaanite mythological threads woven into the tapestry of Israel's early religious history resurface and begin to flower (e.g. Is. 64, Ezek. 28-29). In most of the corpus of Deutero-Isaiah and Trito-Isaiah, the balance between the historical and the eschatological is maintained; there are constraints governing the use of a cyclic (mythic) time frame (Cross 1973:346). The same may be said of Ezekiel. This may represent either a speculative strain of a period in the sixth century after the compilation of Job or an alternative philosophical/theological school whose dates are coeval with that of the final editors of Job. However in Job, as Cross suggested (1973:343-345), the balance is lost and the contextualization of history gives way to the recurring cycle of myth. The crucible of exilic life, the tragedy of national dissolution, and the perplexing questions to which these events gave birth, left the author of Job standing not before the god envisioned by the wisdom teachers, the prophets, or the Deuteronomist—he stood before El and Baal.[312]

Cross proposed that Job stands at the crossroads of Israelite religion. Deutero-Isaiah, Ezekiel, and others carry the theological strain of the book forward and assemble a new form of faith incorporating myth, history, wisdom, and the prophetic heritage. Only in the brief period of the Chronicler

---

[311] See esp. 59 notes 57 and 58, where he discusses the distribution of these names in archaic Hebrew poetry and in the sixth century. Note 60 on p. 60 should also be consulted for a discussion of the use of El as a designation for Yahweh in later Hebrew literature and the reasons accounting for it.

[312] For an assessment of speculative thought in the ancient Near East during the sixth century B.C.E. see Thomas (1961) and Davison (1980).

would an attempt be made to revive the old faith (1973:344 note 2). It is his opinion that this transformation was characterized by three traits: (1) an eschatologizing and democratizing of old prophetic forms and themes; (2) the emergence of a doctrine of two ages (one of "old things," and one of "new things"); and (3) a return to the use of creation myths to frame and give transcendence to history. Israel is prophet and Yahweh is the supreme ruler (1973:346). In Job 38:1-38, however, wise and compassionate El speaks and Baal, lord of the storm, thunders. Job merely stands in awe.

Rejoicing accompanies the creation (v. 7). It is clear that *kwkby bqr* and *bny ᵓlhym* are references to the divine council. In v. 7 they have been cast as astral deities. Gordis (1978:443) shared this opinion and also suggested that older myths (e.g., Gen. 6:4) had possibly become the foundation for a new astral mythology. Evidence suggests that the mythology referred to here is archaic and at home in Canaan and Israel. There is, therefore, no need to suppose that the poet has created a new tradition.

8-11

ויסך בדלתים ים בגיחו מרחם יצא:
בשׂומי ענן לבשו וערפל חתלתו:

way-yassik ba-dalataym yamm	8	1	And (who) fenced in Yamm/Sea with doors,
ba-gīḥō mir-raḥm yiṣiᵓ[313]	7	1	when he burst from the womb,
ba-śūmī ᶜanān lubūšō	8	1	when I made a cloud his garment,
wa-ᶜarapill ḥatullatō[314]	7	1	yea, a heavy cloud as his swaddling band,

Verse Type: Quatrain
Meter: 1:1::1:1

ואשׂבר עליו חקי ואשׂים בריח ודלתים:
ואמר עד־פה תבוא [ ]לא תסיף ופא־ישׂית בגאון גליך:

---

[313] OG reads *hote emiamassen ek koilias mētros autēs ekporeuomenē,* "when it rushed out eagerly, going froth from its mother's womb." LXX^{A,V} read *hote emaiouto kai ek koilias mētros autēs exeporeueto,* "when it was delivered, and went forth from its mother's womb."

[314] OG reads, *ethemēn de autē nephos amphiasin omichlē de autēn esparganōsa,* "and I made for it a cloud as a garment and I swathed it with mist."

wa-ʾišbur ʿalayw ḥuqqī	7	1	and broke my boundary for him,
wa-ʾaśīm birīḥ wa-dalataym[315]	9	1	then placed bars and doors,
wa-ʾōmar ʿad pō tabōʾ[ ] lōʾ tōsīp	10	1	and said, come here but no farther,
wa-pōʾ yašīt ba-gaʾōn gallaykā[316]	10	1	so therefore let (a limit?) be placed on the pride of your waves?

Verse Type: Quatrain
Meter: 1:1::1:1

The reference to the birth of the sea god is not attested elsewhere in Hebrew or Canaanite myth—though there does seem to be reference to it here. It is also possible to treat vss. 8-11 as an allusion to Yamm's battle with Baal (KTU 1.2). Vs. 8b could be translated, "when he burst forth (in battle?) (as though) from the womb," the image being one of a youthful warrior charging recklessly into combat, but one would need to treat this as an example in which a complex syntactic relationship is indicated without particles or prefixed prepositions. The rules of Hebrew syntax would have to be extended considerably to allow for such a construction. A more banal reading is appropriate.

It is also possible to translate v. 10a "and I violated my statute for him." One could infer from this that the creator-god broke an agreement or overstepped established bounds on behalf of Sea. Unfortunately, each of these proposals stretches credulity. The creation motif initiated in vss. 4-6 and continued in vss. 7-8 suggests that one is on more solid ground taking vss. 8-11 simply as a reference to Yamm's birth.

12-15

המימיך צוית בקר ידעתה שׁחר מקמו׃
לאחז בכנפות [ ]ארץ וינערו רשׁעים ממנה׃

ha-miy-yamaykā ṣiwwītā buqr	9	1	Have you ever commanded Morning,

315 OG reads, *ethemēn de autē horia peritheis kleithra kai pylas,* "and I established borders for it, having placed around (it) bars and gates."

316 OG reads *all en seautē syntribēsetai sou ta kymata,* "but within yourself shall your waves be shattered."

yiddaᶜtā [317] šaḥr maqōmō[318]	7	1	directed Dawn to his place,
la-ʾiḥuz[319] ba-kanapōt [ ]ʾarṣ	8	1	indeed, seized the extremities of Earth
wa-yinnaᶜirū[320] rašaᶜīm[321] mimminnā	10	1	so that the rebels were shaken from her?

Verse Type: Quatrain
Meter: 1:1::1:1

תתהפך כחמר חותם ויתיצבו כמו לבוש:
וימנע מרשעים אורם וזרוע רמה תשבר:

tithappik ka-ḥumr ḥōtām[322]	7	1	She transforms herself like sealing clay,
wa-yityaṣṣibū kamō lubūš[323]	9	1	and they stand forth as a garment,

---

[317] Here I follow the *Ketîb* rather than with the *Qərê*.

[318] OG reads *ē epi sou synetacha pheggos prōinon, heōsphoros de eiden tēn heautou taxin,* "did I order the morning light in your presence, and did the morning light see his station for himself?"

[319] OG reads *epilabesthai* (aor., mid., infin.), "to lay hold of."

[320] OG reads *ektinaxai* (aor., act., infin.), "to shake out." Note the absence of the copula before the verb (against the reading of MT). LXX^{A,V} retain the conjunction (perhaps reflecting corrections to bring their readings into agreement with MT).

[321] See BDB:957-958 on the semantic range of *√ršᶜ*.

[322] OG reads "Did you, taking earth (*gēn*) clay (*pēlon*), mold a living creature?" One could treat *gēn pēlon* as a hendiadys, "earthen clay," or, "clay from the earth." The Greek translator has either failed to understand *ḥwtm,* exercised authorial prerogative in order to advance a theological agenda, or both. A reference to the creation of humanity is not a crucial theme within the first thirty-eight verses of this chapter. The focus is, instead, on other cosmogonic and theogonic events.

[323] OG reads "and endowed with speech (*lalēton*—neut., accus., sing.) place (*ethou*—2sg., aor., mid., indic.) him upon earth." LXX^{A,S} have been corrected by an editorial hand to read *auto* (neut., accus., sing.) rather than *auton* (masc., accus., sing.). OG departs radically from MT here as in the previous line. I have followed the reading of MT.

wa-yimmanaᶜ mir-rašaᶜîm ᵓôrām	10	1	but the Light of the rebels is witheld,[324]
wa-zirōᶜ rāmā tiššabir	8	1	indeed, the upraised arm is broken.

Verse Type: Quatrain
Meter: 1:1::1:1

Boqer/Šaḥar represents the deified dawn. The Ugaritic text describing the birth of Dawn and his twin god Dusk—*šalim*—(KTU 1.23) makes no mention of their needing to be directed to their proper station. This does not mean that the reference has originated in the mind of the Hebrew poet, however. Once again we have a reference to material either at home in popular myth, or from a Canaanite/Hebrew source of which we know nothing.

Here, *ᵓrṣ* "Earth" does not refer to the underworld— Sheol.[325] Instead, it is the "olden god," Earth. Heaven and Earth are a theogonic tandem similar in type to other pairs attested throughout the literature of the ancient Near East. They are usually linked in binary combinations. They are not active gods and receive no regular offerings (Cross 1976:330). Frequently they are cited as witnesses to treaties between nations. In the Israelite covenant lawsuit, they are called as witnesses to Israel's treaty violations against Yahweh (Is. 1:2-3) and to hear his case against the nations (34:1-2).

In KTU 1.6, KTU 1.23, Is. 14:9-11, 15, and Ezekiel 28:8 mythological beings descend or are thrown "earthward" for various reasons. In KTU 1.6, Athtar descends voluntarily to assume kingship over the underworld. In KTU 1.23, *mt wšr* is pruned, bound, and cast to the ground. In Is. 14, *hyll bn šḥr* and the king of Babylon are exiled to Sheol. In Ezekiel 28:8, the prince of Tyre is to be slain and thrown into the pit (Sheol). What one finds in vs. 13 does not fit into this pattern. Here, one sees possible traces of a mythology of the old god Earth. She is guilty of harboring the *ršᶜym* either within her womb or beneath her garments. Is it possible that, early in Canaanite myth, Earth assumed the character of protector? What seems clear is that the *ršᶜym* mentioned here have made Earth their refuge. There is also little doubt that those seeking her protection are divine rather than human transgressors.

---

[324] The literal meaning of the root √*mnᶜ* is "withold, hold back" (BDB:586).

[325] Sumerian *KI* and Akkadian *erṣetu* are frequently used to denote the underworld (CAD[4]:310-311, *erṣetu* 2).

Vs. 14 is difficult. Whatever transformation is described, it is such that the *rš^cym* are no longer concealed, but stand forth visibly. Their leader is called "their light." This may indicate that he was an astral god. The "upraised arm" can be treated as a reference to the act of rebellion which caused them to seek Earth's protection. Unfortunately, one is given no hint as to who the *rš^cym* and "their light" are.

The *rš^cym* are a long-standing *crux interpretationis* in the Hebrew Bible. The lexical meaning of the adjective *rš^c* is "wicked, criminal." It occurs frequently as a substantive whose range of meaning encompasses one guilty of a crime—opposite of *ṣdyq* (Ex. 2:13); an individual guilty of hostility against God or God's people (Is. 26:10); or one guilty of sin against humanity or God (Num. 16:26) (BDB:957). Several of the Biblical references cited in BDB in support of this semantic range show strong mythological overtones. The implication is that violation of divine statute or action against Yahweh is understood as rebellion, the offending parties being identified as *rš^cym* "rebels" (or "traitors"). One is led to believe that when reference to them is made in these instances, a symbolic universe grounded in cosmogonic conflict is being drawn upon. Either mythological combat is referred to in which the *rš^cym* battle opposing divine forces, or an earthly confrontation between righteous powers and evil ones is illustrated. In either case, the vindication/victory of those who oppose the *rš^cym* is assumed to have cosmic implications. Yahweh is portrayed unambiguously as vindicator in the earthly setting of those being attacked by the *rš^cym*. This is partially the case in the cosmic setting. At times Yahweh himself seems to be under attack by the "rebels." There are also instances where the temporal and spatial foci of the conflict are blurred; frequently it is unclear just where the conflict is taking place. This could indicate that earthly battle against human "rebels" of various and sundry sorts mirrored that which raged or continues to rage in the cosmos—the defeat of the *rš^cym* never being final (in much the same way that Baal's cosmogonic battle against Mot produced no clear victor).

It is possible that a mythology of divine transgression informed the development of the concept of the righteous (*ṣdyq*) and the wicked (*rš^c*) that receives full expression in the Psalms and Wisdom Literature, and contributed to the eventual application of the designation *rš^c* to human criminal activity against society and/or Yahweh.[326] Texts that seem to reflect a

---

[326] This is a far more reasonable approach than that of Birkeland (1955:93), for example, who believes that evildoers in the Psalms are gentiles in all cases when they

cosmic locus for the activity of the *ršʿym* include the Song of Hannah, Psalms 9 and 11, and Isaiah 13.

16-18

הבאת עד־נבכי־ים ובחקר תהום התהלכת:
הנגלו לך שערי־מות ושערי צלמות תראה:
התבננת עד־רחבי־ארץ הגד אם־ידעת כלה:

ha-baʾtā ʿad nibakê yamm	8	1	Have you been to the springs of the Sea,
wa-ba-ḥiqr tihōm hithalliktā	9	1	or traversed the recesses of the Abyss?
ha-niglū la-kā[327] šaʿarê mawt	9	1	Were the gates of Death shown to you,
wa-šōʿirêṣalmawttirʾe[328]	8	1	or did you see the netherworld's porters?
hitbônantā ʿad raḥabê ʾarṣ[329]	9	1	Have you considered the expanses of the underworld?
haggid ʾim yadaʿtā kullā[330]	8	1	Tell me if you know (about) all of it!

Verse Type: Sestet
Meter: 1:1::1:1::1:1

(the evildoers) are defined as a collective group. He even extends this so as to include those instances when evildoers are spoken of generally.

[327] OG adds *phobōi,* "for/in fear."

[328] OG, "...and did the porters (*pylōrai*) of hell cower (*eptēxan*—1aor., 3pl. indic., act.) seeing you?" I have followed the reading of OG and vocalize *šōʿirê ṣalmawt* "netherworld's porters."

[329] OG reads "...have you been advised (*nenouthetēsai*—2sg., perf., passive, indic.) concerning the breadth of that which is below heaven?" This appears to be an elliptical translation of a Hebrew text not unlike that represented by MT.

[330] OG reads "tell me indeed how great something (*tis*) is!" The Greek gives greater specificity to the Hebrew command. It asks for facts about anything under heaven. MT asks for a demonstration of total knowledge of the expanses (nature?) of Earth (the olden god)—the 3f.s. suffix referring to Earth. Similarly, OG *tis* refers to *tes hyp ouranon.* *ʾrṣ* is feminine and seldom masculine (BDB:75). In OG, MT's mythological reference to deified Earth has been muted.

These verses amount to a quiz on cosmic geography and Job is asked to display his erudition. Only those who have been to the base of the cosmic mountain, traversed the ocean's depths, or descended into the underworld may provide satisfactory answers to these queries. Only the gods could say that they have been to *nbky ym* and traversed the *ḥqr thwm*. Pope was correct in seeing these as parallel to Ugaritic *mbk nhrm* and *apq thmtm* (1955:61-62). Only the dead, astral deities, and chthonic deities may be said to have seen the gates of Death, encountered the porters of the netherworld, and calculated the expanse of the underworld/Sheol. Job fits into none of these categories. Unlike vss. 4-6 which focus on earth as the home of humanity and vss. 13-14 which refer to Earth as olden god, vss. 17-18 refer directly to *ʾrṣ* as the underworld.

In the *Descent of Ištar* (lines 12-62), the goddess Ištar passes through a series of seven gates with the aid of a gate-keeper on her way to the netherworld.[331] This makes the rebuke of Job more pointed. He is neither dead nor a god. He has no access to the world beyond the grave, therefore he is unqualified to question his creator.

19-21

אי־זה הדרך ישכן־אור וחשך אי־זה מקמו׃
כי תקחנו אל־גבולו וכי־תבין נתיבות ביתו׃
ידעת כי־אז תולד ומספר ימיך רבים׃

ʾê ze had-dark yiškan ʾôr	7	1	Which is the way to where Light dwells,
wa-ḥušk ʾê ze maqōmō[332]	7	1	and which is the place of Darkness;
kī tiqqaḥinnū ʾil gubūlō[333]	9	1	that you may take him to his location,
wa-kī tabīn natībōt bêtō[334]	9	1	that you may know the ways to his house?

[331] I have followed the edition of Borger (1979:95-104). Cf. also the translation of Speiser (ANET:106-109).

[332] OG reads *to phōs*, with *skotous*, "darkness." MT *ʾwr* is taken as the original reading.

[333] OG reads *horia auton*, "their country."

[334] *Tribous auton*, "their tracks," is the reading of OG against *ntybwt bytw* "tracks to/of his house," that one finds in MT. Of these alternatives, MT represents the more difficult reading and has been preferred.

yadaʿtā kī ʾaz tiwwalid[335]	8	1	You know because you were born then,
wa-mispar yamaykā[336] rabbīm	8	1	and the number of your days is great.

Verse Type:	Sestet
Meter:	1:1::1:1::1:1

The cosmic quiz continues. Light and Darkness refer either to deified Dawn and Dusk—the Šaḥar and Šalim of KTU 1.23—or to deified Day and Night.[337] The meaning of lines 3-4 of this sestet is perhaps better expressed in the following manner:

> that you may take the former to his location,
> that you may understand the ways/paths to the
> latter's house?

Job is on the receiving end of the creator-god's sarcasm. Asked yet again for evidence of his wisdom, the deity asserts that Job must certainly know these things because he was present at their inception. He is, therefore, compared sarcastically to deified Wisdom, who is said in some myths to have been present with Yahweh at creation (cf. Wisdom of Solomon 9:9).

22-24

הבאת אל־אצרות שׂלג ואצרות ברד תראה:
[ ]חשׂכתי לעת־צר ליום קרב ומלחמה:
אי־זה הדרך יחלק אור יפץ קדים עלי־ארץ:

ha-baʾtā ʾil ʾōṣarōt šalg	8	1	Have you been to the stores of Snow,
wa-ʾōṣarōt barād tirʾe[338]	8	1	or seen the stores of Hail,

---

[335] It is doubtful that OG *oida*, "I know," represents an original reading different from that found in MT. *ydʿt* could have been construed as a defective spelling for the 1cs form of the verb.

[336] *Arithmos de etōn sou*, "and (the) number of your years," in OG is best taken as the translator's interpretation of the idiomatic use of Hebrew *ym*.

[337] Cross called my attention to the list of witnesses in the *Sefireh Treaty*—e.g. Heaven and Earth, Abyss and Sources, Night and Day (personal communication).

[338] The punctuation of OG shows that the translator has overlooked or misunderstood the *hē* interrogative in *hbʾt*. Otherwise, the reading of MT does not differ from

[ ][339] ḥaśaktī laʿitt ṣarr	6	1	which I withhold for time of distress,
la-yôm qarāb wa-milḥamā	8	1	for a day of battle and war?
ʾê ze had-dark yiḥḥaliq ʾôr[340]	8	1	Where is the way where Light is divided,
yapiṣ qadīm ʿalê ʾarṣ	7	1	(where) the East Wind is dispersed over the earth?

Verse Type: Sestet
Meter: 1:1::1:1::1:1

Snow and Hail are treated as a divine pair. One is reminded of other instances in which a god is accompanied by at least two divine attendants. For example, Šullat and Ḫaniš accompany the storm god in tablet XI:97-100 of the *Gilgamesh Epic*:

---

the Hebrew text underlying OG. *Thēsaurous* (accus. pl.) for MT ʾṣrwt (pl.) does not present a major problem.

339 MT ʾšr has been taken as a prosaizing addition and therefore not an original reading. OG has *de*, "and," rather than the expected relative pronoun.

340 The Greek translator has perhaps: (1) misunderstood 24a; (2) been placed at the mercy of a mangled manuscript; (3) decided to exercise license in translation; or (4) retained a reading not preserved in MT. *Pothen de ekporeuetai pachēn*, "whence proceeds (the) hoarfrost," is remotely related to MT, but there is internal evidence indicating this translator's tendency to paraphrase when Hebrew *ʾy zh hdrk* is encountered. In v. 19, OG reads *poia de gē*, "what type of land...." In both instances, idiomatic Hebrew has posed a problem for the translator. The solution in each instance has been the circumlocution of the original text by creative means. *Yḥlq ʾwr* is more difficult. Of OG and MT, the latter represents the more difficult reading and is to be preferred. √*ḥlq* (BDB:323) is found four times in Job with the following Greek equivalents (the letters in parentheses indicate the conjugation in which √*ḥlq* appears):

1. 27:17 (G) *katechein*, "hold back, withhold" (LSJ:926)
2. 39:17 (G) *epimerizein*, "impart, give a portion" (LSJ:518)
3. 38:24 (N) *ekporeuesthai*, "make to go out" (LSJ:518)
4. 21:17 (D) *echein*, "have, hold" (LSJ:749)

It is clear from this list that the translator is either unsure of the meaning of √*ḥlq*, or believes that it has a semantic range as broad as the four verbs used to convey its Greek meaning. The latter choice is improbable.

īlâmma ištu išid šamê urpatum ṣalimtum
^dAdad ina libbīša irtammamma
^dŠullat u ^dḪaniš illakū ina maḫri
illakū guzalê šadû u mātum

A black cloud went up from the foundation of the
heavens,
Adad roars in its midst.
Šullat and Ḫanish go in front,
The throne bearers go upon the mountains and land

In the theophany described in Habakkuk 3:5, Yahweh is accompanied by the divine dyad of Plague and Pestilence:

Before him went Plague,
yea Pestilence followed closely.

Lines 5-6 of this sestet are troublesome. The "light" mentioned here might be Šapaš, the sun goddess. The reference may be to her dispensing of justice, but a specialized meaning for √*ḥlq* would need to be defended. Line 4 may concern the point of origin of the deified East Wind.

25-27

מי־פלג לשטף תעלה ודרך לחזיז [ ]:
להמטיר על־ארץ לא־איש מדבר לא־אדם בו:
להשביע שאה ומשאה ולהצמיח מצא דשא:

mīpillag la-šaṭp t(i/a)ʿalā	8	1	Who opened a watercourse for the Rainflood,
wa-dark la-ḥvzīz [ ][341]	5	b	and a way for Thunder-bolt,

[341] OG has no equivalent for *lḥzyz*. It seems that two ancient variants have been retained by MT that may be reconstructed as follows:

1. *wdrk qlwt*
2. *wdrk lḥzyz*

OG retains the first as the basis for its reading, *hodon de kydoimōn,* "and a way of/for tumults/uproars." MT has conflated the variants. *Wdrk lḥzyz* has been taken as the original reading (against OG). Note the grammatical parallelism between *lḥzyz* and *lšṭp* (both are masculine singular substantives with identical prefixed prepositions). While this alone provides insufficient basis for a decision on the originality of one or the

la-hamṭīr ʿal ʾarṣ lōʾ ʾīš	7	1	to bring rain upon uninhabited land,
madbār lōʾ ʾadam bō	6	b	an uninhabited desert;
la-haśbīʿ šōʾā wa-mišōʾā	9	1	to satiate an utterly desolate place,
wa-la-haṣmīḥ môṣaʾ dašʾ[342]	7	1	and to cause an issuing forth of grass?

Verse Type:	Sestet
Meter:	1:1::1:1::1:1

Here reference is made to the devastating result of torrential rains or violent storms, perhaps to be understood in a manner similar to Akkadian *abūbu* which may designate a flood, a divine title, or a mythical weapon (AHw[1]:8). The duty of providing rain and fertility belongs to Baal.

28-30

היש־למטר אב או מי־הוליד אגלי־טל׃
מבטן מי יצא [ ]קרח וכפר שמים מי ילדו׃
כאבן מים יתחבאו ופני תהום יתלכדו׃

ha-yiš la-maṭār ʾāb	6	1	Does Rain have a father,
ʾô mī hôlīd ʾigalê ṭall[343]	7	1	or who brought forth drops of dew?
mib-baṭn mī yaṣaʾ [ ] qarḥ[344]	6	1	From whose womb did Frost go forth?

---

other of these two variants, one must also consider *lḥzyz* as the more difficult of the two variants. The strength of the combined evidence favors this reading more than the agreement of MT and OG.

[342] Vss. 26-27 are lacking in OG. They were marked with the asterisk in the *Hexapla* and are of little use in reconstructing an original Hebrew text. Origen drew from Theodotion when filling gaps in his Greek text (Orlinsky 1946:55). One is forced to rely exclusively on MT for these two verses.

[343] OG reads *tis de estin ho tetokōs bōlous drosou,* "and who is the one having engendered the lumps of dew."

[344] OG (*ho krystallos*) and MT (*hqrḥ*) appear to agree. LXX^{A,S} omit the definite article. I believe that in this text one is dealing with references to deified natural phenomena rather than with a demythologized meteorological taxonomy. Therefore the definite article is not necessary; it is no doubt a part of editorial efforts to expunge or modify overtly mythological references—a tendency commonly shared by many later Hebrew redactors and, to a greater extent, by Greek translators.

wa-kupōr šamaym mī yaladō	9	1	And who birthed the hoarfrost of heaven,
ka-ʾabn maym yitḥabbaʾū[345]	7	1	(when) the waters hid like a stone,
wa-panê tihōm[346] yitlakkadū[347]	9	1	and the face of the Abyss congealed?

Verse Type: Sestet
Meter: 1:1::1:1::1:1

Lines 1-3 read like a litany of the members of the storm god's coterie, though partially demythologized. In KTU 1.3 III 5-8, one finds three daughters of the storm god Baal mentioned by name: Arṣay ("muddy"), Pidray ("misty"), and Ṭallay ("dewy"):[348]

li-dôdi ʾalʾiyāni baᶜli
yadi pidrayyi bitti ʾāri
ʾahabati ṭallayyi bitti rabbi
dôdi ʾarṣayyi bitti yaᶜabdiri

For the love of Baal the Conqueror,
the hand of Pidray, daughter of light,
the desire of Ṭallay, daughter of rain,
the love of Arṣay, daughter of floods.[349]

In this sestet we have shifted from cosmic geography to important figures in the pantheon and, one suspects, associated meteorological phenomena. Rain, drops of Dew, Frost, hoar frost, and the Abyss are mentioned. To

---

345 OG reads *hē katabainei hōsper hydōr reon,* "which descends like running water," a misreading of the translator's Hebrew text if it resembled what one finds in MT.

346 OG reads *abyssou* (< *abyssos,* "bottomless, unfathomed").

347 OG reads *epēxen* (< *pegnūmi,* "stick, fix in," LSJ:1399). LXX[B] reads *eptexen* (< *ptēssō,* "to scare, alarm"). LXX[S,A] read *etexen* (< *tēkō,* "to melt, melt down"). The translator apparently had little knowledge of the meaning of *√lkd* in the Dt, which occurs here and in 41:9. MT is likely the original reading.

348 In KTU 1.3 I 22-25 Pidray and Ṭallay are called Baal's daughters. Though Arṣay is not mentioned there, she is known to be Baal's daughter from other references—see KTU 1.4 I 9-19, and KTU 1.4 IV 50-57.

349 I have followed Coogan's translation of *yᶜbdr* (1978:91).

what extent one is dealing here with deified forces is a matter of debate. Rain (*mṭr*), Dew (*ṭl*), and Abyss (*thwm*) are etymologically related to deified forces elsewhere in the Ancient Near East, while frost (*qrḥ*), hoarfrost (*kpwr*), and waters (*mym*) are without a comparable referent. However, the language used in vss. 28-30 is anthropomorphic. One is given the sense that sentient beings rather than meteorological phenomena are being spoken of. *ʾgly ṭl* is somewhat problematic since in the text reconstructed above, it is the only entity which is not listed simply as a proper noun. It is possible that an early attempt at demythologization may have led, at some point in the transmission process, to the insertion of *ʾgly*. While one suspects that all of the forces mentioned in these verses are deified, there is *firm* evidence in support of only three of them (Rain, Dew, and Abyss). These three appear to be juxtaposed with non-deified phenomena.

Line	Element	Deified/Natural
1	Rain (*mṭr)*	Deified
2	drops of dew (*ʾgly ṭl*)	Deified
3	frost (*qrḥ*)	Deified?/Natural?
4	hoar frost (*kpwr*)	Deified?/Natural?
5	waters(*mym*)	Deified?/Natural?
6	Abyss (*thwm*)	Deified

Pope's suggestion that *yṭhbʾw* be treated as a dialectal form of *yṭhmʾw* (38:10) meaning "harden" is unconvincing (1965b:254). The translation of vs. 30 offered above, which renders the Hebrew verbatim, is difficult to interpret. It could be that the birth of hoarfrost caused the face of the Abyss to congeal, but the reason for this would remain unanswered.[350] This verse must remain an unresolved *crux criticorum*.

31-33

התקשר מעדנות כימה או־משכות כסיל תפתח:
התציא מזרות בעת<ו> ועיש על־בניה תנחם:
הידעת חקות שמים אם־תשים משטרו בארץ:

---

350 One is reminded of Vergil's *Aeneid* 6.729—*quae marmoreo fert monstra sub aequore pontus* (cf., Fairclough 1986).

ha-taqaššir[351] maʿdannōt kīmā	8	1	Have you bound the Pleiades with fetters,
ʾô môšikōt kisīl tupattiḥ[352]	9	1	or loosed the cords of Orion?
ha-tôṣīʾ mazzarōt ba-ʿitt<ān>[353]	9	1	Can you release the constellations at their time,
wa-ʿayš ʿal banayhā tanḥim	8	1	or lead the Bear to her children?
ha-yadaʿtā ḥuqqōt šamaym	8	1	Do you know the statutes of Heavens;
ʾim taśīm maštarō ba-ʾarṣ[354]	8	1	can you establish his[355] rule over Earth?

Verse Type: Sestet
Meter: 1:1::1:1::1:1

Mzrwt is treated as a dialectal variant of *mzlwt* "constellations" (BDB:561; Pope 1965b:255). The first four lines of the unit refer to deified celestial bodies. The poet contrasts the power of the one who sets in place the heavenly bodies with the human limitations of Job whose role as a mortal, one assumes, is limited to the observation of the heavens.

Lines 5 and 6 are most enigmatic. The meanings of *ḥqwt šmym* and *mšṭrw* are obscure. These may refer to the diviner's ability to interpret the meaning of the stars and to shape human behavior in accordance with the fates which have been decreed. It may also refer to ancient cosmogonic material involving the subjugation of the old god Earth to the rule of the old

---

351 OG reads *synēkas* (< *syniēmi*) "bring or set together," metaph., "to understand" (LSJ:1718). LXX^{A,V} place *synēkas* at the end of the preceding line and read *desmon de pl(e)iados egnōs,* "and did you know the band of Pleiades?" This is a further corruption of what must have been the original reading.

352 OG reads "Did you understand the band of Pleiades and did you open the fencing of Orion?"

353 I have corrected MT *bʿtw* to *bʿtn*. The latter appears to have been the original reading of the text. By contrast, *bʿtw* seems to be an editorial correction prompted by *mzrwt* (which was likely interpreted as a singular form).

354 OG is a paraphrase—"and did you know the turnings/changes of heaven, or the things transpiring together under heaven?"

355 The antecedent here is unclear. One suspects that it is Heavens, but this would necessitate a plural pronominal suffix.

god Heaven.[356] What is clear from this passage is that Job's finite power is being measured against a superior divine force.

34-38

התרים לעב קולך ושפעת־מים תכסך׃
התשלח ברקים וילכו ויאמרו לך הננו׃

ha-tarīm la-ᶜāb qōl-kā[357]	7	1	Can you raise your voice to/in the clouds,
wa-šipᶜat maym[358] tukasse-kā[359]	8	1	and make abundant water cover you?
ha-tušallaḥ[360] baraqīm wa-yilikū	11	1	Can you command lightning bolts so that they come,
wa-yō(ᵓ)marū la-kā hinninū[361]	9	1	and say to you, 'We're here'?

Verse Type: Quatrain
Meter: 1:1::1:1

מי־שת בטחות חכמה או מי־נתן לשכוי בינה׃
מי־יספר שחקים בחכמה ונבלי שמים מי ישכיב׃
בצקת עפר למוצק ורגבים ידבקו׃

mī šat baṭ-ṭuḥḥōt[362] ḥukmā	7	1	Who placed wisdom in Thoth,

[356] The major problem with this suggestion is that there is no evidence from Canaanite or Hebrew lore attesting to the dominance of Heaven over Earth.

[357] OG reads *phonē*, "with/by voice."

[358] OG reads *kai tromō hydatos labrō*, "and/that with a furious trembling/quaking of water...." The connotation is that of a violent rain storm accompanied by thunder.

[359] OG reads *hypakousetai sou*. It is possible that this reflects a Hebrew reading different from that of MT—see the suggestion of Gerlemann (BHS:1269 note 34a). However, I think that MT represents a superior reading.

[360] OG adds *de* , "and."

[361] OG *ti estin* for Hebrew *hnnw* poses no problem. It does not reflect a Hebrew text different from that of MT.

[362] OG *gynaixin hyphasmatos*, "women of the woven robe/weaving women." If the translator has a reading similar to that of MT, it is both obvious and understandable that difficulty was encountered in rendering Hebrew *bṭḥwt*. It continues to generate debate among modern translators.

ʾô mī natan la-śikwī bīnā[363]	9	1	or gave Sikwi understanding?
mī[364] yasappir šaḥaqīm ba-ḥukmā	10	1	Who numbered the clouds with wisdom,
wa-nabalê šamaym mī yaškīb[365]	9	1	and tipped the water jars of the heavens?"
ba-ṣiqt ʿapār la-mūṣāq[366]	7	1	....
wa-ragabīm yudubbaqū[367]	8	1	................................[368]

Verse Type:	Quatrain
Meter:	1:1::1:1::1:1

Presumably, only Baal or one who can exercise the power of the storm god can do those things outlined in the first quatrain. Here, the deity seems to ask, "Do you think that you are the storm god?" This query contrasts once again Job's limitations with the limitlessness of the god who speaks to him. However, one cannot help but see a distant allusion here to Athtar's brief tenure as storm god. It is possible that the poet intended the audience to draw a connection between Job and Athtar. Both have been placed in untenable positions. Job's suffering and Athtar's kingship were decreed by the

---

[363] OG *ē poikiltikēn epistēmēn,* "or embroidering skill." The translator's Hebrew text is in all probability similar to that of MT. The translator must have had trouble finding a suitable Greek equivalent for Hebrew *lśkwy*. It is also possible that the ultimate source of the translation preserved here and in the previous line is an interpretive tradition current within Egyptian circles at the time of translation. I have vocalized the form as a divine name preceded by the preposition *la-*.

[364] OG adds *de.*

[365] OG *ouranon de eis gēn eklinen,* "and (who) inclined heaven toward earth?" The reading of MT is superior to that of OG.

[366] The syntax of OG *kechytai de hōsper gē konia* is difficult. Both *gē* and *konia* are nom. sing. fem. substantives. One might translate the line, "It has been spread out as dust covered/sandy earth," or *gē* might be corrected to *gēs* (following LXX^{A,V}) with the line being translated, "dust/sand has been spread out as earth." In either case, the Greek presents a text which neither departs from nor is superior to MT. The line is possibly an idiomatic reference to primordial reality similar to that found in Gen. 1:2.

[367] OG *kekollēka de auton hōsper lithō kybon,* "and I have glued it as a cube to a stone," seems to be an expansionistic and interpretive translation of a Hebrew text similartoMT.

[368] Job 38:38 is inscrutable. I have, therefore, elected not to attempt a translation.

controlling voice within the divine council. Both are enigmatic—the former because of his divinely decreed suffering which he cannot escape, the latter for his voluntary abdication of authority bestowed by the most powerful of divine patrons.

As a mortal, Job certainly could not hope to fill the storm god's throne. Since ill-fortune has been decreed for him, his vitality as a human is further reduced. In one sense, this makes him the least of humans—an enigmatic turn of events for one purported to be righteous. In this weakened state he can vie with neither man nor god, let alone presume to act in Baal's capacity. He is a human icon of an immutable cosmic enigma—the peculiar nature of the highest of all divine powers and multiplicity of possible responses (divine and human) to it. Like Job, Athtar does not become a replacement for Baal. Moreover, neither Job nor Athtar compete for cosmic dominance. Neither one raises his voice in the clouds or commands lightning. In Job's case, this is the result of the nature which was decreed to him at birth—he is human. For Athtar, it is because he chose to do otherwise.

Pope's suggestion (following J. G. E. Hoffman) that *ṭḥwt* in v. 36 refers to Thoth, the Egyptian god of wisdom has been adopted.[369] His adoption of Hoffman's connection of *śkwy* with the Coptic name for the planet Mercury, *souchi* (Pope 1965b:256) is also appropriate.[370]

The references made to wisdom deserve special mention. One is left to assume that the creative acts described in vss. 36-37 require a god characterized as a wise god. Vs. 37b may reflect old mythological material concerning El and his battle with Heaven, his father; it is El who, in a sense,

---

[369] Against Albright (1968:244-248) who sees the Phoenician hierophant Taauth mentioned by Sanchuniathon lying behind biblical references in the Psalms (51:8) and Job to *ṭḥwt*, rather than his Egyptian prototype Thoth, the ibis-headed god of wisdom.

[370] I do not agree with Albright's reading *škwy* rather than *śkwy* (1968:246). It was his belief that the name meant "mariner, navigator" and was of similar type to Ugaritic *daggayyu*, "fisherman," (< *daggu*, "fish"), and etymologically related Ugaritic *ṯkt* "bark" (Heb. pl. *škywt*). I do not find his identification of this creature with the Galilaean cock (which was given the title "sailor" because of its identification as the fisherman's alarm clock) a convincing one. The poet has not yet shifted his thematic agenda away from the divine world to that of pseudo-deities (hierophants) and animals with special powers (the cock).

ended[371] the folly of his father (i.e., if one takes the references in Sanchuniathon as credible witnesses to Phoenician mythology and if one considers *Šmym*'s behavior as tantamount to folly) and seized control of the pantheon by emasculating the old god.[372] Unfortunately, one would need substantially more information than these verses provide to establish a convincing argument in favor of this reading. Further, the semantic range of *√škb* would have to be extended to make this interpretation viable. Neither of these prerequisites can be met, hence, one must be satisfied with a more banal reading involving the creator-god's ability to provide fertility in the form of rain to the parched earth. Therefore, *nbly* has been rendered "water jars" and line 3 translated, "and tipped (caused to recline) the water jars of the heavens," the implication being that this takes place when the ground is dry and cracked (Pope 1965b:256).

No solution can be offered for the vexing mystery of v. 38. One possibility involves taking the prefixed *bêt* in *bṣqt* to mean, "from (the time) when" or "before." This would then make lines 5-6 reflect pre-human cosmic reality (in other words, that time before "dust was poured into a casting and clods of dust cleaved together" to form the first earthly creatures). However, there are no comparative data from ancient Near Eastern mythological sources to substantiate this proposal. This solution is based solely on the internal witness of v. 38 itself.

It is best, perhaps, to leave this verse untranslated. The tentative reading above is offered merely as an indication of what a conservative translation of the text might yield. The author's intention in vs. 37 is clear, however. His query is intended to indicate to Job that he has the power neither of the one who numbered the clouds (El?), nor of the one who waters the earth (Baal).

7.6.3 Summary

The poet has constructed a divine reply to the queries of Job. It presents a vision of theogonic and cosmogonic events that shaped the world in which both Job and the poet find themselves. The poet speaks of the old gods Heaven and Earth, of Sea's birth, of Dawn, and a host of other divine fig-

---

[371] I have taken the causative of *√škb* to mean, "to cause to (be in a state of) reclination."

[372] See Eusebius' *Preparation for the Gospel* 1.10.15-30 (cf. Attridge and Oden 1981). See also Cross (1974a:251).

ures from the lore of Canaan and Egypt. He also describes the *rš*ᶜ*ym* who sought protection from Earth but were shaken out by the creator-god.

Throughout the poem the language of Canaanite myth obtains. The theophany from the storm cloud is itself highly reminiscent of Baal, while the allusions to wisdom call to mind El, the wise patriarch. With the exception of 38:1, there is no trace of Yahweh, the god who guides the destiny of Israel and no attestation of courtly protocol and practical advice which are generally found in wisdom sources. Instead the creator-god orders the cosmos, gives a guided tour of the recesses of the universe, outlines pivotal events, and introduces a cast of characters at home in the world of ancient Near Eastern myth.

Of these, the figure referred to as the light of the *rš*ᶜ*ym* (vs. 15) is crucial. That which he and the *rš*ᶜ*ym* represent serves as the interpretive and moral paradigm for vss. 1-38. Just as the *rš*ᶜ*ym* are discovered, and just as the "upraised arm"—which has been taken as a symbol of defiance against the creator-god—is broken, so too is there futility in attempting to fathom divine will. In this respect Gordis was correct in seeing Job's error as presuming to judge divine actions from a limited vantage point (1978:559). Questioning unjust suffering in life is not fruitless; it is unwise and ignorant. One is tempted to go so far as to say that such action is rebellious, but this is far too strong. To challenge divine wisdom is as inappropriate as the attempt of the *rš*ᶜ*ym* to flee to Earth for protection from the creator. Insofar as the cosmos is created and ordered by a wise god, it is understandable through wisdom. Yet, like eternal life, supreme wisdom belongs exclusively to the gods, as does authority to apply it.[373]

Can a case be made for linking the *rš*ᶜ*ym* and "their light" in this text with the *npylym* of Genesis 6:1-4. As stated in connection with Isaiah 14, Ezekiel 28:1-10, Ezekiel 28:11-19, and Psalm 82, insofar as rebellion threatens cosmic order, the events narrated in Job 38:1-38 and the *npylym* of Genesis 6:1-4 are symbolic of forces that threaten harmony in the universe (see Mullen 1980:240). Moreover, the post-flight locus of the *rš*ᶜ*ym* in Job 38:12-15 is Earth—although in the this case, it is deified.

Is there indication that the *rš*ᶜ*ym* and "their light" encountered in this text share any similarities with Athtar as he is reflected in Ugaritic literature? Can a linkage be made between Athtar, *mt wšr, hyll bn šḥr*, the unnamed cosmic rebel in Ezekiel 28:1-10, the Cherub and *ʾbny ʾš* of Ezekiel

---

[373] See the following references to El's wisdom: KTU 1.3 V 30-31, KRU 1.4 IV 41-43, KTU 1.4 V 3-4, and KTU 1.16 IV 2.

28:11-19, and the "Shining One" in Psalm 82? Once again, there is no Ugaritic tradition that identifies Athtar as rebel. There is, however, an indication from the *Baal Cycle* that he descended voluntarily to the underworld (*ʾrṣ*) where he ruled. As noted above, the issue of wisdom is important in Job 38 and one is reminded again both of the Athtar epithet *yadiᶜ yilḥan* and of the knowledge (of self or of cosmic principles) that led to his voluntary descent to the underworld. The designation given to the leader of the *ršᶜym*—i.e., *ʾwrm* their "light"—suggests an astral identification which would place this being in possible relationship to *mt wšr, hyll bn šḥr,* the Cherub and the *ʾbny ʾš* in Ezekiel 28:11-19, and the "Shining One" in Psalm 82. It is clear that the *ršᶜym* in 38:13, 15 are not human evildoers. Their activity takes place in a mythological setting and this suggests that they are divine criminals. They are exposed when Earth is seized by the skirts and shaken, after which "their light" is witheld. Without "their light" the "upraised arm" is broken. Context implies that a crime against the creator-god has been committed by the rebels since it is he who pursues and exposes them. It also implies that the "light" is crucial in order for the rebels to function. Thus, the "light" is conceptualized as the leader, guiding principle, or motivating force that enables the rebels to commit their crimes. The first of these seems most likely. Throughout the poem individual characters of mythological import are mentioned. One is, therefore, justified in taking *ʾwrm* as a reference to a particular being rather than as a reference to an ideal or unifying power that inspires and/or informs the actions of the rebels. The poet ascribes no other attributes to this unnamed divine being. As a result, emphasis shifts to *ʾwr* itself. It is possible that the poet is describing an astral god, akin, perhaps, to the *kwkby bqr* mentioned in 38:7. If this is correct, Hebrew *ʾwr* in this instance would fall within the same semantic range as Ugaritic *šr*. This would allow it to be used in describing a celestial god (e.g., planet or star). Therefore, it is possible that reference to Athtar or some other astral god could lie behind *ʾwrm*. The "upraised arm," symbolic of defiance and conflict, could be treated as an euphemism for this crime. One is not able to determine what the crime involved, but it was of sufficient gravity to merit an escape of the "rebels" and "their light" to Earth.

Once again, the fact that there is no Ugaritic evidence of a revolt by either an astral god or a wise god against El is a somewhat unsettling. Still, the mythological allusions in this poem—as is the case with Isaiah 14, Ezekiel 28:1-10, Ezekiel 28:11-19, and Psalm 82—are clearly of Canaanite origin. It could be that Job 38:1-38 is: (1) reflective of a tradition whose

Canaanite prototype has yet to be discovered; (2) a fuller development of the tradition whose fragmentary remains are found in KTU 1.23 (related to *mt wšr*); or (3) an Israelite inversion of the Athtar tradition found in KTU 1.6 similar in purpose to Isaiah 14, Ezekiel 28:1-10, Ezekiel 28:11-19, and Psalm 82—to debase Athtar and other Canaanite gods whose characteristics (e.g., astralization and wisdom in this instance) made them potential rivals of Yahweh.

Von Rad (1966:281-91) was probably correct in seeing a connection between Job 38 and onomastica like that of the Egyptian Amenemope. He believed that its author had reworked an onomasticon and made a poetic composition—a common practice for wisdom teachers.[374] The questioning pattern characteristic of Job 38 corresponded, in his opinion, to the ironical questions found in *Papyrus Anastasi I*, which hails from the catechetical exercises in Egyptian scribal schools. In either case, for him, onomastica underlie both the poetic compositions made by wisdom teachers for didactic purposes (Ben Sira 44-49; Psalm 148; Song of the Three Children vss. 35-68), and the method of inquiry (questions) used to test students. Demands to prepare to be quizzed were at home in wisdom circles, and in Von Rad's opinion serve as a fitting background for understanding 38:1-4.

The only drawback to Von Rad's thesis is that he does not address the problem of mythological allusions in the poem. The argument for an Egyptian background for its form is intriguing but content leads one to suggest a Canaanite background. Job 38:1-38 is a cosmological exercise. Job's knowledge of the cosmos and the extent of his power (i.e., in contrast to that of the gods) are tested. If an onomasticon were used by the author of Job 38:1-38, the original would need to have contained a list of gods and/or divine epithets. Gordis believed that if an onomasticon were used, it was used selectively so as to inspire awe and wonder in the phenomena described rather than to inform (1978:562-563). This presupposes that the poet is unconcerned with teaching. Such does not appear to have been the case.

Poets inspire and inform. The cosmological content of Job 38 is as important as the emotion which the theophany creates. Wisdom is experiential and speculative. The author has taken an established form and, with the addition of archaic folklore, allowed the divine world to reveal its knowledge.

---

[374] If an onomasticon has not been used, one would have to suppose that the poet constructed a literary montage of haphazardly selected themes and characters drawn from Canaanite and Egyptian mythology.

From the rubric beginning the speech one is told that it is Yahweh who speaks. In content and theme one suspects strongly that the poet envisioned Job standing before El and/or Baal. The storm is Baal's mode of theophany. References to knowledge/understanding and the aura of command which the structure of the poem lend to the divine voice speak of El, whose knowledge of the universe is vast because he is the creator of everything.

7.7 Daniel 11:21, 36-39, 45; 12:1-3

7.7.1 Overview

Daniel 11:21-45 is generally held to be an apocalyptic vision inspired by the persecution instigated by Antiochus IV Epiphanes whose regnal years extend from 175 to 163 B.C.E.[375] His military activity against Palestine and Egypt provided the impetus for a resurgence of mythology in this second-century setting. Some of the more important aspects of his foreign and domestic policy included the illicit seizure of temple treasuries to bolster government revenue, the fostering of the Hellenic ideal as a unifying ideology for the empire, the granting to certain select cities the rights of the Greek polis, state-sanctioned religious syncretization (with Zeus and other gods being identified with local divinities), and the promulgation of a royal cult which held the king to be Zeus manifest. This represented a policy shift from the program of Antiochus III, who allowed a degree of Jewish cultural autonomy. This led, initially, to the replacement of Onias III by Joshua (Jason) as high priest and the construction of a gymnasium in Jerusalem. Joshua found himself eventually replaced by Menelaus, and during Antiochus' campaign against Egypt (in 169 B.C.E.), Joshua seized control of the city and caused his rival to flee. Upon his return, Antiochus restored Menelaus and sacked the temple in reprisal for rebellion.

One year later Antiochus' second invasion of Egypt was halted by Roman decree. His forced withdrawal combined with the apparent failure of efforts to Hellenize Judea resulted in the dispatch of Apollonius (his mercenary commander) to Jerusalem and the institution of harsh policies against the civilian populace. Jerusalem was treated as a city under siege and with the construction of an independent and self-governing garrison (the Acra) became, in form and function, the property of a Greek city-state. This latest

[375] For an historical overview of the period see Bright (1981:412-427) and Musti (1984:175-220). Cf., also Collins treatment of Daniel 11-12 (1993:363-404).

sequence of events removed all barriers to the total Hellenization of the region, and with the assistance of Menelaus, a syncretized Yahweh-Zeus cultus was established.

By 167 B.C.E., local religious observations were forbidden and steps had been taken by the state to ensure the success of Antiochus' ideological program. Resistance was met with persecution. Opposition was focused most clearly in the *ḥsydym* "pious ones," and it was the effective insurgency of the Maccabeans which led eventually to the defeat of Seleucid forces and the cleansing of the temple in 164 B.C.E.

Daniel 11:21-45 deals almost exclusively with the evils and excesses of Antiochus IV. In the following exposition, particular interest has been expressed in v. 21 where his rise to power is discussed, vss. 36-39 which recount his break with acceptable religious practice, vs. 45 which details his final act of treachery and demise, and 12:1-3 which contains the cosmic denouement of the earthly persecution of the faithful. Michael the great angel will rise and a time of unprecedented trouble will ensue, after which the righteous will "shine like the brightness of the (heavenly) firmament" (12:3). The eschaton will result in a change in status of the persecuted. They shall be likened to the stars.

Within the text, profound concern was registered over the evils of a single ruler rather than over the general abuses of kingship. Since the combat raging on earth was seen to be a reflection of similar warfare taking place in heaven, the author's perspective was at variance with the military activism espoused by the Maccabees. The political posture assumed by the author was one that placed the fate of the community of the faithful in the hands of Yahweh. Consequently, the *ḥsydym* patiently awaited the outcome of the war (Hanson 1986:344-345).

Archaic material has been incorporated into the apocalyptic vision of 11:21-45 and 12:1-3. The meaning of the text and the nature and function of the mythological references contained therein are the primary exegetical concerns.[376]

---

376 On the date of chapters 7-12 of Daniel and their interpretation, see Collins (1993:26, 274-404).

7.7.2 Analysis

21

ועמד על־כנו נבזה ולא־נתנו עליו הוד מלכות
ובא בשלוה והחזיק מלכות בחלקלקות׃

wa-ᶜamad ᶜal kannō nibze[377]	And one who is despised shall arise in his place,
wa-lōᵓ natanū ᶜalayw hōd malkūt	who has not been granted kingly honor,
wa-baᵓ ba-šalwā	and he will enter quietly,
wa-hiḥzīq malkūt ba-ḥalaqlaqqōt[378]	and seize the kingdom by means of flattery.

The allusion to Antiochus as one despised (*nbzh*),[379] who has assumed his regency illegitimately, is clear.[380] The major difference between the route to kingship depicted above and in Isaiah 14, for example, is that here the usurper is actually said to have secured his regency through intrigue (*ḥlqlqwt*).[381] In the former, a tyrant has fallen because while in office he assumed rights belonging to the highest god. The paucity of adjectives describing him may reflect the author's total disdain for the usurper. The effect

---

[377] OG reads *eukataphronētos,* "(one who is) contemptible" (LSJ:717).

[378] OG reads *en klērodosia autou,* "in/by his distribution of land." Theodotion reads *en olisthrēmasi.*

[379] I disagree with DiLella's assessment that *nbzh* probably refers to the lowly status of the king rather than to the unfavorable opinion of him held by the populace (1978:269). One senses that the author's intention was to express total disdain for the king's legitimacy as heir and complete disgust with regard to his official policies.

[380] DiLella (in Hartman and DiLella 1978:294) has described the process whereby Antiochus IV was freed from his forced exile in Rome by Seleucus IV (who sent his son Demetrius to replace Antiochus in Rome) and assumed the throne by counteracting Heliodorus' plot to seize power and murdering his young nephew whom Heliodorus had placed in power.

[381] Context suggests that allusion is being made to the intrigues that led to Antiochus' assumption of power. *Ḥlqlqwt* in Psalm 35:6 and Jer. 23:12 is used with particular reference to treacherous footing. It seems that the author's intention was to convey the insincerity of Antiochus' intentions and promises. This range of meaning would be similar to that of the root √*ḥlq* in Hosea 10:2 and of the noun *ḥlq* in Proverbs 7:21. Montgomery (1927:450) translates *ḥlqlqwt* as "intrigues."

of this stratagem is that Antiochus is cast as the sum total of his actions rather than as an individual with definable character traits.

36-39

ועשׂה כרצונו המלך
ויתרומם ויתגדל על־כל־אל ועל אל אלים ידבר נפלאות
והצליח עד־כלה זעם כי נחרצה נעשׂתה: ועל־אלהי אבתיו
לא יבין ועל־חמדת נשׁים ועל־כל־אלוה לא יבין כי על־כל
יתגדל: ולאלה מעזים על־כנו יכבד ולאלוה אשׁר לא־ידעהו
אבתיו יכבד בזהב ובכסף ובאבן יקרה ובחמדות: ועשׂה
למבצרי מעזים עם־אלוה נכר אשׁר [יכיר] ירבה כבוד
והמשׁילם ברבים ואדמה יחלק במחיר:

wa-ᶜaśā ka-raṣōnō ham-malk	And according to his will shall the king behave,
wa-yitrōmim[382] wa-yitgaddil ᶜal kull ᵓēl	and he shall exalt and glorify himself above every god,
wa-ᶜal ᵓil ᵓilīm yadabbir niplaᵓōt	and against the god of gods he will say extraordinary things,
wa-hiṣlīḥ ᶜad kullā zaᶜm[383]	and he will prosper until the curse is complete,
kī niḥraṣā niᶜśatā[384]	for what is determined shall be done.
wa- ᶜal ᵓilōhê ᵓabōtayw lōᵓ yabīn[385]	And he will not heed the gods of his fathers,
wa-ᶜal ḥimdat našīm	or the one beloved of women;
wa-ᶜal kull ᵓilōh lō yabīn[386]	neither shall he obey any god,
kī ᶜal kull yitgaddil[387]	because he magnifies himself above all.
wa-la-ᵓilōh maᶜuzzīm[388]	
ᶜal kannō yakabbid	And to the god of fortresses he will give glory in his place,
wa-la-ᵓilōh ᵓašr lōᵓ yadaᶜūhū ᵓabōtayw	and to a god his fathers did not know

[382] OG reads *kai parorgisthēsetai* "and he will be provoked to anger."

[383] OG reads *hēorgē* "temperament, disposition, mood; anger" (LSJ:1246).

[384] OG reads *eis auton yar synteleia ginetai*, "for he is coming to an end."

[385] OG reads *ou mē pronoēthē.*

[386] This line is missing from OG.

[387] OG adds *kai hypotagēsetai autō ethnē ischura*, "and he will subjugate under himself a mighty nation."

[388] This reading is missing from OG.

yakabbid ba-zahāb wa-ba-kasp	will he give honor by means of gold and silver,
wa-ba-ʾabn yaqarā wa-ba-ḥamūdōt	and with precious stones and treasures.
wa-ʿaśā la-mabṣarê maʿuzzīm[389]	
ʿim ʾilōh nikār	And he will attack strong fortresses with (the aid of) a foreign god.
ʾašr yakkīr[390] yarbe kabōd	The ones who honor (him) he shall magnify with honor,
wa-himšīlām ba-rabbīm	and he will cause them to rule (over) many
wa-ʾadamā wa-ḥalliq ba-miḥīr[391]	and the land he will divide for a price,

45

ויטע אהלי אפדנו בין ימים להר־צבי־
קדש ובא עד־קצו ואין עוזר לו׃

wa-yiṭṭaʿ ʾuhalê ʾappadanō[392]	
bên yammīm	and he will pitch his palatial tents between the Seas
la-harr ṣabī qudš[393]	at/on[394] the beautiful holy mount,
wa-baʾ ʿad qiṣṣō wa-ʾên ʿōzēr lō	yet he will come to his end with no one to help him.

The king will regard no external authority in the determination of his actions, shall place himself above all gods, and will make unusual claims against the most important of the gods (*ʾl ʾlym*), presumably Yahweh. His period of prosperity has been fixed and is unalterable. The king is repre-

---

389 OG reads *poiēsei [poleōn] kai eis ochyrōma ischuron hexei,* "he will build cities and he will have a strong fortress."

390 I have adopted the *Qərê* reading.

391 OG reads *eis dōrean,* "for a gift."

392 An equivalent for *ʾpdnw* is not contained in OG.

393 OG reads *tou orous tēs thelēseōs tou agiou,* "the mountain of the pleasure of the holy one."

394 While the sequence *byn...l-* could indicate a location between two points—"between the Seas and the beautiful holy mount" (Waltke and O'Connor 1990:199-201)—in this instance the *lāmed* might also have a locative meaning similar to that found in Ugaritic grammatical usage (cf. UT:97).

sented as a force who has no earthly superior and also thinks himself to be without divine or human peer.[395]

The king will also break tradition—abandoning the ritual practice of his forebears and turning away particularly from the *ḥmdt nšym* "one beloved of women," which some take to be the cult of Tammuz.[396] Again, one is reminded that he will acknowledge the superiority of no god because he places himself above them all.[397]

The king will give cult to the *ʾlh mᶜzym* "god of fortresses." This is, perhaps, a reference to the Acra constructed in Jerusalem by Apollonius and his contingent in the mid-second century B.C.E. The foreign god who is to receive honor in the form of gold, silver, precious stones, and treasure is likely Zeus.[398]

With the aid of Zeus and by means of the Hellenization policy of which this cult is a central part, the king will insure success against enemies, and those who honor him—presumably sympathizers, collaborators, and assimilationists—will receive favorable treatment by him and his administration.[399] They will be given positions of prominence. This reference might include the scandal caused by the sale of the high priesthood to one whose

---

[395] DiLella noted that Antiochus was the first to assume the title *theos* on his coins. He also stated that the name Epiphanes demonstrates the extent to which Antiochus identified himself as a divine figure (Hartman and DiLella 1978:301).

[396] See Hammer (1976:113) for example.

[397] DiLella gives a brief account of scholarly opinion regarding the nature of these offenses. They include the suppression of the cults of local deities (including Tammuz) and the plundering of temple treasuries whenever the crown was suffering through a fiscal crisis (Hartman and DiLella 1978:301-302).

[398] Other suggestions include Jupiter Capitolinus, for whom Antiochus built a temple in Antioch (Hammer 1976:113), Syrian *ᶜazīz, el-ᶜuzza,* Mars, and Roma (see Montgomery 1927:461 for references to the appropriate secondary literature). The author is concerned with the impact of the monarch's Hellenizing policies and their impact on the faithful living in Jerusalem. I have taken this reference and that made in vs. 39 to the *mbṣry mᶜzym* as references to the Acra specifically. Hammer stated that vs. 39 has as its background resistance to the general policy of garrisoning troops in Jerusalem (1976:114).

[399] These should be identified with those who have a vested interest in the maintenance of the religious and political status quo. For a discussion of the sociological background and political dimensions of the exilic period see Hanson (1979:211-220).

sentiments were pro-Greek (e.g., Joshua or Menelaus). The valuation and sale of the land may echo the de-facto ownership of Jerusalem by the self-governing Acra after its construction. We are told in v. 45 that ultimately, the fate of the king is sealed. His attempted siege of Jerusalem, "the beautiful holy mount," is to be the act which results in the appearance of Michael and the armies of Yahweh and the initiation of the final eschatological battle.[400] The author anticipated that the demise of Antiochus would take place at this time. This event marks the culmination of Antiochus' evil reign and the end of the forced Hellenization of Jerusalem. The assault begins to assume cosmic dimensions at this point which will be expanded fully in 12:1-3.

12:1-3

ובעת ההיא יעמד מיכאל השׂר הגדול
העמד על־בני עמך והיתה עת צרה
אשׁר לא־נהיתה מהיות גוי עד העת ההיא
ובעת ההיא ימלט עמך כל־הנמצא כתוב בספר׃
ורבים מישׁני אדמת־עפר יקיצו
אלה לחיי עולם ואלה לחרפות לדראון עולם׃
והמשׂכלים יזהרו כזהר הרקיע
ומצדיקי הרבים ככוכבים לעולם ועד׃

wa-ba-ᶜitt hah-hīᵓ yaᶜmud	And at that time will arise
mīkaᵓēl haś-śar hag-gadōl[401]	Michael the great prince,
haᶜ-ᶜōmēd ᶜal banê ᶜammakā	the one in charge of the children of your people.
wa-hayītā ᶜitt ṣarrā	And it will be a distressful time,
ᵓašr lō nihyatā mih-hvyōt gōy[402]	such as has never been since there was a nation
ᶜad haᶜ-ᶜitt hah-hīᵓ	until that very time;

---

[400] For a summary of proposed solutions to *byn ymym* see Montgomery (1927:467). DiLella takes this as a reference to the Mediterranean and *hr ṣby qdš* as a reference to Mt. Zion (Hartman and DiLella 1978:273).

[401] OG reads *pareleusetai Michaēl ho aggelos ho megas,* "Michael the great angel shall come forward/pass by."

[402] I have treated *oia ouk egenēthē aph ou egenethēsan eōs tēs hēmeras ekeinēs,* "which has not transpired since they were created until that day," as a paraphrase of an OG *Vorlage* similar to MT.

wa-baᶜ-ᶜitt hah-hiᵓ yimmaliṭ ᶜammakā	but at that time your people will be saved,
kull han-nimṣāᵓ katūb bas-sipr	all (those) found written in the book.
wa-rabbīm miy-yōšinê	And many who sleep
ᵓadamat ᶜapār[403] yaqīṣū	in the earth's dust shall awaken;
ᵓille la-ḥayyê ᶜôlām	some to eternal life,
wa-ᵓille la-ḥarapōt la-dirraᵓōn ᶜôlām	and some to disgrace and eternal abhorrence.
wa-ham-maśkīlīm yazhīrū	But those who have understanding shall shine
ka-zuhr har-raqīᶜ	like the splendor of the firmament,
wa-maṣdīqê har-rabbīm[404]	and those who turn many toward uprightness,
ka-kôkabīm[405] la-ᶜôlām wa-ᶜēd	as the stars for all eternity.

Once stationed at the holy mount, a time of unequaled distress will begin, but the faithful will be protected by their champion, Michael. Those found listed in the book (i.e., those who have maintained their allegiance to pure Yahwism as opposed to its syncretized form) will be spared the coming cataclysm. The dead will awaken, those who have kept themselves free from Hellenism's taint will awaken to eternal life, while those who have collaborated and adopted assimilationist attitudes will rise only to face everlasting disgrace. Those who have understanding (perhaps those who have knowledge of this coming time of trouble, or those who comprehend the true nature of Antiochus' policies) will shine (*yzhyrw*) like the sky above and like the stars (*kwkbym*) eternally.[406]

7.7.3 Summary

Antiochus, as monarch and as the personification of the Hellenization process, is the central concern for the apocalyptic community which produced

---

[403] OG reads *en platei tēs gē*, "in the breadth of the earth."

[404] OG reads *hoi katischontes tous logous mou*, "the possessors of my word."

[405] OG reads *hōsei ta astra tou ouranou*, "as the stars of heaven."

[406] Hammer treated this as a reference to the religious leaders who had distinguished themselves as martyrs and teachers during the time of persecution (1976:116). On the issue of astral immortality and its relationship to this text, see Collins (1993:393-394).

Daniel. His promulgation of a cult of divine-kingship, assault on the integrity of the priesthood, reduction of Jerusalem's status, and syncretization of the religious cult were quantifiable offenses against Yahweh. They represented a challenge to the claim that Yahweh was cosmic ruler. As such, they could be interpreted only as acts of rebellion from the perspective of those who resisted Hellenistic assimilation. That this should result in the resurgence of apocalyptic eschatology should not come as a surprise.[407]

The eschatological import of the monarch's actions against the faithful have been described in this text using mythological imagery similar to that encountered in Isaiah 14, Ezekiel 28, Psalm 82, and Job 38 above. The following common elements have been isolated that require comment: (1) in vs. 21, questions are raised about the legitimacy of the king's reign—the implication is that he has not achieved his status by acceptable means; (2) in vs. 36ff. the king is said to have disdain for all gods, including the god of gods; (3) in vs. 45, it is said that the king will come to his end when he pitches his tent between the seas (*byn ymym*) at/on the beautiful holy mount (*hr ṣby qdš*); (4) in vs. 12, cosmic conflict ensues with Michael, called *hśr*, engaging in battle on behalf of the pious ones; and (5) in 12:3 it is said that the *mśklym* will shine (*yzhr*) like the *zhr hrqyᶜ* and that the *mṣdyqy hrbym* will shine like the *kwkbym*.

The king's right to rule is questioned here just as the authority of the king of Babylon and the aspirations of *hyll bn šḥr* are questioned in Isaiah 14. The disdain which the king displays for all the gods, including the *ʾl ʾlym*, in Daniel 11 is similar to the sentiment expressed by *hyll bn šḥr* toward the authority of Yahweh (*ᶜlywn*). Neither showed deference to superior power, or to the foremost of all divine powers. In Isaiah 14:13, *hyll bn šḥr* says that he will be seated on the assembly mount (*hr mwᶜd*) in the "far reaches of the north." In Daniel 11, the despised king will meet his end when he encamps between the seas at Mt. Zion.[408] It is said that Michael "the great prince" will rise in defense of the faithful. It is possible that the form *śr* "prince" is in fact meant to be read "shining one," or that a dual

---

[407] See Hanson (1979:211-220, 402-409) for a discussion of the sociological background for the growth of apocalyptic visionary movements and an assessment of the key features of apocalyptic eschatology.

[408] The place of the cosmic battle is described using language reminiscent of El's abode (*byn ymym* and *hr ṣby qdš*). See the description of El's abode in KTU 1.4 IV 21-24.

sense is intended in which both were to have been understood in this instance and in 10:13, 20, and 21.

Can a case be made for linking the *nbzh* in this text with the *npylym* of Genesis 6:1-4. Once again, as stated in connection with Isaiah 14, Ezekiel 28:1-10, and Ezekiel 28:11-19, Psalm 82, and Job 38, insofar as rebellion threatens cosmic order, the *nbzh* and the *npylym* of Genesis 6:1-4 are symbolic of forces that threaten harmony in the universe (see Mullen 1980:240).

Is there indication that this *nbzh* shares any similarities with Athtar as he is reflected in Ugaritic literature? Can a linkage be made between Athtar, *mt wšr, hyll bn šḥr,* the unnamed cosmic rebel in Ezekiel 28:1-10, the Cherub and *ʾbny ʾš* of vss. 11-19, the "Shining One" in Psalm 82, the *ršʿym* and *ʾwrm* "their light" of Job 38, and this divine usurper? Once again, there is no Ugaritic tradition that identifies Athtar as rebel. In the *Baal Cycle,* Athtar's descent to the underworld is voluntarily and the process by which he becomes king in KTU 1.6 is in no way similar to the events described in Daniel 11-12. Athtar is strange—even enigmatic—but he is neither braggart nor boaster.

The astral connotations of 12:1-3 are certainly reminiscent of characters, events, and allusions in the Ugaritic and Hebrew texts encountered thus far—e.g., *mt wšr, hyll bn šḥr,* the Cherub and the *ʾbny ʾš* in Ezekiel 28:11-19, the "Shining One" in Psalm 82, and the *ršʿym* and *ʾwrm* "their light" in Job 38.

The fact that there is no Ugaritic evidence for a revolt by any god against El does not pose an insurmountable obstacle to understanding the mythological background of Daniel 11-12. The allusions in these chapters and in each of the Hebrew texts cited above are clearly of Canaanite origin. It is possible, therefore, that the myth around which Daniel 11-12 is built is either (1) reflective of a tradition whose Canaanite prototype has yet to be discovered; (2) a fuller development of the tradition whose fragmentary remains are found in KTU 1.23 (related to *mt wšr*); or (3) an Israelite inversion of the Athtar tradition found in KTU 1.6 intended to appropriate the tradition of Canaanite astral deities in order to create a binary opposition in the author's construction of the universe. Old Canaanite astral deities and the rebel Antiochus are found on one end of the cosmic continuum while the righteous are on the other. The righteous are promised a transformation that will make them "shine" (√*zhr*). The semantic relationship between this reference and that of *mt wšr, hyll bn šḥr,* the Cherub and the *ʾbny ʾš* in Ezekiel 28:11-19, the "Shining One" in Psalm 82, and the *ršʿym* and *ʾwrm* "their light" in Job 38 is apparent.

The author made use of a myth similar to that in Isaiah 14 to illustrate and/or give eschatological significance to the crimes of Antiochus IV. While the divine rebel's identity is withheld, his heavenly adversary, Michael, is named. This is not unexpected. As stated above, the author has depersonalized Antiochus and one should expect similar treatment for his mythological counterpart. The language used to describe the fate of the righteous in juxtaposition to that of the king leads one to suspect this. The former were to shine like heavenly bodies. The latter was to die with no one to assist him.

As part of a hermeneutical program with practical application for the marginalized community that produced Daniel, this imagery accents the positive transmutation of the oppressed community into something more than human. Unlike Antiochus, whose assumption of divine prerogative was against the will of Yahweh, the faithful will be rewarded for their righteousness, perseverance, and understanding. The implication is that those who have died and those who presently devote their lives to furthering the cause of the non-collaborators will be given *a measure* of that which the king sought. Though they will not be given kingship of the cosmos, they will share at least one of the characteristics of Yahweh's divine subordinates who administer the affairs of heaven and earth. Thus, the author speaks of the birth of a new order in the cosmos in which those who have suffered persecution will become luminaries, though of a lesser sort, in the assembly of the divine king, Yahweh.

CHAPTER EIGHT

SUMMARY OF HEBREW EVIDENCE

This study has established that Genesis 6:1-4, Isaiah 14, Ezekiel 28:1-10, Ezekiel 28:11-19, Psalm 82, Job 38, and Daniel 11-12 reflect mythological patterns that are remarkably similar. In each text, criminal activity against a divine monarch (on earth and in the cosmos) is narrated, alluded to, or employed as a part of the background information for understanding the text.

In Isaiah 14 and Ezekiel 28:11-19, one is given the identity of the mythological characters compared to the kings of Babylon and Tyre. The content of each may be outlined as follows:

Isaiah 14

> *Hyll bn šḥr* desires to: (1) ascend; (2) set his throne above El's stars; (3) sit on the assembly mount; (4) ascend above (ride?) the clouds; and (5) make himself like the "Highest." *Hyll* is brought down to Sheol.

Ezekiel 28:11-19

> The Cherub was: (1) perfect and (2) stationed in Eden—on the holy mount, where he enjoyed favored status (as an astral god?). Fault was found with him and he was cast from the holy mountain and driven from the "stones of fire."

Note should be taken of the fact that in both texts, the holy mount—the place of the meeting of the divine assembly—is mentioned specifically. In Isaiah 14, it is one of the objects of Helel's desire. In Ezekiel 28:11-19, it is the place where the Cherub lived before he was driven out by Yahweh/El.

In Ezekiel 28:1-10 and Daniel 11-12 the mythological figures in question are not expressly identified (in the latter instance he is called a *nbzh*). Patterns similar to those cited above are discernible nonetheless. The interweaving of historical and mythological elements makes separating them quite difficult. Listed below is the outline of the myth as it may be reconstructed from the evidence in these two texts.

Ezekiel 28:1-10

> A god whose wisdom and pride are substantial: (1) claims to be El and (2) desires to reside in El's dwelling place. He is/will be thrust into Sheol for his presumptions.

Daniel 11—12

> (1) One god makes claims against all the gods and against the *god of gods*; (2) he establishes a battle encampment at the holy mount; and (3) the commander of Yahweh's army rises up and combat ensues.

In each of these texts, the scene is the mount of assembly and the principal character is a god who assaults the highest god in the pantheon verbally and/or physically. If this reconstruction is correct, Daniel 12 retains memory of the mustering of the high god's armies in response to this challenge, but records no outcome. Ezekiel 28 notes the outcome but lacks details of the conflict which preceded the usurper's fall.

From the foregoing analysis, it can be seen that in each of these texts: (1) a god is described who possesses one or more of the following traits—an astral nature, wisdom, beauty, or pride; (2) this god is said to have enjoyed favorable status within the divine assembly at some point in time[409]; (3) a verbal or physical attack is made against the chief-god; (4) the holy mount functions in one or more of the following capacities—(a) as the desired dwelling place of the usurper, (b) as the site of cosmic conflict, or (c) as the original home of the usurper; (5) the reversal of fates is expressed in one of the following ways—(a) in the descent of the usurper to Sheol, (b) in the expulsion of the usurper from the holy mount, or (c) in the mustering of the armies of the chief-god in response to the usurper's attack[410]

The presence of these elements indicates that one is not dealing with several different myths. It suggests instead the possibility that one is dealing with a single myth which has assumed varied forms. The interpretive agenda of the poets who mediated the myth certainly helped to determine the shape that it took. For example, Isaiah 14 seems particularly concerned with the downfall of kingship as an institution. Ezekiel 28:1-10 is concerned with the abuses of wisdom and the excesses of princely ambition. Ezekiel 28:11-19 deals with hegemonic offenses caused by wealth and pride. Daniel 11-12 directs attention to the fate of the faithful in the eschaton and the fall of Antiochus Epiphanes.

Genesis 6:1-4, Job 38, and Psalm 82, are also helpful in understanding the mythology behind Isaiah 14, Ezekiel 28, and Daniel 11. The references made to the *npylym* in Genesis 6:1-4 and "Shining One(s)" in Psalm 82 are

---

[409] In Isaiah 14:12ff., the fate of *hyll* would have little significance unless he held a position from which he could "fall."

[410] See Daniel 12:1-3.

symbolic of chaos and disorder. In terms of semantic range, they are no doubt related to *mt wšr* (KTU 1.23), *hyll bn šḥr*, the Cherub and the *ʾbny ʾš* in Ezekiel 28:11-19, the *ršʿym* and *ʾwrm* "their light" in Job 38, and the events narrated in Daniel 11-12.

The density of Canaanite mythological elements found in these biblical texts and their thematic congruence suggest that there did exist a single old Semitic tale of cosmic rebellion and that this myth came to Israel by way of Canaan. The combination of Ugaritic and Hebrew evidence points toward: (1) the possible identification of Athtar as the combatant against El in the original myth and (2) a connection between Athtar and the "Shining Ones" referred to elsewhere in Ugaritic and Hebrew literature. While Athtar is cast neither as usurper nor rebel in known Ugaritic sources, it is not implausible to conclude that such tradition did in actual fact exist, even though the earliest controllable extant witnesses are confined to the Hebrew Bible. Canaanite mythological allusions are ubiquitous in Hebrew literature[411] and can be utilized productively in reconstructing certain elements of older Canaanite tradition.

Equally plausible are the suggestions made above in connection with each of the Hebrew texts examined—that: (1) they represent a fuller development of the tradition whose fragmentary remains are found in KTU 1.23 (related to *mt wšr*); or (2) they reflect an Israelite inversional adaptation of the Athtar tradition found in KTU 1.6—one that interprets Athtar's *otherness* negatively and *demonizes* him (a practice that was apparently continued in Jewish, Christian, and Islamic tradition).

Nonetheless, the evidence cited seems to indicate that there did in fact exist an old Canaanite myth that told of sedition against the high god of the pantheon. Isaiah 14:12 presents the strongest evidence in support of identifying Athtar as divine anti-hero in that myth. The astral imagery there and in Ezekiel 28:11-19 and Job 38:13-15 also support this claim. The desire of *hyll bn šḥr* to make himself like "the Highest" echoes the boast *ʾl ʾny* placed on the lips of the prince of Tyre in Ezek. 28:2, as does the accusation made against Antiochus in Daniel 11:37—that he elevated himself to divine status ("he will magnify himself over all"). These data suggest that the texts in question had a common progenitor—one that this study has designated Proto-CR^{A}. It is virtually impossible to establish with any precision the era and the socio-political and/or religious setting that gave birth

[411] For example, the connection between the Israelite and Ugaritic serpentine traditions is well-known.

to Proto-CR^A. It is probable that its plot and cast of characters were set at least by the sixth century B.C.E. (and probably much earlier). This coherence in form and content no doubt facilitated the further adaptation of the myth in later Jewish, Christian, and Muslim intellectual circles.

The influence of this myth in Israel was pervasive and is attested by the distribution of its reflexes across a broad temporal spectrum and in texts representing a variety of socio-political settings and genres. It appears to have been a particularly malleable myth. Its didactic value in matters ethical, moral, and practical, allowed its incorporation within the primeval cycle of Genesis (for purposes of background), the poetry of Isaiah 14, the oracles of Ezekiel, the reflections of the unknown hymnodist who authored Psalm 82, the Yahweh Speeches of Job, and the semiotic universe of Daniel. Remnants are also prevalent in Apocryphal, Pseudepigraphic, Jewish, Christian, and Islamic literature from the third century B.C.E. onward. It seems fairly certain that in these latter sources, Proto-CR^A is mediated primarily—*though not exclusively*—via biblical texts. While this study did not address the issue of archaic survivals in these later sources, it is certainly an area in need of investigation.

Evidence from the biblical texts examined suggests that each one can be treated as a *reflex* of Proto-CR^A. One should not expect to find strict agreement in structure, detail, plot, purpose, or characters in so great a variety of sources. Allowance must be made for those transformations of the myth engineered by literary artists who made use of the material in meeting specific social, religious, political, and other agenda. Selective memory and poetic license must also be factored into the transmission equation. Thus, it is prudent to look closely at the relationship between any single purported *reflex* of the myth and its immediate context.

CHAPTER NINE

PROTO-CR^{A}—A PRELIMINARY RECONSTRUCTION

There are dangers inherent in the harmonization of literary witnesses, even when one has as a goal the reconstruction of a tentative outline of a myth for the purpose of further consideration and discussion. It was mentioned at the beginning of this study that solid precedent exists for such an endeavor. Thus, the following is offered as a preliminary reconstruction of Proto-CR^{A} based on the analysis of the biblical reflexes and other data examined in this study.

After having enjoyed primacy of place within the pantheon as one of the creator's most perfect entities—endowed with wisdom and beauty (cf. Ezekiel 28:3,-3, 12b, 15, 17)—Athtar conspired to make war against El and wrest control of the pantheon and the cosmos from him. He was corrupted by the very characteristics that made him unique among his divine peers (Ezekiel 28:2, 5, 15-17) and this hubris led him to claim equality with El (Ezekiel 28:2, 6, 9; Isaiah 14:14). He boasted of sitting in El's throne (Ezekiel 28:2), of being in possession of a wisdom comparable to that of his wise patron and benefactor (Ezekiel 28:5), and, indeed, of being El (Ezekiel 28:9). He had honorable status on El's mountain (Ezekiel 28:13) where he communed with other astral gods before corruption led to his demise (Ezekiel 28:13-18). He aspired to rise above the circumpolar stars, to set his throne on El's mountain in the far north, to mount the clouds like Baal, and to make himself like Elyon (El) (Isaiah 14:13-15).[412] He declared war against El and pitched his battle encampment at El's tent-shrine (Daniel 11:45). He was defeated,[413] driven from his place on the holy mount (Ezekiel 28:16), and exiled to the underworld (Psalm 82:7; Isaiah 14:9-11, 14-19; Ezekiel 28:8).[414]

---

[412] The author of Daniel 11 has muted, to some extent, the mythological material related to the crimes of the cosmic rebel and has made general comments about the criminal's boasts (11:21, 36).

[413] Job 38:13-15 may represent an intermediate stage in the myth when Athtar and his band fled to Earth for protection after being defeated by El's forces and before being sentenced to the underworld.

[414] If one follows Daniel 12:1-2, then one may assume that the defeat came at the hands of the commander of El's celestial army.

CHAPTER TEN

CONCLUSION

This study has established that: (1) Hebrew literature retains evidence of Proto-CR^A; (2) similarities in plot shared by Isaiah 14, Ezekiel 28:1-10, Ezekiel 28:11-19, Job 38, and Daniel 11-12 and allusions made in Genesis 6:1-4 and Psalm 82 suggest these biblical texts contain reflexes of this myth; (3) mythological motifs in these texts are reminiscent of those found in Ugaritic lore—in particular, it appears that the original myth involved a revolt against El by a member of his divine council; (4) the events which form part of the revolt myth as it is attested in Hebrew literature have no immediate counterpart in Ugaritic lore; (5) the exploits of Athtar found in the *Baal Cycle* in no way indicate that Athtar initiated or participated in a revolt against El—though they do cast him as quite enigmatic; (6) descriptions of the divine anti-hero in Isaiah 14, Ezekiel 28:11-19, and Job 38, along with the description of the fate of the faithful in Daniel 12:1-3—suggest that this rebellious figure was an astral god, perhaps even a member of El's celestial army.

To the extent that a convincing linguistic argument can be established linking Athtar and *mt wšr* on the one hand, and *hyll*, the Cherub, the *ʾbny ʾš*, the *ršʿym* and their "light," and the "Shining One(s)" known from Hebrew literature on the other, one may suggest tentatively that an *astralized hypostasis* of Athtar is the protagonist in the reflexes of Proto-CR^A found in Isaiah 14, Ezekiel 28, Job 38, and Daniel 11-12—and that this myth provides the background against which Genesis 6:1-4 and Psalm 82 are to be understood. These texts also make clear that the goal of Athtar's attempted coup was to secure kingship of the cosmos from El.

The dwelling place of Yahweh/El, the cosmic mountain, is the locus of activity in the myth. It is described variously in the biblical reflexes as: (1) the desired dwelling-place of the usurper; (2) the site of cosmic conflict; or (3) the rebel's original home.

Finally, if one theme can be said to predominate in Proto-CR^{A}, it is perhaps that of the reversal of fortune that results from inappropriate boundary crossing. The rebel desires to be monarch. His reward is cosmic exile.

APPENDIX A

KEY ELEMENTS IN PURPORTED BIBLICAL REFERENCES OF PROTO-CR^{A} AND SELECTED UGARITIC TEXTS[415]

	K^{A}	K^{B}	K^{C}	K^{D}	Gn	Is	Ez^{A}	Ez^{B}	Ps	Jb	Dn
Rš^{c}ym						X			X	X	
Npylym/√npl		X(?)			X				X		
Rebel's Presumption						X	X	X			X
Earth as Refuge[416]										X	
Sheol/ Underworld		X	X			X	X	X			
Rebel's Initial Status[417]								X			
Michael										X	
Athtar as King	X										
Astral Imagery[418]	X	X	X			X		X	X	X	X
Athtar Epithets	X	X	X(?)	X		X(?)		X(?)	X	X(?)	X(?)
Rebel's Attributes[419]						X	X	X		X	X
El's Abode						X	X	X	X		X

---

[415] Key: X=element found in text; K^{A}=KTU 1.2; K^{B}=KTU 1.6; K^{C}=KTU 1.23; K^{D}=KTU 1.24; Gn=Genesis 6:1-4; Is=Isaiah 14:4b-20a; Ez^{A}=Ezekiel 28:1-10; Ez^{B}=Ezekiel 28:11-19; Ps=Psalm 82; Jb=Job 38:1-38; Dn=Daniel 11:21, 36-39, 45; 12:1-3.

[416] The existence of an intermediate stage in the revolt (when Athtar and his rebel band fled to Earth for protection after the failed coup) is assumed here.

[417] Descriptions of the rebel's pre-revolt status (i.e., as a favored member of the divine court or privy to certain cosmic events) are included here.

[418] This category includes stars and other astral deities.

[419] Chiefly involved here are his wisdom, beauty, pride, boastfulness, etc.

APPENDIX B

UGARITIC ELEMENTS—PROTO-CR^A BIBLICAL REFLEXES

Genesis 6:1-4

bny [ ]ʾlhym
[ ]npylym

Isaiah 14:4b-20a

šʾwl
hyll bn šḥr
kwkby ʾl
hr mwʿd
yrkty ṣpwn
yrkty bwr
bmty ʿb
ʿlywn
ʾbny bwr

Ezekiel 28:1-10

ʾl
mwšb ʾlhym
blb ymym
dnʾl

Ezekiel 28:11-19

gn ʾlhym
hr qdš ʾlhym
ʾbny ʾš
hr ʾlhym

Psalm 82

ʿdt ʾl
bny ʿlywn
[ ]śrym

Job 38

kwkby bqr
bny [ ]ʾlhym
ym
thwm
šḥr
bqr
šʿry mwt
šʿry ṣlmwt
ʾrṣ
šmym
mṭr
ʾgly ṭl
kymh
ksyl
mzrwt
ʿyš
ṯḥwt
śkwy

Daniel 11:21, 36-39, 45; 12:1-3

ʾl ʾlym
byn ymym
hr ṣby qdš
kwkbym

BIBLIOGRAPHY

Ackerman, James

1966 An Exegetical Study of Psalm 82. Th.D. dissertation, Harvard University.

Aistleitner, J.

1974 *Wörterbuch der ugaritischen Sprache*. Berlin: Akademie Verlag.

Albright, W. F.

1932-33 The North-Canaanite Epic of ᵓAlᵓêyân Baᶜal and Môt. *JPOS* 12:185-208.

1946 *Archaeology and the Religion of Israel*. Baltimore: Johns Hopkins Press.

1948 Review of L'épithète divine Jahvé Səba'ôt: Étude philologique, historique et exégétique, by B. N. Wambacq, O. Praem. Bruges (Belgium): Desclée De Brouwer, 1947. *JBL* 67:377-381.

1969 *Yahweh and the Gods of Canaan*. Garden City, NY: Anchor Books.

Alter, Robert

1985 The Art of Biblical Poetry. San Francisco: Basic Books.

Attridge, Harold W. and R. A. Oden (eds.)

1981 *Philo of Byblos. The Phoenician History: Introduction, Critical Text, Translation, Notes*. Catholic Biblical Quarterly Monograph Series 9. Washington, DC: Catholic Biblical Association of America.

Aufrecht, Walter E.

1989 *A Corpus of Ammonite Inscriptions*. Ancient Near Eastern Texts and Studies, 4. Lewiston/Queenston/Lampeter: Edwin Mellen Press.

Barton, G. A.
1934 A Liturgy for the Celebration of the Spring Festival at Jerusalem in the Age of Abraham and Melchizedek. *JBL* 53:61-78.

Birkeland, H.
1955 *The Evildoers in the Book of Psalms.* Oslo: I Kommisjon Hos Jacob Dybwad.

Blau, Joshua
1972 Marginalia Semitica, II. *IOS* 2:57-82.

Blenkinsopp, Joseph
1983 *A History of Prophecy in Israel.* Philadelphia: Westminster Press.

1992 *The Pentateuch: An Introduction to the First Five Books of the Bible. Anchor Bible Reference Library,* D. N. Freedman, gen. ed. New York: Doubleday.

Borger, Rykle
1979 *Babylonisch-Assyrische Lesestücke, 2., Neubearbeitete Auflage, Heft I. Analecta Orientalia 54.* Roma: Pontificium Institutum Biblicum.

Briggs, C. A., and Briggs, E. G.
1907 *The Book of Psalms,* Vol. 2. *International Critical Commentary,* S.R. Driver et al., eds. Edinburgh: T. and T. Clark.

Bright, John
1981 *A History of Israel,* 3rd. ed. Philadelphia: Westminster Press.

Brown, F., S. R. Driver, and C. A. Briggs.
1951 *A Hebrew and English Lexicon of the Old Testament.* Oxford: Clarendon Press.

Caquot, A.
1958 Le dieu Athtar et les textes de Ras Shamra. *Syria* 35: 45-60.

Caquot, A., Sznycer M., and Herdner, A.
1974 *Textes ougaritiques, I, mythes et légendes.* Littératures anciennes du Proche-Orient 7. Paris: Les Éditions du Cerf.

Cassuto, U.
1961 *A Commentary on the Book of Genesis: From Adam to Noah.* Jerusalem: Magnes Press.

1971 *The Goddess Anath,* trans. Israel Abrahams. Jerusalem: Magnes Press.

Charles, R. H.
1913 *Apocrypha and Pseudepigrapha of the Old Testament,* Vols. 1 and 2. Oxford: Clarendon Press.

Charlesworth, James H.
1983-85 *The Old Testament Pseudepigrapha,* Vols. 1 and 2. Garden City, NY: Doubleday.

Chase, Debra
1994 *Baᶜl Šamêm: The Epigraphic Evidence.* Ph.D. Dissertation, Harvard University.

Childs, Brevard
1960 *Myth and Reality in the Old Testament.* London: S.C.M. Press.

Clifford, R.
1972 *The Cosmic Mountain in Canaan and the Old Testament.* Cambridge: Harvard University Press.

Clines, D. J. A.
1979 The Significance of the 'Sons of God' Episode (Genesis 6:1-4) in the Context of the 'Primeval History' (Genesis 1-11). *JSOT* 12: 33-46.

Collins, Adela Yarbro

1976 *The Combat Myth in the Book of Revelation.* Harvard Theological Review Harvard Dissertations in Religion, 9. Missoula: Scholars Press.

Collins, John

1993 *Daniel. Hermeneia—A Critical and Historical Commentary on the Bible,* F. M. Cross, Jr., ed. Minneapolis: Fortress Press.

Coogan, Michael D.

1978 *Stories From Ancient Canaan.* Philadelphia: Westminster Press.

Cooke, G. A.

1936 *The Book of Ezekiel.* The International Critical Commentary. Edinburgh: T. and T. Clark.

Cobb, W. H.

1896 The Ode in Isaiah XIV. *JBL* 15:18-35.

Craigie, P. C.

1973 Helel, Athtar and Phaeton (Jes. 14:12-15). *ZAW* 85:223-225.

Cross, F. M.

1953 The Council of Yahweh in Second Isaiah. *JNES* 12:274-277.

1961 The Development of the Jewish Scripts. *The Bible and the Ancient Near East,* ed. G.E. Wright. New York: Doubleday, pp. 133-302.

1962 Yahweh and the God of the Patriarchs. *HTR* 55: 225-259.

1971 El. *Theologisches Wörterbuch zum Alten Testament,* Vol. 1, ed. G. J. Botterweck and H. Ringgren. Berlin: W. Kohlhammer.

1973 *Canaanite Myth and Hebrew Epic: Essays in the History of the Religion of Israel.* Cambridge/London: Harvard University Press.

1974a El. *Theological Dictionary of the Old Testament,* eds. G. J. Botterweck and H. Ringgren, trans. J. T. Willis. Grand Rapids: Eerdmans. Vol. 1:242-261.

1974b Prose and Poetry in the Mythic and Epic Texts from Ugarit. *HTR* 67:1-9.

1976 The Olden Gods in Ancient Near Eastern Creation Myths. *Magnalia Dei,* eds. F.M. Cross, W. E. Lemke, and P. D. Miller, pp. 329-338. New York: Doubleday.

1983a The Epic Traditions of Early Israel: Epic Narrative and the Reconstruction of Early Israelite Institutions. In *The Poet and the Historian: Essays in Literary and Historical Biblical Criticism,* ed. Richard E. Friedman. HSS 26. Chico: Scholars Press.

1983b Studies in the Structure of Hebrew Verse: The Prosody of Lamentations 1:1-32. In *The Word of the Lord Shall Go Forth: Essays in Honor of David Noel Freedman in Celebration of His Sixtieth Birthday,* eds. C. L. Meyers and M. O'Connor, pp. 129-155. Winona Lake: Eisenbrauns.

1983c Studies in the Structure of Hebrew Verse: The Prosody of the Psalm of Jonah. In *The Quest for The Kingdom of God: Studies in Honor of George E. Mendenhall,* eds. H.B. Huffmon, et al., pp. 159-167. Winona Lake: Eisenbrauns.

Cross, F. M. and D. N. Freedman
1952 *Early Hebrew Orthography.* American Oriental Series, Vol. 36, J. B. Pritchard, ed. New Haven: American Oriental Society.

Culley, Robert C.
1985 Exploring New Directions. *The Hebrew Bible and its Modern Interpreters*, D. A. Knight and G. M. Tucker, eds., pp. 167-200. Chico: Scholars Press.

Dahood, M.
1958 Ancient Semitic Deities In Syria And Palestine. *Le antiche divinità semitische.* Rome:65-94.

1968 *Psalms II. The Anchor Bible*, W.F. Albright and D. N. Freedman, eds. Garden City: Doubleday.

Dalley, Stephanie
1991 *Myths from Mesopotamia: Creation, The Flood, Gilgamesh, and Others. The World's Classics.* Oxford: Oxford University Press.

Davison, Jean M.
1980 The Oikoumene in Ferment: A Cross Cultural Study of the Sixth Century. *Scripture in Context: Essays on the Comparative Method.* C. D. Evans et al. eds. Pittsburgh Theological Monograph Series, 34. Pittsburgh: Pickwick, 197-221.

Day, Peggy
1988 *An Adversary in Heaven, śāṭān in the Hebrew Bible.* HSM 43. Atlanta: Scholars Press.

Deutsch, R. and M. Heltzer
1994 *Forty New Ancient West Semitic Inscriptions.* Tel Aviv-Jaffa Israel: Archaeological Center Publication.

Dietrich, M., Loretz, O., and Sanmartín (eds.)
1995 *The Cuneiform Alphabetic Texts from Ugarit, Ras Ibn Hani and Other Places* (KTU: second, enlarged edition). Abhandlungen sur Literatur Alt-Syrien-Palästinas und Mesopotamiens, 8. Münster: Ugarit-Verlag.

Donner, H. and Rollig, W.
1962-64 *Kanaanäische und aramäische Inschriften.* Wiesbaden: O. Harrassowitz.

Driver, S. R. and G. B. Gray
1921 *Job.* International Critical Commentary, eds. S.R. Driver, A. Plummer, and C.A. Briggs. Edinburgh: T. and T. Clark.

Driver, S. R.
1904 *The Book of Genesis.* London: Methuen and Co.

1956 *An Introduction to the Literature of the Old Testament.* Meridian Books, Inc.

Eichrodt, W.
1970 *Ezekiel: A Commentary.* Old Testament Library. C. Quin, trans. Philadelphia: Westminster Press.

Eilberg-Schwartz, Howard
1990 *The Savage in Judaism: An Anthropology of Israelite Religion and Ancient Judaism.* Bloomington: Indiana University Press.

Elliger, K. and W. Rudolph (eds.)
1977 *Biblia Hebraica Stuttgartensia.* Stuttgart: Deutsche Bibelgesellschaft.

Elliott, J. K.
1993 *The Apocryphal New Testament.* Oxford: Clarendon Press.

Ember, Melvin and Carol
1993 *Anthropology,* 7th ed. Englewood Cliffs, NJ: Prentice Hall.

Evans, Elizabeth
1969 *Physiognomics in the Ancient World.* Transactions of the American Philosophical Society, New Series—Vol. 59, Part 5. Philadelphia: American Philosophical Society.

Fairclough, H. Rushton (ed.)
1986 *Virgil, Vol. 1 (Eclogues, Georgics, Aeneid I-VI). Loeb Classical Library.* Cambridge: Harvard University Press.

Forsyth, Neil
1987 *The Old Enemy: Satan and the Combat Myth.* Princeton: Princeton University Press.

Frazer, James G.
1919 *Folk-lore in the Old Testament.* London: MacMillan.

Gaster, T. H.
1938 On a Proto-Hebrew Poem from Ras Shamra. *JBL* 57:81-87.

1941 Ezekiel and the Mysteries. *JBL* 60:289-310.

1946 A Canaanite Ritual Drama. *JAOS* 66:49-76.

1947 The Canaanite Poem of the Gracious Gods, line 12. *JAOS* 67:326.

1950 *Thespis.* New York: Henry Schuman.

1962 Angel. *Interpreter's Dictionary of the Bible, Vol. 1.* G. A. Buttrick et al., eds. New York/Nashville: Abingdon Press.

Gelb, I. J., et al., (eds.)
1958 *The Assyrian Dictionary of the Oriental Institute of the University of Chicago,* Vol. 4. Chicago: Oriental Institute.

1977 *The Assyrian Dictionary of the Oriental Institute of the University of Chicago, Vol. 10 (Part II).* Chicago: Oriental Institute.

Gibson, J. C. L. (ed.)

1976 *Canaanite Myths and Legends.* Edinburgh: T. and T. Clark.

1971 *Textbook of Syrian Semitic Inscriptions, I.* Oxford: Oxford University Press.

1975 *Textbook of Syrian Semitic Inscriptions, II.* Oxford: Oxford University Press.

1982 *Textbook of Syrian Semitic Inscriptions, III.* Oxford: Clarendon Press.

Ginsberg, H. L.

1938 Women Singers and Wailers among the Northern Canaanites. *BASOR* 72:13-15.

1939 Two Religious Borrowings in Ugaritic Literature, I. A Ḫurrian Myth in Semitic Dress. *Orientalia* 8:317-327.

Ginzberg, L.

1909 *The Legends of the Jews,* Vol. 1, trans. H. Szold. Philadelphia: Jewish Publication Society.

1925 *The Legends of the Jews,* Vol. 5. Philadelphia: Jewish Publication Society.

Goetze, A.

1941 The Nikkal Poem from Ras Shamra. *JBL* 60:353-374.

Gordis, R.

1978 *The Book of Job: Commentary, New Translation, and Special Studies.* New York: Jewish Theological Seminary.

Gordon, C. H.

1937 A Marriage of the Gods in Canaanite Mythology. *BASOR* 65:29-33.

1965 *Ugaritic Textbook.* Analecta Orientalia 38. Rome: Pontifical Biblical Institute.

Gowan, D.
1975 *When God Becomes Man: Humanism and Hubris in the Old Testament.* Pittsburgh Theological Monograph Series, No. 6. Pittsburgh: Pickwick Press.

Gray, John
1949 The Desert God ^{c}Aṯtr in the Literature and Religion of Canaan. *JNES* 78: 72-83.

1965 *The Legacy of Canaan. The Ras Shamra Texts and their Relevance to the Old Testament. SVT* 5. Leiden: Brill.

Grelot, P.
1956 Isaïe XIV 12-15 et son arrière-plan mythologique. *RHR* 149: 18-48.

Gröndahl, F.
1967 *Die Personennamen der Texte aus Ugarit.* Studia Pohl 1. Roma: Pontificum Institutum Biblicum.

Guillaume, A.
1968 *Studies in the Book of Job,* ed. Supplement II to The Annual of Leeds Oriental Society. Leiden: Brill.

Gunkel, H.
1895 *Schoepfung und Chaos in Urzeit und Endzeit.* Göttingen: Vandenhoeck and Ruprecht.

1964 *The Legends of Genesis* (Originally the Introduction to *Genesis. Göttinger Handkommentar zum Alten Testament, I.* Göttingen, 1901) W. H. Carruth trans. New York: Schocken Books.

Hackett, J.
1989 Can a Sexist Model Liberate Us? *JFSR* 5:65-76.

Hahn, Herbert F.
1966 *The Old Testament in Modern Research*, exp. ed. Philadelphia: Fortress.

Hammer, R.
1976 *The Book of Daniel.* The Cambridge Bible Commentary. New York: Cambridge University Press.

Hanson, Paul
1977 Rebellion in Heaven, Azazel and Euhemeristic Heroes in 1 Enoch 6-11. *JBL* 96:195-233.

1979 *The Dawn of Apocalyptic.* Philadelphia: Fortress Press.

1986 *The People Called: The Growth of Community in the Bible.* San Francisco: Harper and Row.

Harris, Z.
1939 *Development of the Canaanite Dialects.* AOS 16. New Haven: American Oriental Society.

Hartman, L. F., and DiLella, A.
1978 *The Book of Daniel.* The Anchor Bible, Vol. 23. Garden City: Doubleday and Co., Inc.

Heidel, Alexander
1952 *The Babylonian Genesis, 2nd. ed.* Chicago and London: University of Chicago Press.

Heimpel, Wolfgang
1982 A Catalog of Near Eastern Venus Deities. *SMS* 4:8-22.

Hendel, Ronald
1987a *The Epic of the Patriarch: The Jacob Cycle and the Narrative Traditions of Canaan and Israel. HSM* 42. Atlanta: Scholars Press.

1987b Of Demigods and the Deluge: Toward and Interpretation of Genesis 6:1-4. *JBL* 106: 13-26.

Herdner, A. (ed.)
1963 *Corpus des tablettes en cunéiformes alphabétiques.* Paris: Paul Geuthner.

Herrmann, W.
1968 *Yariḫ und Nikkal und der Preis der Kuṯarāt-Göttinnen.* Berlin: Verlag Akfred Töpelmann.

Huehnergard, J.
1986 *Ugaritic Grammar Notes-Fall 1986* (Unpublished). Harvard University.

1987 *Ugaritic Vocabulary in Syllabic Transcription. HSM* 32. Atlanta: Scholars Press.

Huehnergard, J. and Lambdin, T. O.
1985 *Historical Hebrew Grammar Notes-Spring 1985* (Unpublished). Harvard University.

1990 *Introduction to the Comparative Study of the Semitic Languages—Outline.* Cambridge, MA: Harvard University, Department of Near Eastern Languages and Civilizations.

Jacobsen, T.
1968 Babylonia and Assyria: V. Religion. *Encyclopedia Britannica.*

1976 *The Treasures of Darkness.* New Haven: Yale University Press.

Jakobson, R.
1966 Grammatical Parallelism and its Russian Facet. *Language* 40:399-429.

Jamme, A.
1962 *Sabaean Inscriptions From Maḥram Bilqîs (Mârib).* Publications of the Foundation for the Study of Man. Baltimore: Johns Hopkins Press.

Jantzen, J. Gerald
1985 *Job.* Interpretation: A Bible Commentary for Teaching and Preaching. Atlanta: John Knox Press.

Jastrow, Morris, and Clay, A. T.
1920 *An Old Babylonian Version of the Gilgamesh Epic. YOSR 4 (3).* New Haven: Yale University Press.

Kapelrud, Arvid S.
1952 *Baal in the Ras Shamra Texts.* Copenhagen: G. E. C. Gad.

1962 Tyre. *Interpreter's Dictionary of the Bible*, Vol. 4: 721-723, G. A. Buttrick, ed. Nashville: Abingdon.

Kautzsch, E.
1910 *Gesenius' Hebrew Grammar.* Edit. and enl. by A. E. Cowley. Oxford: Clarendon Press.

Kissane,
1941 *The Book of Isaiah, Vol. 1.* Dublin: Richview Press.

Koehler, Ludwig and Baumgartner, W.
1967-<1983> *Hebräisches und aramäisches Lexikon zum Alten Testament, 3. Aufl.* Leiden: E. J. Brill.

Kraeling, E. G.
1947 The Significance and Origin of Genesis 6:1-4. *JNES* 6: 193-208.

Kugel, James
1981 *The Idea of Biblical Poetry: Parallelism and its History.* New Haven: Yale University Press.

Labat, R.
1935 *Le Poème babylonien de la création.* Paris: A. Maisonneuve.

Langhe, R. de

1958 Myth, Ritual and Kingship in the Ras Shamra Tablets. In *Myth Ritual and Kingship,* S. H. Hooke, ed. Oxford: Clarendon Press.

Leidlmair, Adolf (ed.)

1962 *Hermann von Wissmann Festschrift.* Tübingen: Selbst verlag des Geographischen Instituts der Universität Tübingen.

Leslau, Wolf (ed.)

1987 *Comparative Dictionary of Ge^{c}ez.* Wiesbaden: Otto Harrassowitz.

L'Heureux, C.

1979 *Rank Among the Canaanite Gods.* HSM 21. Missoula: Scholars Press.

Lichtenstein, M.

1971 Psalm 68:7 Revisited. *JANES* 4:97-111.

Liddell, H. G., Scott, R., and Jones, H. S. (eds.)

1940 *A Greek English Lexicon*, new ed. Oxford: Clarendon Press.

Margolis, Baruch

1972a The Kôšārôt/kṯrt: Patroness-saints of Women. *JANES* 4:53-61.

1972b A Reply to M. Lichtenstein. *JANES* 4:113-117.

May, H. G. et al. (eds.)

1977 *The New Oxford Annotated Bible With The Apocrypha (Revised Standard Version).* New York: Oxford University Press.

McKay, J. W.

1970 Helel and the Dawn Goddess. *VT* 20: 451-464.

Miller, Patrick D., Jr.
1970 Animal Names as Designations in Ugaritic. *UF* 2:180.

1987 Aspects of the Religion of Ugarit. *Ancient Israelite Religion: Essays in Honor of Frank Moore Cross*, P. D. Millet et al., eds. Philadelphia: Augsburgh Fortress.

Montgomery, J.
1927 *The Book of Daniel.* International Critical Commentary. Edinburgh: T. and T. Clark.

1935 Ras Shamra Notes IV: The Conflict of Baal and the Waters. *JAOS* LV:268-277.

Moor, J. C. de
1970 The Semitic Pantheon of Ugarit. *UF* 2:187-228.

1971 *The Seasonal Pattern in the Ugaritic Myth of Ba*ᶜ*lu according to the Version of Ilumilku.* Kevelaer/Neukirchen-Vluyn.

1987 *An Anthology of Religious Texts from Ugarit.* Nisaba: Religious Texts Translation Series, Vol. 16. M.S.H.G. Heerma van Voss, et al. eds. Leiden: E. J. Brill.

Moore, Patrick
1956 *The Planet Venus.* London: Faber and Faber Limited.

Morgenstern, J.
1939 The Mythological Background of Psalm 82. *HUCA* 14: 29-126.

Mullen, T.
1980 *The Assembly of the Gods.* HSM 24. Chico: Scholars Press.

Musti, Domenico
1984 Syria and the East. *Cambridge Ancient History*, 2nd. ed., Vol. 3, Part 1—*The Hellenistic World*, F. W. Walbank, ed. Cambridge: Cambridge University Press.

Niditch, Susan
1993 *Folklore and the Hebrew Bible.* Guides to Biblical Scholarship—Old Testament Series, G. M. Tucker, ed. Minneapolis: Fortress.

Nielsen, D.
1936 *Ras Šamra Mythologie und Biblische Theologie.* Leipzig.

Nougayrol, J. et al. (eds.)
1968 *Ugaritica V.* Paris: Paul Geuthner.

O'Connor, M.
1980 *Hebrew Verse Structure.* Winona Lake: Eisenbrauns.

Oldenburg, Ulf
1969 *The Conflict Between El and Baal in Canaanite Religion.* Leiden: E.J. Brill.

1970 Above the Stars of El: El in Ancient South Arabic Religion. *ZAW* 82:187-208.

Pagels, Elaine
1995 *The Origin of Satan.* New York: Random House.

Pardee, D.
1982 *Handbook of Ancient Hebrew Letters.* Chico: Scholars Press.

Petersen, D. L.
1979 Genesis 6:1-4, Yahweh and the Organization of the Cosmos. *JSOT* 13: 47-64.

Petersen, D. L. and Kent H. Richards
1992 *Interpreting Hebrew Poetry.* Guides to Biblical Scholarship—Old Testament Series, Gene M. Tucker, ed. Minneapolis: Fortress.

Pope, Marvin
1955 *El in the Ugaritic Texts. SVT* 2. Leiden: E.J. Brill.

1965a Athtar. *Wörterbuch der Mythologie*, H. W. Haussig, ed. Stuttgart: Ernst Klett Verlag.

1965b *Job.* The Anchor Bible. Garden City, NY: Doubleday and Co., Inc.

Pritchard, J. B. (ed.)

1969a *Ancient Near Eastern Texts Relating to the Old Testament,* 3rd. ed. with Supplement. Princeton: Princeton University Press.

1969b *The Ancient Near East in Pictures,* 2nd. ed. with Supplement Princeton: Princeton University Press.

Rad, Gerhard von

1966 *The Problem of the Hexateuch and Other Essays.* E. W. Trueman Dicken, trans. New York: McGraw-Hill.

1963 *Genesis.* Old Testament Library. Philadelphia: Westminster Press.

Rahlfs, Alfred

1935 *Septuaginta, id est Vetus Testamentum Graeca iuxta LXX interpretes.* Stuttgart: Privileg. Württ. Bibelanstalt.

Reiner, Erica, et al., (eds.)

1992 *The Assyrian Dictionary of the Oriental Institute of the University of Chicago,* Vol. 17, Part II. Chicago: Oriental Institute.

Ringgren, Helmer

1973 *Religions of the Ancient Near East.* London: S.P.C.K.

Roberts, J. J. M.

1972 *The Earliest Semitic Pantheon.* Baltimore and London: Johns Hopkins Press.

Rummel, S., (ed.)

1981 *Ras Shamra Parallels, III.* Rome: Pontificum Institutum Biblicum.

Russell, Jeffrey Burton

1977 *The Devil: Perceptions of Evil from Antiquity to Primitive Christianity*. Ithaca and London: Cornell University Press.

1981 *Satan: The Early Christian Tradition*. Ithaca and London: Cornell University Press.

Segert, S.

1984 *A Basic Grammar of the Ugaritic Language*. Berkeley/Los Angeles/London: University of California Press.

Seymour-Smith, Charlotte

1986 *Dictionary of Anthropology*. Boston: G. K. Hall.

Sievers, Eduard

1904 *Metrische Studien II, Das Hebräische Genesis*. Leipzig: B. G. Teubner.

Skelton, Robin

1971 *The Practice of Poetry*. New York: Barnes and Noble, Inc.

Smith, Mark

1984 Divine Travel as a Token of Divine Rank. *UF* 16:359.

1986a Baal in the Land of Death. *UF* 17:311-314.

1986b Interpreting the Baal Cycle. *UF* 18:313-339.

1994 *The Ugaritic Baal Cycle*, Volume 1. *SVT* 55. Leiden: E. J. Brill.

1995 "The God Athtar in the Ancient Near East and His Place in KTU 1.6.I." *Solving Riddles and Untying Knots: Biblical, Epigraphic, and Semitic Studies in Honor of J. C. Greenfield*, Z. Zevit et al. eds. Winona Lake: Eisenbrauns.

Smith, W. Robertson
1969 *The Religion of the Semites*, 3rd. edition, with Introduction and Additional Notes by S. A. Cook (Reprint of 1927 edition). The Library of Biblical Studies. New York: KTAV Publishing House.

Soden, W. von (ed.)
1965 *Akkadisches Handwörterbuch, Band I.* Wiesbaden: Otto Harrassowitz.

1972 *Akkadisches Handwörterbuch, Band II.* Wiesbaden: Otto Harrassowitz.

1981 *Akkadisches Handwörterbuch, Band III.* Wiesbaden: Otto Harrassowitz.

Speiser, E. A.
1964 *Genesis.* The Anchor Bible. Garden City, NY: Doubleday.

Strugnell, John
1959 The Nabatean Goddess Al-Kutbaʾ and Her Sanctuaries. *BASOR* 156:29-36.

Thomas, D. Winton
1961 The Sixth Century B.C.: A Creative Epoch in the History of Israel. *JSS* 6:33-46.

Tsevat, M.
1952 The Ugaritic Goddess Nikkal wīb, *JNES* 12:61-61.

Tsumura, D. T.
1974 A Ugaritic god Mt-w-Šr and his two weapons. *UF* 6:407-413.

Van Leeuwen, R. C.
1980 *ḥôlēš ᶜal gwym* and Gilgameš XI, 6. *JBL* 99:173-184.

Virolleaud, C.
1936 Hymne phénicien au dieu Nikal et aux déeses Košarôt. *Syria* 17:209-228.

1957 *Le Palais royal d'Ugarit, II. Textes en cunéiformes alphabétiques des Archives Est, Ouest, et Centrales.* Mission de Ras Shamra, 7. Paris: Imprimerie Nationale.

Walls, Neal
1992 *The Goddess Anat in Ugaritic Myth.* SBLDS 135. D. L. Petersen, ed. Atlanta: Scholars Press.

Waltke, Bruce and M. O'Connor
1990 *An Introduction to Biblical Hebrew Syntax.* Winona Lake: Eisenbrauns

Weiser, A.
1962 *The Psalms: A Commentary.* H. Hartwell, trans. Old Testament Library. London: S.C.M. Press.

Wellhausen, Julius
1885 *Prolegomena to the History of Ancient Israel.* J. S. Black, trans. Edinburgh: Adam and Charles Black.

Westermann, C.
1984 *Genesis 1-11: A Commentary.* J. J. Scullion, trans. Minneapolis: Augsburg.

Widengren, G.
1958 Early Hebrew Myths and their Interpretation. In *Myth Ritual and Kingship,* S. H. Hooke, ed. Oxford: Clarendon Press.

Wilson, R. R.
1987 The Death of the King of Tyre: The Editorial History of Ezekiel 28. *Love and Death in the Ancient Near East: Essays in Honor of Marvin H. Pope,* J. H. Marks and R. M. Good eds. Guilford, Conn.: Four Quarters Publishing Co.

Zimmerli, W.
1979 *A Commentary on the Book of the Prophet Ezekiel, Vol. 2. Hermeneia: A Critical and Historical Commentary on the Bible.* J. D. Martin, trans. Philadelphia: Fortress.

INDEX

Ugaritic Texts

Biblical Texts